Ideology and politics in Britain today

MANCHESTER
UNIVERSITY PRESS

Politics today

Series editor: Bill Jones

Ideology and politics in Britain today

Ian Adams

Manchester University Press
Manchester and New York
distributed exclusively in the USA by St. Martin's Press

Published by Manchester University Press
Oxford Road, Manchester M13 9NR, UK
and Room 400, 175 Fifth Avenue, New York, NY 10010, USA

Distributed exclusively in the USA by
St. Martin's Press, Inc., 175 Fifth Avenue, New York, NY 10010, USA

Distributed exclusively in Canada by
UBC Press, University of British Columbia, 6344 Memorial Road,
Vancouver, BC, Canada V6T 1Z2

British Library Cataloguing-in-Publication Data
A catalogue record for this book is available from the British Library

Library of Congress Cataloging-in-Publication Data
Adams, Ian. 1943–
   Ideology and politics in Britain today / Ian Adams.
     p.   cm. — (Politics today)
   Includes bibliographical references and index.
   ISBN 0–7190–5055–3 (cloth). — ISBN 0–7190–5056–1 (pbk.)
   1. Political science—Great Britain.   2. Ideology—Great Britain.
I. Title. II. Series.
JA84.G7A33   1999
320.5'0941'09049—dc21   98–28386

ISBN 0 7190 5055 3 *hardback*
    0 7190 5056 1 *paperback*

First published 1998

05 04 03 02 01 00 99 98   10 9 8 7 6 5 4 3 2 1

Typeset in Photina
by Northern Phototypesetting Co. Ltd, Bolton
Printed in Great Britain
by Biddles Ltd, Guildford and King's Lynn

In memory of Henry Tudor
(1937–97)

Contents

Part III: The fringe

Part IV: The future

Preface

We live in a confused and changing world where traditional political doctrines are constantly being reformed and challenged by new ones. To understand what is happening involves understanding how we arrived at our present situation, how traditions of political thought have shaped and continue to influence how we think about and make sense of the present political world.

The purpose of this book is to examine the variety of ideas, values and doctrines that influence British politics today in the light of how they developed and arrived at their present state. In contemporary politics, two people both claiming to be conservatives may nonetheless have very different understandings of what conservatism is, and the same is true of socialists, liberals and the believers in a variety of other doctrines. Only with an understanding of the development of these sets of beliefs can we understand the part they play in political life.

Most of this book will be taken up with examining the development of these doctrines individually. However, the first section consists of three chapters that look at different aspects of the wider context. The first discusses the nature of political doctrines or ideologies and their role in politics. The second looks at the British constitution and how one ideology – liberalism – has been especially important in shaping it. The third looks at the role of economic theory in modern politics and how it connects with, while at the same time cutting across, different ideologies.

The main body of the book looks at individual ideologies, broadly grouped into two categories: 'mainstream' – conservatism, socialism, liberalism and nationalism – and the 'fringe', including the 'greens', the far left and right, and miscellaneous others. Finally, a short section considers what the role of ideology might be in the politics of the future.

I would like to express my thanks to all those who have helped me.

Part I

Background

1

Politics and ideology

Political ideologies are central to the whole nature of modern politics. This is not always recognised, since people are often influenced by ideologies without realising it. Understanding politics today involves, therefore, some understanding of their nature and influence. It is important first of all to see how ideology, which is essentially a matter of ideas and theory, fits into the very practical business of politics.

What is politics?

Politics is surprisingly difficult to define. At first thought it may seem obvious to identify politics with government, with the business of running a country. But then we have to account for the fact that we also talk, apparently without baffling ourselves, of the politics of many things quite remote from affairs of state: university politics, office politics, church politics and even family politics.

Collective decision-making

There are various and sometimes contradictory theories about the nature of politics: such as that it is essentially about power, or about the peaceful settlement of disputes. But perhaps the simplest and most straightforward way to think of it is to say that politics is essentially about collective decision making, and in particular making decisions about policy. Any organisation needs to make collective decisions about what to do next and what general policy to adopt, including upon what basis it will conduct its business, what aims it will pursue, and to what principles it will adhere.

What to do next is always a problem, individually or collectively, for we can never be sure how things will turn out, what effects our actions will have. We can never be certain that our best laid plans will not end in

1

disaster. For this reason alone there are usually many opinions of the best thing to do, what policy to adopt.

In all politics, but especially modern democratic politics, there will be dis-agreement over the right thing to do. And the more complex the society, the greater the scope for disagreement. Indeed the whole idea of democracy is that, in principle at least, all potentially may participate or have influence, despite numbers that may run into hundreds of millions. Arriving at author-itative decisions in these circumstances is an immense task, involving parties and pressure groups and a great array of institutions and procedures, linked together in systems so extensive and so intricate that entire professional aca-demic lifetimes are spent simply studying them.

Interests and values

The scope for disagreement and contention in a democratic society is end-less. However, the sources of political conflict tend to fall into to two broad categories: interests and values. A modern complex society generates an infinite number of overlapping interests, as is clear from Britain's many thou-sands of interest groups. In consequence there is almost nothing a govern-ment can do that is not bad for somebody's interests. We would all agree that ending pollution is a good thing, but whenever laws are proposed to control it, there is always fierce protest from those who claim they would be put out of business by, for example, the cost of making their factories non-polluting, and from, among others, those who are liable to lose jobs or business as a consequence. Many conflicts of interest are permanent: workers and employ-ers, manufacturers and consumers, pedestrians and motorists, developers and environmentalists, and so on.

In addition to interests, values are important sources of political disagree-ment and conflict. This is because in politics, as in other aspects of life, we are concerned not merely with what is effective but what is right. An effec-tive solution to a problem might be to kill those causing it, but in any civilised society that would be morally unacceptable. However, while there may be a broad moral consensus on many things we know that in detail people's beliefs about what is right and wrong differ enormously, and this can produce some of the most bitter and intractable of political conflicts. These may be over individual values and issues, such as abortion or nuclear disarmament. However, these values are often set within a wider framework of moral beliefs, such as religions and ideologies, which are capable of afflict-ing whole nations with conflicts that cannot be reconciled.

Systems and constitutions

The scope for conflict is endless, especially in a modern democracy where there is such variety of interest and belief. Unless there was some system of reconciling all these conflicts society could not exist, a country could not function. The purpose of the political system is to try to take all these conflicting ideas into account and come up with the best decision for the country as a whole. There have to be endless compromises and adjustments to try satisfy as many people as possible. But in the end authoritative decisions have to be made or we would never get anything done.

It is vital that the decisions made are authoritative so that all can accept them. Every organisation worthy of the name has some kind of system for taking and implementing authoritative decisions. In modern states this is the government, which is charged with making the final decisions and has the ultimate responsibility for running the country. Deciding who the government shall be is a central part of politics, with many institutions and organisations, elections and other procedures involving the electorate, the media, pressure groups and many others. In democracies we have rival teams with rival outlooks, which change from time to time. But the business of influencing government goes on permanently.

Conflict is inevitable in politics, and in modern democratic politics it is perfectly natural, normal and healthy; provided, that is, everybody abides by the political rules. So long as the rules of the political game are observed by all who participate, we are safe. It is when people go beyond the rules that we have much to fear, for the only real alternative is violence. In a sense it does not matter how much conflict there is so long as people stay within the rules.

The rules in question here are simply the constitution, the way the political system works. A constitution is the set of basic rules by which any human association is organised and run. Whether the constitution is for a state or an amateur dramatic society, the basic elements are much the same: institutions; officers and how they get their position; rules for changing the constitution; rules for membership, and for determining the rights and duties of members.

In a modern political system, what is meant by playing by the rules is simply following the usual legal means of political activity – elections, political parties, pressure groups, protests and so on – and accepting the decisions reached, at least until such times as they can be changed by further political activity. Many people are distressed by the amount of political conflict in democracy. They sometimes say that if only people of good will could sit down and sort things out, everything could be amicably resolved. But this is naive. In the nature of things there will always be issues about which people feel strongly. But if the rules are observed a great deal of conflict can be accommodated, even involving those who disagree with the constitution itself.

The danger comes when people feel that nothing can be achieved in this way, or that their cause is so morally righteous that it justifies the use of violence to change things. In Northern Ireland, for example, we have in the Social Democratic and Labour Party (SDLP), a party committed to constitutional politics, even though it is opposes to the constitution. This contrasts with the violence of the Provisional IRA who have traditionally refused to abide by the constitution, being convinced that the justice of their cause entitled them to wage war against it (although hopefully Republican attitudes are now changing). Major divisions in society – such as those over religion, race, political beliefs, nationality, language or way of life – are capable of causing conflict so fierce that the political system cannot contain it, and the resulting violence can cause the collapse of government and civil war.

Politics, then, refers to the process of decision-making for human associations. But there needs to be some kind of formal organisation or constitution which members recognise, otherwise decisions will have no authority. Thus, states, political parties, churches, amateur dramatic societies and other organisations may engage in politics to decide the policies of the organisation. When we talk of 'office politics' or 'family politics' where no explicit process exists for reaching authoritative decisions, we do not speak of politics in the full sense of the word.

The nature of ideology

If this is the nature of politics, then what kind of thing is ideology and how and where does it fit into the political process? We have seen that politics is not just about what will be effective but also about what will be right. Above all in politics people feel the need for a sense of direction, some conception of the better society we would like to live in and an idea of how we might achieve it. Ideology is above all concerned with these overall aims, and it is for this reason that political parties are associated with ideologies, because parties want to attract voters with visions of how they can improve the world.

Ideologies are, therefore, sets of ideas which contain a particular view of what society ought to be like and how politics ought to achieve it. Such sets of ideas include liberalism, conservatism, socialism, nationalism and similar political doctrines that are often give their names to parties devoted to furthering the their aims. However, ideologies are complex sets of ideas, composed of several elements.

Moral visions and ideal worlds

First of all, ideologies are about values or ideals: things which are important, desirable and good. Any ideology has a set of positive values, making up a conception of what we should strive for, as well as a conception of what is bad, what we must avoid or fight against. Different ideologies stress different values, such as freedom, equality, order, justice, national self-determination, harmony with nature and many others. Some values are common to several ideologies, like freedom and social justice, but often they mean different things in the respective ideologies. Other values may be confined to one alone, such as racial purity. These values come in different forms and in different combinations. Thus, even within the same ideological tradition, there may be different versions. There are very different notions of freedom to be found among liberals, different ideas of equality among socialists, and so on. Each ideology, or version of an ideology, has its own set of values. These are principally about what is good, but also cover what is bad: such as ignorance and irrationality, alienation, class division, imperialism or patriarchy, according to the ideology.

For each ideology these sets of values are closely bound up with its own particular conception of human nature. That is, the values sum up what is good and bad for human beings as such; what hinders and what is conducive to human flourishing. Thus, human nature is conceived in such a way that it can only flourish when people are free, or equal, or in harmony with nature, or not subject to coercion, or foreign domination, or some such state of affairs.

From this follows a conception of an ideal world where society represents the optimum conditions for human flourishing. That is, a society where people are free or equal, or in harmony with nature, or where patriarchy has been eliminated, or where races are integrated, or separated, or whatever social form best embodies the positive values of the ideology and eliminates their opposites.

These three elements of values, conception of human nature and ideal society are so intimately connected as to form a unit, what might be called the moral vision of an ideology.

Explanations and prescriptions

Armed with its moral vision it is then possible for an ideology to apply this vision to our present world so that our present situation can be evaluated in its light. Needless to say, in some way or other, and to a greater or lesser extent, the present always falls short of the ideal. We are not free or equal, or we are out of harmony with nature, or patriarchy rules, or in some way what the doctrine deems to be bad prevails.

Ideologies then need to explain how we got into this state. If being free or equal is essential to human flourishing, then why are we not free or equal? The explanation is bound up with the moral vision, if the good for man is bound up with reason and freedom, then the explanation will be in terms of ignorance and authoritarianism. Such explanations often involve the identification of enemies. In the view of liberalism, for example, human progress was held back by ignorance, but it has been in the interests of certain enemies to keep the people in ignorance. The traditional villains in the liberal account, were kings and priests who sought to keep their subjects in awe with superstitions and false doctrines (although in the twentieth century, liberals have found a new enemy in totalitarianism). If the ideal is equality, then ruling classes are the enemy; if national independence is the ideal then the enemy is imperialistic foreigners; if female emancipation, then it is the domineering male that must be dealt with, and so on.

This leads to what in many ways is the culmination of ideological theorising, the prescriptions. In a way, the whole point of all this sometimes vast theoretical apparatus is to prescribe action, to tell us what we must do. What the ideology tells us is how to get from our present unsatisfactory situation to the ideal society. It may be by means of revolution, as with Marx; or by rolling back the state and giving the free market free scope, as with the New Right; or it could be abolishing the state, as with anarchism; or by nationalising industries as with traditional socialists.

In most cases one can see the past present and ideal future as a continuum that constitutes a theory of history. Sometimes the whole process is deemed to be necessary and inescapable, as with Marx's theory. Other thinkers have no such idea of historical inevitability, and warn that if we do not act, humanity will destroy itself. Either way, the human world, past, present and future, is encompassed in an overall theory and described and evaluated in the ideology's own distinctive vocabulary.

These elements of values, conceptions of human nature and ideal societies, explanations, evaluations and prescriptions, appear to be the essential structural features of ideology. We can illustrate this by looking at three contrasting examples: Nazism, Greens and traditional conservatism.

Three examples

At the centre of national socialist ideology is a moralised conception of human nature in which race is the key factor. There is a natural hierarchy of races determined by their relationship to culture and ethical value. At the top is the Aryan race, the only one fully capable of creating culture and all that is morally worthwhile in human life. Other races can only enjoy and transmit what has been created. All, that is, except the Jews, who come at the bottom of the hierarchy, since they are an inherently culture-destroying race. Culture has some mysterious relation to territory, and the fact that Jews did not possess any territory of their own was taken as evidence that they are an essentially parasitic people. History is conceived as a race war between Aryan and Jew, a war that Hitler argued was coming to a crisis in his own generation.

In this view, the ills of racially determined humanity are explicable in terms of a disordering of the natural hierarchy of races, and an overcoming of those ills and the creation of a justly ordered world is to be accomplished by the restoration of the natural hierarchy, which is the ideal society in which humanity may truly flourish. The war between Aryan and Jew, Hitler insisted, came to a head in the twentieth century with Germany's near destruction during the First World War. But, he believed, the drama was about to enter its last act with the final destruction of the just and the establishment of the German Aryans as the master race.

To take another example, the ills of modern humanity, according to the Green movement, derive from humanity's disordered relationship with nature. Greens see humankind as having a specific place in nature, and the ability to live happily as long as this is recognised. But now, because of exploitation and greed, humankind is destroying nature, the environment at a suicidal rate, though modern industry and commerce. However, the fundamental problem is seen to go back to much older attitudes developed in the West, in the Bible and among the ancient Greeks, that nature is there for out benefit and he can exploit it at will. As a result of this, in modern times we are alienated from our true relationship with the natural world, and this alienation is expressed in our obsession with economic growth, that can only result in self-destruction. Humanity can only flourish if that lost harmony with nature is restored. We must therefore stop economic growth and create a society which is in balance with the environment and not depleting the world's resources.

A third example is traditional British conservatism of the pre-Thatcher sort. This has particular features that do present something of a problem to the view of ideology that has just been outlined. In the First the doctrine claims to eschew theory altogether and, secondly, appears to have no ideal society towards which we ought to work. In fact, we have no need to take seriously conservative claims to be non-theoretical. Burke's *Reflections on the Revolution in France* [1790] (1969) is a work of political theory. Conservative claims to base their ideas on common sense are no more convincing than Marxist claims that their theory is fully scientific. There is more of a problem with the question of an ideal society. This is not the case with continental versions of conservatism, where saw the ideal in terms of the re-creation of some past order. But this has never been the case with the British version, which specifically rejects some stated theoretical ideal, and identifies the ideal more or less with the present order which has to be defended. On the other hand, the present cannot be entirely satisfactory, since there would be no point in the conservative thinker putting pen to paper if that were the case. In other words, while Conservatives tend to uphold the present order, they perceive it to be threatened. It is threatened by people who do not understand the necessity of that order, and the point of conservative writing is to demonstrate that the present order needs defending and those that disagree need to be educated. A society without such threats is presumably more ideal than the present one. All the other attributes of an ideology outlined above hold true of traditional conservativism.

Ideological traditions

When we speak of major ideologies, such as liberalism, conservatism or socialism, we are speaking of great traditions of thought that have evolved over time. As they do so, different versions of the ideology emerge. These different versions sometimes contradict each other, while remaining within the broad tradition. This may give rise to fierce controversy as to what is the 'true' version of the ideology. In the 1950s there were disputes within the Labour Party as to whether social democracy was 'genuine socialism'. There are many other examples, as we shall see.

As ideologies evolve there is no control. They change according to intellectual fashion, or the need of a party to increase its vote, or one of several other reasons, but they are always striving to convince potential believers. For example in the mid-nineteenth century, Darwin's theory of evolution made a powerful impact on the intellectual scene. It was soon used by theorists to 'prove' that their particular ideological belief was 'scientific' and 'true'. Thus, liberals, conservatives, anarchists, socialists and others wrote books claiming that evolutionary theory supported their particular political prescriptions.

Ideologies have to move with the times and adapt to popular opinion. Sometimes different ideologies move closer together, and even overlap. This was true of certain forms of liberalism and socialism in the late nineteenth century.

Problems and exceptions

There are perhaps some difficulties with the above account of the nature of ideology, with certain ideologies that seem incomplete. This can be so in two different senses. Take, for example, nationalism. Assuming that its ideal world is one divided up into nation-states, with no nation denied self-determination, what then? It hardly amounts to an answer to human ills, or guarantees the optimum conditions for human flourishing. Nationalism needs to supplemented by something else, like socialism or liberalism, which will say how society should actually be organised. A similar example, is animal liberation, which again needs to be part of some wider ideological system, usually some set of Green ideas.

Nationalism provides partiality in another sense. While nationalism can be a universal doctrine, in practice it often is not. It may be aggressive and deny to others what it claims for itself. Again, gay liberation and other movements based on locality, ethnicity, sexuality, age group, religious or semi-religious cults of various kinds, often seem to lack a general picture of mankind as a whole. Perhaps the most salient feature of most doctrines of this kind is their recency. It might be linked to a general intellectual retreat from universalism that is deemed by some thinkers to be symptomatic of what they call our 'postmodern' age. This will be discussed in the final chapter. It does seem that some doctrines are only partial ideologies. Yet it remains true that the major ideologies are characterised by universality and a conception of humanity as a whole even when associated with a political party of narrow appeal.

Ideology and political parties

Ideologies are practical doctrines aimed at changing the world, and as such in the modern world it is political parties that are the chief vehicles. The major ideologies – such as liberalism, socialism, nationalism and conservatism – have parties based upon them, yet the relationship between doctrine and party is far from simple.

Official party doctrine

Because parties have to keep an eye on popularity to get themselves elected, there is a constant process of ideological renewal. Parties may have to adopt policies that are popular but at odds with official doctrine; sometimes the doctrine itself is modified; and occasionally a party adopts an ideological position that belongs, or used to belong, to another party.

This last is a rather drastic measure, yet examples abound. After the French Revolution the Tories adopted the Whig-liberal ideas of Edmund Burke; in the 1950s they accepted the prevailing policy consensus which was social democratic, a mild form of socialism; while in the late 1970s they adopted Thatcherism, which is an updated version of mid-nineteenth century liberalism, and substantially at odds with traditional conservatism. Similar changes can be found in the histories of the Liberal Party and the Labour Party. Under Tony Blair the Labour Party has undergone just such a rethinking of its doctrine. The Labour 'modernisers' claimed to be remaining true to traditional socialist principles, a claim which many in the party dispute. In fact, it is usual for parties changing their doctrine to make similar claims to be true to their past: Thatcherites also claimed to be fully in line with traditional conservative principles, which also was disputed by some Conservatives.

There is, therefore, no necessary correspondence between a party and the ideology associated with its name. Parties evolve independently of ideologies in order to survive, while at the same time ideological traditions develop independently of parties.

Ideological and non-ideological parties

The fluid, changing nature of the relationship between parties and ideologies applies largely to parties seriously engaged in seeking office. That is, the mainstream parties in Britain and most democratic countries. But there are other parties for whom ideology is more important, and indeed all-important. These tend to be extreme or fringe parties, which, because they are not dependent on public opinion and have no hope of office, set greater store by ideological purity. This is true of both the Marxist far left and the fascist far right. It is one of the reasons why they so frequently split and reform, with each sect claiming greater ideological purity than the others.

In recent years some Green parties in Britain and elsewhere have manifested similar tendencies. This seems to be characteristic of parties which have little chance of power.

Finally, ideological consensus can take issues and ideas, and their embodiment in policies and institutions, effectively out of party politics because everyone agrees with them. This is true of the basic framework of liberal democracy in Britain as elsewhere. This is the subject of the next chapter.

2

British liberal democracy

Anyone studying the role of ideas and ideologies in British politics must recognise that there is one ideology – that of liberalism – which is built into the very structure and fabric of the British political system. This is clear from the fact that the British system is classified as a liberal democracy. Liberal ideas and values are part of the framework within which British politics is conducted. Curiously enough this has not given the modern Liberal Party, or its successor, the Liberal Democrats, any particular advantage. Indeed, these parties (like similar parties in Europe) could be said to be victims of the success of liberal ideology, since all mainstream parties accept the core liberal values and so make it difficult for a specifically liberal party to sustain an identity on the basis of liberal ideas alone.

This chapter will concentrate on how liberal ideas came to shape Britain's constitution and much of the taken-for-granted part of the political system. But first it is necessary to see liberalism in the broader context of modernity.

Liberalism and modern history

Liberalism is the primary political ideology of modern times. It was the first modern ideology to emerge and that emergence was part of the development of the modern outlook from the medieval. Liberal values such as freedom and equality, toleration and democracy are now the taken-for-granted values of the world today. By the end of the twentieth century all the main rivals of liberalism, such as fascism and communism, have been defeated and reduced to political insignificance. Liberal democracy is the dominant form of government for most of the world, while domestic politics in those democracies may be seen as primarily a contest between parties subscribing to different versions of liberalism. Thus, liberalism is built into our whole conception of the modern world, as part of the common sense of our age.

11

Medieval to modern

Liberalism was the first modern political ideology to emerge and the only one that was part of the great transition from medieval to modern. This transition took several centuries and involved a whole series of revolutions and developments including the Renaissance, the Protestant Reformation, the rise of capitalist enterprise and of the sovereign nation-state, and the development of modern science. A fundamental theme of many of these movements is an emphasis on individualism, the capacity of individuals to make of their own lives what they will, to find their own relationships with God, to use their own reason. Liberalism was the social expression of this individualism and involved a very different conception of the human condition than that which prevailed in the Middle Ages.

We need only think of a typically medieval conception of human beings as wretched, sin-ridden, God-dependent creatures whose greatest needs were discipline and hierarchical order. Individuals were presumed to need a lord to tell them what to do and a priest to tell them what to think. Liberalism had a conception of man (and in fact it was a long time before women were considered in equal terms) as a rational being, capable of thinking for himself and choosing how he should live his own life. The liberal view of human beings is, therefore, distinctly individual, in contrast to the medieval view which saw people in terms of their social status within an organic society. Liberals saw an individual's status as capable of changing through his own efforts, and by using his own reason; and not as something given by God and fixed for life within a God-given hierarchy. Civil society (that is, politically organised society) is seen as an artificial entity constructed for human benefit which can be changed for human benefit.

However, liberalism is not simply a reaction against the Middle Ages. It is in part also a reaction against one of the modernising movements just mentioned. That is, the rise of the modern, centralised sovereign state. Absolute monarchy, expressed above all in the theory of the divine right of kings (the concept that the right to rule derives from God and that kings are answerable to God alone), was widely thought of as modern and efficient. It was the divine right pretensions of the Stuart kings in Britain that was largely responsible for the English Civil War and the Glorious Revolution of 1688, and it was these events that stimulated the development of liberal ideas in Britain.

Early liberal values

There are a number of liberal ideas and themes that can be traced to earlier periods, such as Ancient Greece. But as a self-conscious political doctrine, liberalism really crystallises in the mid-seventeenth century and principally in England in the events surrounding the Civil War and its aftermath.

(Although it should be remembered that the word 'liberalism' itself was only coined much later.) The basic values of early liberalism included:

- individual liberty
- natural rights (especially liberty and property)
- limited constitutional government
- government by consent
- subordination of the executive to a representative legislature
- equality before the law
- religious toleration

These views revolve around a picture of the rational individual capable of determining his own destiny, for which freedom is required. But this freedom needed protection from what were considered the greatest threats to freedom at that time, namely the state and the church. Hence the liberal demand for limited government and civil rights. Property rights were also seen as a crucial element in defending freedom. These sum up the ideals of early liberalism, which do not, it should be noted, include democracy as we understand it today. They were articulated in the liberal theory that developed mainly in England in the late seventeenth century. In the following century they spread to America and Europe and helped to stimulate the great political revolutions of the late eighteenth century, which together with the economic revolutions of the same period, ultimately created today's political and economic world.

The age of revolutions

The era of revolutions at the end of the eighteenth century saw the emergence of new forms of liberal thought and new liberal values. Some of these have remained contentious among liberals while others have been absorbed into the stock of values now common to liberals and to other ideologies in the modern world.

The industrial revolution that began in Britain saw the development of economic liberalism. That is, first of all, the belief that the free market was the optimal form of economic life, providing the greatest prosperity for all, and necessitating maximum economic freedom for everyone. This went hand in hand with a wider view of liberty which saw the maximisation of social freedom as the best way to run society in general. It was this version of liberalism that was the first to be actually called 'liberalism', which was in the early nineteenth century. It is better known by the name '*laissez-faire* liberalism', although it is also sometimes called 'classical liberalism'. Its main features are a belief in maximum individual freedom, the free market and the minimal state; that is, the minimum of state interference in society in general and the economy in particular. Economic freedom and minimal state are particular values which this form of liberalism has added to the stock of liberal values, though they remain contentious.

The French Revolution, at the end of the eighteenth century, was fought out in the name of liberal values. The revolutionaries had a particular version of those values, which included not only human rights, but also democracy, equality and the nation. These were much more contentious in their day than economic liberalism, since initially they were too much associated with the horrors of the Jacobin 'terror'. There was, for example, strong resistance to democracy in Britain (not least from many liberals) and it only gradually gained ground. Today it is democracy that is taken for granted while the values of social equality and economic liberalism are contested.

The growth of liberal ideas has been an integral part of the growth of the modern world, initially in the West, and then the world as a whole. Britain has had a central role in this process, with the development of liberal ideas closely related to the development of the British constitution.

Achieving a liberal democratic constitution

The British constitution has famously developed over a thousand years. However, there have been two periods in modern history that have been critical in determining the direction of Britain's constitutional development. The first was in the seventeenth century, when a prolonged constitutional crisis set Britain on the road towards a liberal constitutional development quite different from that of most of continental Europe. The second was during the later nineteenth century, which decisively pointed constitutional development in the direction of full democracy.

The seventeenth-century crisis

Most peoples undergo some kind of crisis in their fortunes which is a constitutional turning point, such as the moment of independence from foreign domination or a great revolution. The great conflicts of the seventeenth century that culminated in the Civil Wars and the Glorious Revolution was such a time for Britain. It was during these conflicts, and stimulated by them, that liberal doctrine began to crystallise. And it was these conflicts that set Britain on the road to the gradual creation of a liberal constitution, quite different from the dominant European model.

The seventeenth century was a period of almost continual constitutional conflict. King and parliament were at loggerheads from the beginning of the Stuart dynasty, when James I ascended the throne in 1603. The new monarch was an upholder of the fashionable continental doctrine of divine right of kings and had written a book on the subject. The English parliament was decidedly unimpressed with these newfangled ideas and stood by its traditional rights and privileges. James I's son, Charles I, tried to rule without parliament and the resulting conflict was only settled by two civil wars and the execution of the king.

Parliament won a decisive victory, and although the king was restored, parliament's dominance was preserved. Charles II and James II both attempted to restore the power of the monarchy, James by overt means that provoked a further revolution. This was happily bloodless, hence 'Glorious Revolution'. The upshot was the final establishment of parliamentary supremacy. The Bill of Rights of 1689 and subsequent legislation meant that parliament would sit permanently and that the monarch was entirely dependent upon it for finance and the right to raise an army. Other rights were guaranteed. There was religious toleration, at least to the extent that nobody was persecuted, although discrimination against Catholics and dissenters remained.

The Glorious Revolution and its aftermath constituted a general settlement that was to last more or less until the 1830s, during which time limited royal government gave way to government by prime minister and cabinet, although they were still chosen by the king. Nonetheless, the constitution following the Glorious Revolution was distinctly liberal compared with continental practice. In Europe royal absolutism, supported by the theory of divine right of kings, was the norm and France, the most powerful state in Europe, was the exemplar. The French king was deemed to be answerable to no-one but God, and no parliament could criticise, no judiciary frustrate and no feudal magnate could insist upon influence. By comparison Britain had a semi-representative government: government had limited powers and the people had a range of civil rights.

Democracy was not an issue. The Whig ideal came in fact from the Ancient world. Thinkers and historians of Ancient Greece and Rome had extolled the virtues of the 'mixed constitution' that would combine the virtues of monarchy, aristocracy and democracy while avoiding the disadvantages of each. The Roman Republic was deemed to have had just such a constitution, and it was universally regarded as the key to Rome's rise to greatness. Enthusiasts of the eighteenth-century British constitution, including Whigs and foreign admirers, believed that Britain had just such a constitution, with the House of Commons providing a democratic element (although only a small fraction of the population could vote), the Lords supplying the aristocratic element and the king the monarchic element. Indeed among the greatest admirers of the British constitution were the American colonists who rebelled against British rule. In the President, Senate (not originally elected) and House of Representatives, they were attempting to create their own version, only without the hereditary principle.

When the idea of full democracy was seriously put forward, it was invariably regarded as a dangerous radicalism, as 'rule by the mob'. Jean-Jacques Rousseau was the first major European thinker to extol the virtues of democracy in his *The Social Contract* [1762] (1973). His Jacobin followers made it central to European politics in the great cataclysm of the French Revolution.

Revolution to democracy

Fear of Jacobinism by the ruling class in Britain put reform (let alone democracy) off the political agenda for a generation. But immense social and economic change, the need to deal with social problems generated by industrialisation and urbanisation, the corruption of the old political system, and simply distance of time from the Jacobin 'Terror', eventually created such pressure for reform of the political system by the 1830s as could no longer be resisted without the danger of revolution.

Famously the Great Reform Act of 1832 opened the door to an age of reform. It did not in fact extend the franchise by much (about 5 per cent to about 10 per cent of the adult population), but above all it redistributed seats in a manner that destroyed the old corruption and made MPs independent of aristocratic patrons and dependent on their voters as they had not been in the past.

To many of those engaged in politics, including most of the Whig Party who had pushed the Great Reform Act through, that was the end of the matter as far as constitutional reform was concerned. The old system had become corrupt and the Great Reform Act had restored the balanced constitution of king, Lords and Commons that was their true ideal. So when pressure for further reform built up again in the 1860s much of the opposition came from liberals.

The 1867 Reform Act greatly increased the franchise and gave the vote for the first time to some working-class men (householders) in the towns. But its significance was more than that. It could not be viewed simply as a readjustment of the old balanced constitution, but a clear move towards democracy. And an arbitrary move, since there was no particular justification for a certain proportion of working-class men to have the vote rather than a different proportion. To most, whether supporters or opponents of the Act, it was only the beginning of a process that would inevitably lead to greater democracy in the future.

The Representation of the People Act of 1884 brought the franchise in the countryside in line with the towns, and the secret ballot was introduced in 1870, but the major move to democracy came in 1918 when all property qualifications were dropped, and so all men over twenty-one years of age could vote. Furthermore, women were given the vote for the first time, but only women aged over thirty years. The age limit for women was lowered to twenty-one, the same as men, in 1928, and then lowered for everyone to eighteen in 1969.

Adult suffrage was the major part of the democratisation of the British system of government, but there also had to be institutional changes. The most important institutional impediment to democratic advance in the nineteenth century was the House of Lords. It retained full powers to change or block any legislation passed to it from the House of Commons. It did this frequently, including, for example, rejecting Home Rule for Ireland which had been passed by the Commons in 1893. By convention the Lords did not interfere with financial legislation, which was deemed the proper sphere of the Commons. But it broke this rule in 1909, when it rejected the Liberal government's Budget. By threatening to use the king's power to create peers, the Liberal government forced the Lords to accept the Parliament Act of 1911. This Act prevented the Lords from interfering with any financial legislation, while limiting its power over other legislation to a mere delaying power of two years (later reduced to one), which effectively destroyed the power of the House of Lords for good.

After the Second World War, a liberal democratic constitution was fully in place and, with two exceptions, there was little constitutional change for more than fifty years. One exception was a further extension of civil rights, particularly in respect of sexual discrimination. The second exception was Britain's joining of the European Community in 1973, which gave the Community a right to legislate in certain areas. Fundamental change to Britain's constitutional system only became a prospect again with the election of a Labour government in 1997, supported on this issue by the Liberals. Devolution to Scotland and Wales, major reform of the composition of the Lords, and a referendum on changing the voting system for Westminster were among the measures proposed.

Liberalism and modern politics

That British politics has for several centuries been conducted within the framework of a liberal constitution, and since the mid-nineteenth century an increasingly democratic one, implies a considerable degree of consensus between the political parties over liberal principles. But this suggests two conundrums. In the first place, different political parties are supposed to stand for different things, so how is it possible for them to do this if they all subscribe to liberal values? In the second place, if liberal principles dominate our political system, why is the Liberal Party or its successor not the dominant party of the state? Why, for most of the twentieth century has it not even been one of the country's two main parties?

Liberalism and the political parties

By the time of the French Revolution the theologically based divine right doctrine of the old Tory Party was no longer viable. The revived party adopted the ideas of the Whig politician, Edmund Burke, with their emphasis upon tradition and conservation. The constitution to be conserved, together with the political tradition to be upheld, had by that time strong liberal elements of constitutional government, civil liberties and a degree of toleration. In this way, liberal values became part of conservative values. Later in the century, the Conservative Party absorbed many businessmen who had left the Liberal Party. Along with them came their free-market ideas, which added a further liberal element to conservative thinking.

The reason for this change of allegiance among businessmen was the rise of the working class as a political force, a rise that was eventually to culminate in the creation of the Labour Party. And as with conservatism, socialist ideas in Britain contained strong liberal elements. With few exceptions, there was a general acceptance of constitutional government and civil rights. In the British tradition of socialist thought, the view has predominated that socialism is the only effective means to realise liberal ideals. Indeed many, such as the early Fabians, believed that liberalism would naturally evolve into socialism.

The arrival of the propertyless classes in politics occasioned a general realignment of the parties, with the Conservatives representing the propertied classes and Labour representing the propertyless. The Liberals tried to appeal to both sides and fell between the two.

However, none of this is to say that the British Labour and Conservative parties are pure liberal parties. They do take certain liberal values for granted, but they also interpret them – and indeed the constitution – in different ways. Besides, liberalism itself is not a monolithic doctrine. There are different varieties. Indeed, one might say that what divides the Labour and Conservative parties today is different varieties of liberalism. and this is true of the wider world.

The wider world

Party realignment, the decline of specifically liberal parties, and the absorption of liberal ideals into class-based parties, also occurred in many parts of Europe, although generally the process took longer than in Britain. In many cases it was only after the Second World War, with the rise of the Christian Democrats and of non-Marxist left wing parties, that there was an unequivocal commitment to liberal ideals in Europe.

At the end of the twentieth century liberalism is by far the most important ideology in the world. Major rivals, particularly communism and fascism, are no longer a serious challenge. It has even been argued that free-market liberal democracy has triumphed to such a degree that it will dominate the political world for ever more (Fukuyama, 1989). And although this view is open to serious criticism (see Adams, 1991), it is certainly true that free-market liberal democracy is dominant in the world today, at least for the time being.

On the other hand, this does not mean, as some would say, that ideology has in any sense ended. Apart from what might be called Asian capitalism (notably illiberal), militant Islam (even more so) and nationalism, there remains within the framework of liberal democracy huge scope for ideological difference.

It has to be recognised that liberalism itself is not monolithic. Within the basic liberal-democratic-capitalist framework there is great political variety. Indeed it might be said that in a broad sense, politics in the Western world, and certainly in Britain, turns upon the debate between various forms of free market liberalism and what might be called social liberalism. Or, put another way, between those parties and ideologies that have absorbed major parts of the liberal inheritance. And this still leaves room for wider ideological differences among Conservatives, Socialists, Liberal Democrats, Greens, Nationalists, Marxists and a variety of others such as single issue parties and groups, as well as extremes beyond the scope of serious politics.

In Britain, beyond the taken-for-granted liberal framework, ideology has a major role in politics. However, before looking at the development and role of the various doctrines that contribute to British politics today, we need to look at another area of consensus that, like the constitution, cuts across ideological lines. This is the field of economic policy.

3

Economics and consensus

As the previous chapter has shown, British politics has for several centuries operated within a constitutional consensus broadly based on liberal values. Constitutional changes have been contentious from time to time, but once they have been made other issues have predominated. At any one time there may be a consensus on one or more areas of policy: defence, or social policy or foreign relations. However, the most important area of policy where consensus has tended to prevail over long periods, and sometimes formed the foundation of other policy agreements, is economic policy.

There have been two major periods of economic consensus in the past and a third is in the process of developing at the end of the twentieth century. Towards the middle of the nineteenth century free market economics became the official wisdom behind government policy and remained so, no matter who was in power, up to the Second World War. After the war a new economics became the orthodoxy, but also became the foundation of a much wider and quite unprecedented consensus on economic and social policy among all the major parties that dominated British politics for a generation. That consensus broke down in the 1970s, and one of the central questions of British politics since has been the extent to which a new economic and social consensus has been developing following the impact of Thatcherism in the 1980s.

The age of *laissez-faire*

The economic transformation of Britain in the late eighteenth century, of which industrialisation was the central feature, was accomplished partly because of, and partly in spite of, prevailing economic conditions and attitudes. The standard economic outlook of governments of that time was known as 'mercantilism', a regime of restriction and control. Foreign trade was heavily regulated, and many aspects of the domestic economy were restricted through official monopolies, labour laws, and the like. On the other hand, British domestic economic conditions were far less restrictive and far more conducive to free economic activity than in most other European countries, especially Britain's major rival, France.

Mercantilism worked on the belief that there was a finite amount of wealth around and the different national economies had to compete for it. But more generally, the attitude prevailed that the economy had to be regulated and controlled just like every other aspect of national life. The notion that people could be left to do what they wanted was inconceivable, it would obviously lead to chaos.

The great challenge to the general belief in the necessity of economic control was Adam Smith's *The Wealth of Nations* of [1776] (1970). He argued precisely the opposite case: that if people were simply allowed to pursue their own interests, bound only by the rules of honesty and fair dealing (backed by law), then their activity would produce optimum prosperity for all. In succeeding decades these ideas became ever more widely accepted, until by the middle of the nineteenth century they had became standard orthodoxy among governments of every party. Economic liberalism was held to be the foundation of Britain's rise to economic supremecy and was rapidly making Britain the richest and most powerful state, with the biggest empire, that the world had ever seen. Thereafter, a free economy at home and free trade abroad became government orthodoxy for practically a century.

When *laissez-faire* economics became the accepted orthodoxy in the mid-nineteenth century, it seemed to many to be inextricably bound up with a wider conception of general freedom of society, whereby, within general conventions and laws, people could do just what they liked. The corrolary of this was a doctrine of minimal government, that everything, including every social problem, can be safely left to the free market for optimum solution. However, in the last quarter of the nineteenth century this doctrine was severely tested by economic recession.

In the mid-1870s the long Victorian boom came to an end in slump. A worse slump followed in the mid-1880s with widespread social distress. All parties began to respond with policies to deal with the social problems. But faith in free market economics remained largely unimpared.

The inter-war years

After the First World War Europe was economically exhausted and suffered from deep recession with mass unemployment. These conditions were greatly compounded by the loss of markets. Other parts of the world had begun to make their own ships, textiles and other goods, instead of importing them from Britain and Europe.

America, however, was enjoying a huge post-war boom in the 1920s and provided a vital market for European goods. But then, in 1929, the Wall

Street crash crippled the American economy. Unemployment was suddenly a massive problem in the USA, which in turn made worse the situation in Europe. After a decade of unemployment, the number of unemployed soared in the early 1930s. This was the period of the Jarrow Crusade, when unemployed men from the Northeast of England marched on London to demand work.

Governments of all parties stuck to orthodoxy and waited for an upturn. There was real poverty and distress on a massive scale and, of course, there was at that time no welfare state to relieve it. Calls for state expenditure, imperial preference and other schemes were ignored. In continental Europe, where the distress was even worse, communism and fascism seemed to be working, and each movement had some following in Britain. In America things were so desparate that despite being elected in 1932 on a platform of economic orthodoxy, Roosevelt defied the orthodoxy and spent on public works, borrowing the money to pay for it. This policy, known as the New Deal, certainly boosted morale, but did not solve the recession, which was only ended by the Second World War.

The experience of the inter-war years discredited the old orthodoxy, and although the Keynesian alternative did emerge in that time, it only made headway during and after the war. It then became the basis of a powerful and comprehensive consensus that dominated British politics for a generation.

The post-war consensus

Between the late 1940s and the mid-1970s British politics was dominated by a broad consensus on policy. The left wing of the Labour Party and a few right-wing Conservatives were not very happy with this but, apart from them, acceptance among politicians and the electorate was almost universal. To understand British politics in the last fifty years of the twentieth century we need to know something about this consensus: what it was, how it came about and why it fell apart.

Three elements

The consensus consisted of three main elements which together provided a framework for economic and social policy. These were:

- the managed economy
- the mixed economy
- the welfare state

A 'managed' economy means that the government manipulates demand through fiscal means (taxation, interest rates, etc.) and through public expenditure in order to maintain a steady demand for goods and therefore full employment. A 'mixed' economy is one where there is a substantial publicly owned sector (i.e. nationalised industries) as well as a free-enterprise private sector. Finally, the welfare state is a wide range of social policies on issues including social security and health, housing and education, which are designed to ensure that nobody is denied these basic essentials because of lack of means.

In the 1950s, 1960s and early 1970s the differences between the parties in these areas (and other policies, such as defence) were largely matters of detail and emphasis within the agreed framework. In fact, the public often complained that the main parties differed so little that it was hardly worth voting. To understand how this consensus was reached it is necessary to look at each element in turn.

The managed economy

The most fundamental of these elements was the managed economy. This was based on the theories of the English economist John Maynard Keynes (1883–1946) which he developed in response to the conditions of the 1930s.

During the economic depression that affected the whole western world in the inter-war years, with its mass unemployment, poverty and other social ills, governments, for the most part, did nothing. The accepted wisdom was that given time the free market would solve its own problems and government interference would only make things worse. Keynes challenged this belief and argued that it was the proper responsibility of government to prevent both booms and slumps in order to maintain gradual economic growth and permanent full employment.

This could be done by manipulating taxation, credit and public expenditure. If the economy was growing too fast then money (and therefore demand) could be taken out of the economy by higher taxes, lower government spending and by making it harder to borrow money. If there was recession and growing unemployment then the government could put money (and therefore demand) into the economy through lower taxes, higher public expenditure and easier credit. If, as a result, there was more money in people's pockets then more would be spent on goods and more people would be needed to make the goods to fulfil the extra demand, and this would reduce unemployment. There is an obvious difficulty with cutting taxes and increasing spending at the same time, but Keynes argued that the government must borrow; restoring full employment was much more important than balancing the books in the short term.

Keynes set out his theories in his book *The General Theory of Employment, Interest and Money*, published in 1936 (1983). It came too late to affect government policy. The great depression of the 1930s was only ended by the Second World War. When it was over there was a widespread feeling that Britain must not go back to the unemployment of the pre-war years, and Keynesian ideas, which had grown in influence during the war, seemed to show how it could be prevented. Keynsian economics were adopted by governments all over the Western world, which proceeded to enjoy nearly thirty years of unprecedented prosperity.

The welfare state

The welfare state was the second major element of the post-war consensus. During the war people began to think about what kind of world they wanted after the war was won. It was widely felt that when the fighting was over Britain had the chance to build a better society, free of the poverty and other social problems of the pre-war years. A certain amount of welfare provision (some old age pensions and very limited social security for a few) had been introduced by the Liberal government before the First World War, but by the outbreak of the Second World War even this provision was in a chaotic state. The government asked an expert on these matters, Sir William Beveridge, to try to make the existing system more orderly. In fact he ignored his brief and in 1942 produced a blueprint for a comprehensive welfare state, which became known as the 'Beveridge Plan'. What the plan advocated was:

- a system of social security (national insurance), guaranteeing substantial benefits to compensate for loss of earnings due to unemployment, sickness or old age, which covered everybody in the land, rich or poor
- child benefit for all, rich or poor
- a free national health service for all, rich or poor
- better education for everyone, rich or poor
- improved housing
- policies to maintain full employment

All this went far beyond what the government had asked Beveridge to do, but his ideas caught the public imagination and were extremely popular.

During the first post-war election, in 1945, Labour promised to implement the Beveridge Plan in full, and this promise helped to give Labour its landslide victory. Most of the plan was put into effect by the Attlee government (1945–51) and has been the basis of British social policy ever since.

The mixed economy

The mixed economy was also created by the post-war Labour government. But the extensive programme of nationalisation – coal, steel, railways, etc. – was not initially conceived of in terms of setting up a mixed economy, but rather as the first stage, along with physical planning (that is, the government deciding how much of what will be produced), in the creation of a socialist economy. But by the time Labour lost office in 1951 physical planning had been dropped in favour of Keynesian economic management, and the dominant right wing of the party were arguing that nationalisation had gone far enough: the mixed and managed economy was the ideal. Further nationalisation (i.e. beyond the 1945 programme) did not reappear in Labour manifestos until the mid-1970s.

All-party agreement

When the Conservatives returned to power in 1951 they did not take the opportunity to reverse all that Labour had done. Instead they accepted the mixed and managed economy and the welfare state, and did not seriously question these policies until the arrival of Margaret Thatcher in the mid-1970s. The Liberal Party also supported the consensus. In the post-war years the Liberals were electorally insignificant, although the two main architects of consensus policies, Keynes and Beveridge, had both been Liberals.

Looking at it from a broader point of view, consensus policies were a kind of compromise between capitalism (supported by Conservatives and Liberals) and the socialist ideas of Labour. It was a bit of both, a half-way house, a step towards socialism that mitigated the worst effects of capitalism without destroying the freedom that goes along with it. This compromise was supported by those in the Labour right who became known as 'social democrats' (as distinct from left-wingers who called themselves 'democratic socialists') and consensus policies are sometimes referred to as the 'social democratic compromise' as a result. These policies were also known in the 1950s and 1960s as 'Butskellism' after the right-wing Labour leader, Hugh Gaitskell, and the Conservative chancellor of the exchequer, R. A. Butler. The left of the Labour Party, which wanted more nationalisation and state planning, was actively opposed to the consensus, especially during the 1950s, but the social democratic view prevailed.

In terms of government policy, the one notable break with the consensus came in 1970 when Edward Heath came to power with a set of policies that put more stress on the free market and less government intervention. The result was rising unemployment, regarded as the great economic evil during the consensus years, at which the government reversed its policies (known as the 'U-turn') and went back to the consensus.

The decline of consensus

Consensus policies of the mixed and managed economy and the welfare state gave Britain, and many other countries, considerable prosperity for many years. However, this consensus eventually disappeared. Throughout the 1960s the British economy had been in gradual decline relative to other countries, but it was in the mid-1970s that things really started to go wrong for a number of reasons:

- a sudden rise in oil prices plunged the western world into a recession
- there was growing unemployment accompanied by growing inflation (known as 'stagflation')
- government attempts to deal with unemployment by standard Keynesian means (pumping money into the economy to stimulate demand) simply did not work. Increased expenditure merely seemed to fuel inflation without stopping unemployment from rising.

The managed economy was really the lynchpin of the consensus, and when it no longer seemed to work the parties had to radically rethink their economic policies and look for new answers.

The end of Keynesian policies

In October 1976 Jim Callaghan, the prime minister, made a speech to the Labour Party conference that really spelt the end of Keynesianism as the dominant theory behind government policy. He said:

> We used to think that you could spend your way out of recession and increase employment by cutting taxes and boosting government spending. I tell you in all candour that that option no longer exists, and that insofar as it ever did exist, it only worked on each occasion ... by injecting a bigger dose of inflation into the economy, followed by a higher level of unemployment as the next step.

But if pure Keynesianism was abandoned, it was not clear what was in its place. The Labour government struggled on, trying to achieve Keynesian objectives using methods that were partially Keynesian and partially something else. Meanwhile the left in the party were demanding more socialism. When the 1979 election came, it was Margaret Thatcher who had a clear and consistent economic strategy based on clear and consistent theory.

1979: the end of consensus

Under Margaret Thatcher (who became leader in 1975) the Conservatives had shifted to the right in the direction of extreme free market economics or 'monetarism', while Labour was shifting to the left in the direction of more nationalisation and state planning. In a sense the consensus dissolved into its constituent parts, with the Conservatives moving towards pure capitalism, and Labour towards pure socialism. The Conservative 'wets' and the Labour right still hankered after the old consensus policies, but they each increasingly became a minority in their respective parties. In fact much of the right wing of the Labour Party left to create their own Social Democratic party, which, together with their Liberal allies, became the chief advocates of those consensus policies which the other main parties had largely left behind.

A new consensus?

The old consensus essentially broke down because Keynesian economics seemed to be unable to cope with the economic crisis of the 1970s, and in particular the combination of rising unemployment and rising prices (according to Keynesian theories you could have either one or the other but not both at the same time). In the eighteen-year period of Conservative government after 1979 a new economic orthodoxy was established which argued that Keynesian economic analysis was mistaken and that economic policy ought to be conducted on a different basis. This view was the foundation of Thatcherite economic policy after 1979.

Economic labels

One of the curious and confusing features of the economic ideas that have dominated British policy since 1979 is that they go by a number of different names: supply-side economics, neo-classical economics, monetarism, neo-liberal economics and New Right economics. They mean roughly the same things, but with subtle variations. They all, however, reject Keynesian analysis and policy, and they all advocate a renewed faith in the operation of the free market as prevailed in the century or more before Keynes. We will look at each of these labels in turn.

1 **Supply-side economics**   This is the most general, technical and ideologically neutral of the terms. It is simply the belief that certain policies will produce a more prosperous economy than alternative policies. It gets its name because Keynesians tend to believe that if the demand side of the economy is right then everything else will fall into place, whereas supply-side economists tend to believe that getting the supply (i.e. production) side of the economy right is the key to success. This essentially means making sure the free market operates with maximum efficiency and minimum distortion. Government policy should be directed to removing those things that tend to distort the effective working of the market, including:
   - inflation
   - excessive government interference (planning, regulation, financial inducements to do this or that, etc.)

- excessive taxation
- excessive trade union power
- monopolies

This outlook is not necessarily linked with a particular vision of an ideal society, and parties and governments are free to adopt some measures and not others, because they have other priorities as well (e.g. eliminating poverty). Thus, by the 1990s the Labour Party had to a considerable degree been converted to supply-side economics.

2   **Neo-classical economics**   This means much the same as supply-side economics. The term emphasises that these ideas are essentially a modern version of the classical economics that prevailed before Keynes.

3   **Monetarism**   This is a version of supply-side economics that puts special emphasis on inflation. Essentially it is a technical theory about the causes of and cure for inflation. It argues that while there may seem to be a number of contributory causes of inflation, the root cause is too much money in the economy. Money is like blood in the body which circulates and keeps everything healthy. If there is too little relative to the size of the economy then the economy cannot work as effectively as it should. Too much is also bad, since it causes inflation, and is easy to induce but extremely hard to eliminate.

Monetarists believe that the main cause of excessive money in the economy is governments spending too much, borrowing too much and printing too many notes. They are especially prone to do this when pursuing Keynesian policies of stimulating demand. The cure of inflation is also in the hands of governments and is indeed their prime economic responsibility. It can be done by reducing public expenditure, borrowing and the amount of money (cash and credit) in circulation, steadily over several years (too quickly would create dislocations) according to targets that are publicly known so that expectations are lowered (e.g. of those making pay claims).

Monetarists are usually the most thoroughly committed to supply-side policies in general, and tend to be neo-liberals as well.

4   **Neo-liberal economics**   This term refers not so much to economic theory, as to economic policies that contribute to a society based on free-market, minimal government and maximum individual freedom and responsibility. These include supply-side and monetarist policies, but also policies thought to contribute to creating the 'enterprise culture': such as sale of council houses, sale of privatisation shares to ordinary consumers, encouragement of private medicine, etc, and the general view that there are 'market solutions' to all social problems as well as economic ones.

Neo-liberal ideas are not associated with the Liberal Party, or even with traditional Conservatives, but with a new breed of free-market Conservatives represented by Margaret Thatcher in Britain, Ronald Reagan

and the right of the Republican Party in the USA and others elsewhere, sometimes known collectively as the New Right. For this reason the term
5 **'New Right economics'** is sometimes used as an alternative to 'neo-liberal economics'.

These five terms can be used fairly interchangeably to refer to the economic thinking of the Thatcher era. However, when they are used more broadly the subtle differences between some of them means that it is sometimes appropriate to use one term but not another. Thus, Edward Heath's government came to power in 1970 with broadly supply-side policies, but not monetarist ones. The Labour government after 1975 adopted some monetarist measures, although the rest of its economic policies were not really supply-side at all. Again, since 1983, the Labour Party has increasingly adopted supply-side policies, while entirely rejecting monetarism. None of these could be said to be neo-liberal or New Right. These only apply to the policies of Margaret Thatcher and her followers, as do the rest of these terms; although the commitment to the purest form of monetarism (what the Labour deputy leader, Dennis Healy liked to call 'sado-monetarism') was somewhat watered down after 1982 and subsequently abandoned..

Labour and supply-side economics

During the 1980s the Thatcher revolution pressed on, and the other parties were left trailing in its wake. The Labour Party's shift to the left proved an electoral disaster from which it struggled to recover, while the Liberal/Social Democrat Alliance rose to prominance only to crumble away. After heavy defeats in 1983 and 1987, Labour began to shift its economic policy in a Thatcherite direction. But it was not until the arrival of Tony Blair in 1994 and his radical programme of 'modernisation' that in the opinion of many the party began to look electable in its own right (rather than by the default of Conservative unpopularity). However, for much of the left of the party 'modernisation' has meant little more than adopting more and more of Thatcherism. Be that as it may, it is certainly true that in many areas, not least economic, the Labour government elected in 1997 presented a number of policies very similar to those of the outgoing Conservatives, such that it is appropriate to talk of a new consensus.

It is undoubtedly true that 'new Labour' has abandoned Keynesian economics of demand management in order to maintain full employment in spite of there being some Keynesian economists and politicians still active in the party. New Labour under Tony Blair and Gordon Brown has opted instead for the Thatcherite supply-side economics of controlling inflation and creating the conditions in which the free market can flourish. However, this is not the rigid 'monetarist' version of the early Thatcher years, but closer to the more mellow version of the later Thatcher and Major periods. For example, one of the first economic policy decisions of the Labour government elected in 1997 was to give greater independence to the Bank of England to control inflation, a move urged on the previous Conservative government by some of the most vigorous supply-side supporters.

Furthermore, all talk of nationalisation or renationalisation has ceased. There is, indeed, the possibility that the Labour government may itself privatise state controlled services.

Welfare state

For some time before the 1997 election, new Labour was signalling that drastic changes would be necessary in welfare, and especially in the field of social security payments. The policy is still being developed, but it is clear that much of the right's analysis of the problems has been accepted. This includes the belief that the country can no longer afford the comprehensive provision of previous years because the burden will be crippling in the future. Further, that an open-ended commitment to benefit leads to 'dependency', which is unacceptable on any large scale. The implications of this were not always spelt out in opposition, but after coming to power in 1997, the Labour government began a programme of welfare cuts, a wide ranging review of welfare, suggesting further cuts in the future, and a new emphasis upon work as the answer to poverty. The policies are still being worked out, but in principle anyone capable of work should no longer be able to live permanently on welfare payments. These are arguments and principles hitherto associated with the right.

Of the three main elements of the old consensus, it is the welfare state that has proved the most durable. Despite being antithetical to the underlying beliefs and values of Thatcherism, none of its essential elements have disappeared. It may, as many claim, have become run down and dilapidated; and it may become more subject to market forces, but it is still there and is likely to remain.

A new consensus

A new consensus can be said to have emerged in economic and social policy. Among the official policies of the main parties supply-side free market principles and the need to keep Britain competitive in a global economy, are common ground. And this consensus goes beyond controlling inflation and government non-intervention, extending to policies on trade unions, taxation, privatisation and much more. Furthermore, it accepted that the costs of welfare must be reduced, and benefit payments reorientated towards work rather than dependency.

On the other hand, this consensus is unlikely to have the same status as the post-war consensus in its heyday. Despite a common outlook on many issues there does remain a fundamental difference in outlook that did not exist in the 1950s and 1960s. An important part of the Thatcher legacy is a hostility to the state, now widely shared among Conservative supporters. This contrasts with the Labour view of the state as, potentially, an instrument of good. Labour sees a more positive role for the state, in such areas as education and infrastructure, and in making Britain fit to cope with global market, than do the Conservatives. Furthermore, other issues have become important in the 1990s, such as Europe and the constitution, which do not quite fit into the old consensus framework and are a major source of disagreement between the parties.

There is a new consensus, and one that seems likely to be with us for some time. Nevertheless, it is not as strong or as comprehensive as that of the postwar years.

Part II

Mainstream

4

Whigs and liberals

Liberal ideas are central to political thinking in the modern world. Liberalism is not, however, a single coherent doctrine, but a broad tradition of thought that encompasses many different and sometimes contradictory strands. An earlier chapter showed how certain liberal ideas of individual rights and constitutional government have become part of the British political system, upheld not only by various forms of liberal theory but also by a range of other ideologies influenced by liberal values. This chapter and the next examine more closely the differing versions of liberalism as they have emerged and evolved in the context of British politics over the last three and a half centuries.

Levellers and Whigs

As we have seen, the rise of liberal ideas was part of a wider series of changes that marked the transition from a mediaeval outlook to a modern one. England was among the countries most affected by the social and intellectual changes of the time, and it was in England, assisted by the catalyst of civil war, that liberal ideas gradually developed. It was later, in the Eighteenth century, that these ideas reached a wider European and American audience.

The English Civil Wars

The English Civil Wars of the middle of the seventeenth century were a conflict for supremacy between king and parliament, although complicated and exacerbated by religious differences. Parliament won, but the victory had to be consolidated a generation later by the Glorious Revolution of 1688. However, behind the struggle between ancient institutions and ancient claims to rights and privileges were new ideas: liberal ideas of freedom, rationality and individuality that would come to challenge the authority of tradition. The medieval outlook tended to see people in terms of their social position and the community to which they belonged. Claims to freedom and toleration challenged the traditional authority of the king who knew what was best for his subjects, and the Church who told them what to think.

Liberalism would ultimately develop as a rejection of tradition in the name of reason. However, the seventeenth century was still an age when tradition possessed great authority and both sides in the Civil Wars sought to appeal to it, even though both were using novel ideas. The early Stuart kings believed in the relatively new theory of divine right of kings that it had become fashionable in Europe, whereas those who rebelled against the king wanted an authority for parliament than it had never hitherto possessed.

The English Civil Wars were as much wars of words as of killing and destruction. The nature of society and how it should be organised and run was at the heart of the conflict and it was accompanied by a flood of pamphlets about how these things ought to be. Ideas ranged from advocating absolute power by anyone who could maintain it, to various kinds of theocracy (rule by the church), to a variety of democratic solutions; some pamphleteers even ignored politics altogether to prepare for the Second Coming.

The pamphlet war was facilitated by the absence of royal censorship. When the war was over parliament sought to revive censorship. This called forth one of the most famous defences of religious toleration and freedom of speech from the poet John Milton (1608–74), in his *Aeropagitica* of 1644. In this pamphlet he defended freedom of the press based on the right of everyone to make moral and religious judgements for themselves having heard the arguments.

Among the more cogent political radicals were the Levellers, a group in Cromwell's army who advocated limited democracy. They demanded the vote for all men who were not servants, and claimed freedom and equality for all: referred to by contemporaries as 'social levelling', hence their name. They did not want the abolition of property, but a more equitable distribution. A society of independent farmers and artisans was their ideal.

With the restoration of the monarchy in 1660 came the restoration of the old social order and such ideas soon appeared remote and obscure. Nevertheless, Civil War divisions to some extent remained, especially since the king still harboured ambitions of absolute royal power. Opinion divided between royal supporters (Tories) and those who upheld parliamentary authority (Whigs). The upshot was the driving out of King James II in 1688 in the Glorious Revolution and the consolidation of parliamentary supremacy. The Whig writer whose work provided a theoretical justification for the revolution was John Locke (1632–1704).

Locke and the Glorious Revolution

Locke's ideas, set out in his *Two Treatises of Government* of 1690 (1960), owed a certain amount to the Civil War radicals, but he created a more coherent and less iconoclastic theory. Basically, all individuals are endowed by God with reason, by means of which men could discern what is right and wrong and how they should live. This was the old medieval theory of Natural Law which stressed everyone's social obligations. What was new was Locke's individualist interpretation of it. His central idea was that God endowed every man with certain 'natural rights', most importantly the rights to life and liberty and property. Locke also maintained that, even without God, Natural Law and natural rights would still be true (a view still held by some today, though disputed). From this picture of essential human nature he derived his theory of government.

Initially, Locke argued, people lived a perfectly adequate social life – with communities, churches, etc. – but without any government. They lived in a 'state of nature', guided only by their reason. However, this presented certain difficulties in dealing with criminals, serious disputes and other problems. To overcome these difficulties people agreed to a 'social contract' to create government as a trust, for the sole purpose of protecting their pre-existing rights. Above all government existed to protect the property and person of individuals. Government must, therefore, be based upon the consent of the governed, expressed in representative institutions. If government does not fulfil its trust, by, for example, attacking property (such as confiscation or taxation without consent), the people are free to remove the government and replace it with one that will do a satisfactory job. In later writings, Locke supplemented these ideas by advocating religious toleration, although a toleration somewhat limited by modern standards.

Locke is generally regarded as the first major liberal thinker. He expounded most of the main themes of subsequent theorists: human rights, individual liberty, minimal government, constitutional government, the executive subject to the people's representatives, sanctity of property, civil liberties and toleration. On the other hand, he was no democrat. What he wanted above all was to have the king's government permanently subject to the control of parliament. He thought that the franchise should be confined to those of substantial property. He had no desire to change existing society in any way. Locke represents the moderate Whig wing of liberalism, while the Levellers and related groups, who did want social change, represent the radical democratic wing.

Whigs in power

During the late seventeenth and most of the eighteenth century, the Whigs were the dominant force in British politics. The system Locke had defended became progressively more corrupt, with the landed aristocracy controlling the Commons more and more. The Whig Party was dominated by a number of great aristocratic families who regarded their own rights and freedoms as the bulwark of the rights and freedoms of all Englishmen. Locke himself was somewhat ignored. His thoughts began to have more impact in America and France.

The Whigs in power developed their own version of liberalism, which avoided Locke's stress upon the natural rights of every individual, their equality and freedom, as well as on the collective rights of the people in the form of government by consent and the right of rebellion. The rights the eighteenth century Whig rulers defended were, in their view, not universal God-given rights belonging to all human beings, as in Locke, but the traditional rights of Englishmen, that had slowly developed over centuries. They held a more traditionalist and aristocratic view. Those of substantial property, and the landed aristocracy in particular, were the principle defenders of the rights and liberties of the people against the possibility of royal tyranny. This had always been so, but was established decisively by the Glorious Revolution and its aftermath, which put the authority of parliament over the monarch into final legal form. The sovereignty of parliament was a central Whig doctrine.

The British constitution was, in the Whig account, thus seen as having achieved some kind of perfection. It was deemed to exemplify the classical ideal of a mixed constitution which, as all educated persons were taught, was the root cause of the greatness of Ancient Rome, the most civilised and best-governed empire the world had ever known. That is, a constitution that manages to combine the good points of each of the three types of government: monarchy, aristocracy and democracy (the rule of the one, the few and the many) while avoiding their respective defects. For this reason the British constitution was greatly admired in France, America and elsewhere.

The ideal was not democracy but a 'balanced constitution' that had a 'democratic element'. We may find it surprising today that democracy was so little advocated. But they took the view of all the great philosophers of the ancient world that democracy was rule of the mob. We take democracy today to be the guarantee of our freedom, but in the seventeenth and eighteenth centuries it was property that was seen as the bulwark of liberty and also as a defence against the anarchy of the rabble. With property the individual was independent and had a natural commitment to preserve good order. Those of inherited wealth were seen as the guardians of English liberties and as society's natural rulers. They were fitted for this role by birth and education and had the time and leisure to devote to national affairs.

Apart from a few years in the reign of Queen Anne, the Whigs enjoyed a virtual monopoly of power for almost a hundred years after 1688. Theirs became an ideology of power: the outlook of an establishment that for the most part saw little need for change, even though the system had many distortions. For example, there were the 'rotten boroughs' whose population had declined to such an extent that their parliamentary seats (normally two) were in the control of the local landowner who could choose the MPs himself. These were justified on the grounds of providing opportunities for those of talent but no wealth to rise through the patronage of those who had wealth. This establishment Whig view of the constitution was most famously expressed by Edmund Burke in his *Reflections on the Revolution in France* of 1790 (1969).

Throughout the eighteenth century, however, there were Whigs who saw things differently. There were radical Whigs who, from time to time advocated the rights of man, and remained true to the Lockean Whig tradition (as distinct from the establishment Whig tradition), and even to some degree advocated the ideas of the Civil War radicals. Often these were religious dissenters, such as Joseph Priestly, who traditionally allied themselves to the Whigs, but who were still discriminated against. However, with the American and French revolutions, there was an upsurge of radical ideas and sentiment.

Revolutionaries and radicals

The late eighteenth century and early nineteenth century was an age of revolutions which transformed Western thought and politics. Liberal ideas played a central role in all these transformations, but liberalism was itself transformed in the process.

The American Revolution

The American Revolution was in many ways surprisingly English. The initial rebellion was on the basis of the good English principle of refusing to be taxed without being represented. The rebels were supported by many Whig politicians, including Edmund Burke, and when it came to formulating their basic principles, the Americans turned to Locke. The *Declaration of Independence* of 1776 was an epitome of Locke's political theory. It was based upon a belief in natural rights, in the prime function of government to protect the rights of citizens, and in the collective right of the citizens to remove a government that is not fulfilling its role.

Finally, the American constitution of 1787 is substantially modelled on the British, albeit without the hereditary principle. It was meant to be a 'balanced' constitution combining the rule of monarchy (in the sense of the rule of the one) in the Presidency; aristocratic rule represented by the senate (originally a nominated not elected body) and a democratic element in the House of Representatives (elected on a limited franchise based on property). Indeed, a number of the Founding Fathers were ardent admirers of the British constitution.

Jacobin liberalism

The French Revolution which began in 1789 was initially concerned with replacing absolute monarchy with constitutional monarchy, but the early revolutionaries were soon outflanked by the more radical Jacobins. They were influenced by Rousseau's *The Social Contract* [1762] (1973), with its notion of radical democracy in which there would be total unity. In order to defend the revolution, the Jacobins, led by Robespierre and Saint-Just, instituted the Terror, with its orgy of bloodshed and its massacre of much of the French aristocracy. They did not have the time to develop their vision of post-revolutionary France before being overthrown; but their ideal was, like Rousseau's, a society of small farmers, artisans and shopkeepers. Property was still seen as essential for liberty, but they regarded equality of property, with nobody rich or poor, as just as important. However, Rousseau's notion of democracy was very different from any notion that we would recognise today.

Jacobin liberalism, with its stress on democracy, equality, unity and nationalism, was very different from the Whig liberalism of Britain or even the American revolutionaries. Although they were closer to some of the radicals of the English Civil Wars.

Burke and the Tories

When the French Revolution began, and before there was any bloodshed, the Whig party divided between a right wing which abhorred what happened in France, and those such as the leader, Charles James Fox, who welcomed the events in France and were willing to contemplate modest reform at home. As the Revolution became more fierce and bloody it increasingly polarised the politics of Britain, and indeed all Europe.

The response of the right-wing Whigs was crystallised in the writings of Edmund Burke, who fiercely attacked the early revolutionaries and predicted the bloodshed and chaos to come. With the coming of the Terror, Burke was hailed as a prophet and became the darling of the royal court and the Tory Party. It was he who turned out to be more in tune with popular opinion, and certainly the opinion of the ruling class, than the reformist Whig leaders.

Burke articulated and expounded the establishment Whig view of politics and society with brilliant eloquence, and gave it a theoretical foundation more solid than before, although it was a view taken up by the Tories (see Chapter 6). In his defence of property, tradition, the organic society, and his hostility to radical change and to abstract theory, Burke is still influential among Conservatives today.

Paine and the radicals

Those who ardently supported the Revolution and thought Britain should undergo a similar political and social transformation (though without the bloodshed) were known as radicals. They stressed democracy and human rights. The leading radical in Britain during the 1790s was Tom Paine (1737–1809) who, remarkably, also played a significant role in both the American and French Revolutions. His main book, *The Rights of Man* [1791] (1969), advocated radical democracy, the abolition of the monarchy and all social privilege. Similar to the radicals of Paris, he was concerned with equality and advocated what we would call welfare state measures. He could not, however, be called a socialist. Similar to almost all radicals of the time his theme was the rights of man, and Paine followed Locke in insisting that among the most fundamental of such rights was the right to property, including the rights of inheritance. However, to the ruling class, Paine's militant atheism, republicanism and hostility to the hereditary principle made him and his followers appear dangerous subversives bent on bringing Jacobinism to Britain.

After the Napoleonic Wars the radicals agitated for parliamentary reform, but met with repression. The British establishment was badly shaken by the French Revolution and suppressed all public protest, banned trade unions and turned a deaf ear to appeals to deal with the appalling social problems that were being thrown up by the Industrial Revolution. When political and social reform did really begin, with the Great Reform Act of 1832, the outcome was decidedly whiggish and far removed from any such radicalism. However, by this time a new dimension of liberalism had developed that was linked to a less threatening kind of radicalism. It was influencing educated opinion, different parties and even making an impact on the thinking and actions of governments. This was *'laissez-faire'* liberalism.

Free market or *laissez-faire* liberalism

Liberal ideas lay behind both of the great political revolutions of the late eighteenth century, ideas that were principally concerned with matters of civil rights and constitutional government. The other great revolution of the age, which was even more central to the creation of the modern world, was the Industrial Revolution. Liberal ideas were important here as well, and indeed it is against the background of this economic revolution that a version of liberalism developed that has arguably been the most successful, and which many regard as the definitive form of liberalism.

The Industrial Revolution and Adam Smith

The break-up of the medieval world, with its feudal system and guilds, allowed people more economic freedom and made possible the early growth of capitalism. Nevertheless, governments still had a great deal of control over economic activity in manufacturing and trade. The case for economic liberalism, when it began to be argued in Britain in the eighteenth century, made the startling claim that if everyone was simply left to their own economic devices, then the result would not be chaos but a harmonious society of ever growing prosperity.

Experience seemed to bear this out. In the eighteenth century there were less restrictions on British commerce and manufacturing than in France and most other countries. The economy boomed to such an extent that in the 1780s Britain began to embark upon the world's first industrial revolution and become the first industrial society. The thinker who analysed what was happening and advocated even greater freedom was the Scottish philosopher, Adam Smith (1723–90).

The Enlightenment aspiration to create a rational science of man, parallel to Newton's scientific account of the universe, did not have much success. The nearest anyone came was in the field of economics. In 1776 Adam Smith published his great work, *The Wealth of Nations* (1970) which laid the foundations of modern economic theory. Above all, it revealed the wonders of the free market and demonstrated the overall benefits of the unrestricted movement of goods, capital and labour. Smith argued that the free market, without any government interference, would produce maximum prosperity for the whole nation. Everyone pursuing their own selfish economic self-interest would in fact work out to be for the maximum benefit of all.

The government policy of non-intervention, or *laissez-faire*, that Smith was advocating was at odds with the economic practice of most governments of his day, which sought to control economic activity in great detail. They protected home industry with high import duties, granted legal monopolies, and allowed a multitude of internal barriers to trade to exist between regions.

It took time for Adam Smith's ideas to influence government. But such influence was inevitable in the long run, since they chimed so well with the wishes of the new class of industrialists who were creating Britain's Industrial Revolution. To a great degree, it was the followers of this group that gave a new radical liberalism (though not of the revolutionary kind) a certain respectability in the early nineteenth century.

Laissez-faire liberalism

It was the coming together of the ideas of Adam Smith and later economists who followed his ideas (known as the 'classical economists') with the traditional Whig-liberal ideas of civil rights and limited government, that created the foundations of laissez-faire liberalism, sometimes called 'classical liberalism'. Economic *laissez-faire* combined with notion of civil rights and toleration implied a wider vision of people being free in all aspects of their lives; which, like economic freedom, would be for the ultimate benefit of all. The vision was of a society based upon voluntary agreement between free rational beings; that is, a society based upon contract instead of upon traditional authorities, hierarchies and ways of doing things. The picture is of a free society of self-reliant, responsible, productive individuals, possessed of equal rights, creating a prosperous society with the minimum of government involvement.

This is a very different picture of an ideal society from that of establishment Whig thought where traditional hierarchies based on wealth and social status are the guardians of the people's rights. Free market liberals saw no need for such paternalism, nor for the aristocratic privileges that went with it; and least of all for the kind of aristocratic government of the few that this implied. The government of a free, self-reliant people would be representative of, and responsible to, the people, according to a constitution.

In brief, *laissez-faire* liberalism adheres to three basic principles:

- the free market
- the minimum state
- maximum freedom and responsibility for every individual

It has been a profoundly influential idea and is still so today. In the immediate term it was a view particularly strong among the new class of manufacturers and businessmen thrown up by the Industrial Revolution. Passionate about the free market, free trade and personal freedom, they were resentful at not being adequately represented in parliament and suspicious of aristocratic privilege. And since many were nonconformist, they were also resentful about the religious discrimination that still debarred them from universities and public office.

Bentham and the philosophical radicals

Although the term 'liberalism' has been used freely up to now, it was not until the early nineteenth century that the word began to be used to denote a political doctrine. The name began to be adopted at that time by some of the more progressive members of the Whig Party, and by those pressing for substantial parliamentary reform in the Commons, who were known as 'Radicals'.

The radicals of the revolutionary period, such as Tom Paine, were regarded as dangerous subversives bent upon destroying the social order. But in the years after Waterloo, the term 'radical' became gradually attached to anyone seeking parliamentary reform. These new Radicals were somewhat different from the earlier radicals of the revolutionary period. The sanctity of property was as essential to this form of radical liberalism as it was to the Whig version. It was a more 'respectable' radicalism. A small number were elected to the old pre-reform parliament. These were a mixed group but mostly elected by industrial constituencies and representing the new manufacturing class. Those who emphasised the free market and free trade as the answer to everything came to be known as the 'Manchester School' or 'Manchester Liberals'. But the most consistent and theoretical group of radicals were the followers of Jeremy Bentham (1748–1832). They called themselves 'Philosophical Radicals'.

Bentham founded a system of ideas known as utilitarianism. This was based on the idea that all human psychology could be reduced to the pursuit of pleasure and the avoidance of pain, from which it followed, according to Bentham, that all good was essentially pleasure and all bad was pain. It was further supposed to follow that the ultimate good for which we can strive is the greatest happiness of the greatest number. Bentham appeared to think that we all go about our lives making little calculations that set so many units of pleasure against so many of pain in deciding all that we do. People only behave badly, he thought, because they made bad calculations: they thought in the short instead of the long term.

The importance of all this for government, Bentham believed, was that it provided a means of evaluating good and bad laws, and good and bad institutions. The good government, armed with this knowledge, could make calculations of the amount of pleasure or pain caused according to what Bentham called the 'felicific calculus' (from 'felicity', meaning 'happiness'), and could then pass laws and create institutions that could shape and mould human behaviour for the common good. He believed that all existing laws, institutions and practices could be assessed according to these principles and, if found wanting, could be immediately replaced by better ones. He had no time for ideas of tradition and continuity that were so important in the political thinking of the day. The good society, he thought, could be set up very easily by using his ideas.

Originally, Bentham's ideal form of government had been benevolent autocracy, simply on grounds of greater efficiency. But when governments ignored his ideas he changed his mind. Influenced by his friend James Mill, Bentham became converted to popular government sometime around 1806.

Each individual, Bentham and Mill insisted, was the best judge of his or her own happiness. People should be as free as possible to pursue their own interests, which meant minimal government and minimal legislation; they believed that fewer laws automatically meant greater freedom. This included economic freedom, for they were also devoted to Adam Smith's free-market economics. People should vote on a wide, though not quite universal, franchise, for their representatives, who would then be mandated delegates: there to express the people's wishes. There would be no monarchy or House of

Lords. Many working men would have the vote, although Mill believed that they would vote for middle-class representatives, the professional and business middle classes being the most intelligent and competent section of society.

Bentham and James Mill, therefore, developed a distinct version of liberalism that was radical and democratic; although not in the French sense of deliberately changing society in order to make it more equal. It also differed from previous radical versions of liberalism in dismissing the idea of natural rights, which Bentham thought was not only nonsense, but 'nonsense on stilts'.

Bentham believed his system to be firmly based upon the empirical science of human behaviour; in fact a doubtful contention, although a common one at the time. There were other difficulties with his theories. For one thing, he believed totally that the greatest happiness of the greatest number would always coincide with free market liberalism. But what if it could be proved that the greatest happiness could be achieved by state intervention or the abandonment of other basic principles? This was an ambiguity at the heart of Benthamism, but it only became apparent later in the century.

In the early nineteenth century, Benthamism was the leading edge of a free market liberalism that was to dominate Victorian England and give it much of its essential character. It was the dominant creed of the rising commercial and industrial middle classes. The ideas of Bentham and Mill were disseminated by a body of disciples, including several influential MPs, who called themselves Philosophical Radicals. They met regularly and constituted a kind of early nineteenth-century 'think tank', giving public lectures, writing books and articles, and generally spreading the word. Benthamism was central to mid-nineteenth century liberalism, providing arguments and ideas, which influenced many who did not share the whole doctrine.

Laissez-faire liberalism and social class

Not all *laissez-faire* liberals were Benthamites. Partly this was because the age was a deeply and overtly religious one and many combined *laissez-faire* liberalism with evangelical Christianity. The atheism and soulless conception of human nature of Bentham and many philosophical radicals was unacceptable to considerable numbers who were nonetheless committed to the general *laissez-faire* doctrine. However, although *laissez-faire* liberalism also penetrated all parties and social classes, it was especially associated with the rising manufacturing and commercial classes that were becoming ever more economically and socially important. A number of theoretical developments within classical economics reinforced this class identification.

One of Adam Smith's most distinguished followers was the economist Thomas Malthus (1766–1834), famous for his *An Essay on the Principle of Population* of 1798 (1971). He argued that the growth of population would always outstrip the growth of the food supply. Thus, ameliorating the lot of the poor would always be self-defeating since they would simply have more children, which would keep them poor. Malthus' treatise was a deliberate counter to the utopian thinking and belief in progress common in some circles following the French Revolution. He demonstrated that such hopes were facile. He believed that Adam Smith had indeed perceived in economic freedom the means to the optimum prosperity for society as a whole, but he was less sanguine about the possibility of everyone sharing in it.

However, Malthus later put increasing stress on the possibility of population control through 'moral restraint', and the poor improving their condition by being more industrious, sober and acquiring the habits and outlook of the commercial middle classes. In general, the vision of a good society common among the free market liberals is one of independent responsible citizens, all equal and all pursuing their self-interest. It is a vision of a one-class society, with no poor and dependent class on the one hand, and no privileged class on the other.

Following Malthus (whose ideas became rapidly absorbed into free market liberalism) it was widely believed by liberals that the working class needed to be made industrious and independent, and this is why the Victorian Poor Law system was made deliberately harsh. It was made so awful that the poor who experienced it would eagerly change their way of life and become sober, responsible citizens.

At the other end of the social scale were the landed aristocracy, who saw their privileges as the reward for past merit and the continuance of their status and privileges as necessary to the stability and good running of the country. But increasingly Radical liberals saw things differently. They were influenced in this view by the economics of David Ricardo (1772–1823). Ricardo systematised the classical economics of Adam Smith, making it more rigorous and mathematical. He settled upon labour as the basis of all value (as a permanent feature of an object as distinct from its price), which was later influential in the Labour movement in ways Ricardo had not foreseen.

Ricardo, like Malthus, also discovered reasons for doubting that *laissez-faire* would automatically bring ever-increasing progress and prosperity for all. His analysis of the workings of the free market economy led him to conclude that land was a commodity like no other, and had the peculiarity that it was fixed. Consequently, as the economy grew and demand for land grew with it, owners of land could simply increase their rents; and since collectively they were in a monopoly position they could charge what they liked. Thus, in the long term all the wealth created by the energy and enterprise of those operating in the free market would tend to gravitate to landowners who had taken no risk and had not exerted themselves at all.

Ricardo's views tended to cast the land-owning class in a parasitic light, contrary to the traditional Whig view as the upholders of English liberties and good order. Ricardo's observations came at a time when the landed aristocracy, because of their dominance of parliament, had just passed a protectionist and anti-liberal trade measure which forbade the importation of the cheap foreign corn that undermined the high prices of British corn: the Corn Laws of 1815. This was blatantly a class measure which denied the working class cheap food and required industrial employers to pay more for labour and incur higher costs. The Corn Laws were seen by free market liberals as an abuse of power and privilege by the landed class.

This view of a selfish and parasitic aristocracy chimed with the view the rising commercial middle classes had of themselves as the most intelligent, productive and useful section of the population. James Mill extolled their virtues in just this manner. They were increasingly resentful at their exclusion from the political life of the country because of the electoral system, and the exclusion of many from public office and higher education by religious discrimination. They tended to see unjustifiable aristocratic privilege as the obstacle to progress and the creation of a good society. This was why people were not as free as they should be. It was the aristocracy who wanted to keep things as they were, to maintain their privilege and keep the people subservient. Further, they maintained that because the aristocratic system tended to breed subservience, instead of independence and self-reliance, there was a massive problem of poverty. The poor needed to be taught hard work and thrift and to value the benefits of independence, not subservience. In addition, wars and international conflict were associated with the aristocratic military ethic, while peaceful commerce would bring mutual benefit and understanding to all nations.

The 1832 Great Reform Act signalled a shift of power, away from the countryside and the landed class in favour of the urban and industrial elite, a shift reinforced by the abolition of the Corn Laws in 1846. The leaders of the Anti-Corn Law League, Richard Cobden and John Bright were both manufacturers and Radical MPs who embodied the new urban commercial and professional classes. Their outlook was by this time increasingly coming to dominate British society and British politics. It was the urban-based Radicals from these classes, especially the nonconformists, who were instrumental in the formation of the new Liberal Party and its programme.

The formation of the Liberal Party

These new industrial middle classes were poorly represented in parliament in the early part of the century. Only a handful of MPs, known as Radicals, sat for constituencies in those ancient boroughs that happened to have become industrial towns (like Oldham). Most industrial towns, including the largest, such as Manchester, Birmingham and Sheffield, had no MPs, while the middle classes in the counties were excluded from voting by a franchise restricted to landowners. However, by 1830 the Whigs at least had understood the need to enfranchise the new industrial classes, and Radicals and Whigs combined to push through the Great Reform Act of 1832, although Whigs and Radicals were often at odds thereafter.

By this time *laissez-faire* liberal ideas in general were influencing both the main parties, especially the Whigs who eventually became the Liberal Party. Traditionally, the Whigs were the party of liberal ideas, the party of moderate reform and of religious dissent, although its leadership was still dominated by Whig aristocrats who were suspicious of democracy. But the Tories were also influenced by liberal ideas. Their leader, Robert Peel, tried to modernise the party to attract the new commercial classes, but split it over the eminently liberal measure of abolishing the Corn Laws in 1846 in favour of free trade. By 1859 the Whigs, Radicals and Peelite Tories joined forces in what became the Liberal Party.

The union of Radicals and Whigs was a rather odd marriage. The Whigs tended to be aristocrats, while the *laissez-faire* liberals tended to attribute all the ills of the system to aristocratic influence. To *laissez-faire* liberals, aristocratic privilege was the greatest obstacle to the creation and the proper workings of the single-class society of independent prosperous citizens that they desired. Needless to say, the Whigs saw things rather differently and they held on to the party's leadership. Despite its rather aristocratic leadership, the new Liberal Party was very much the party of business people. Yet they still shared much with the industrial middle classes, such as a belief in the sanctity of property, which enabled the two elements to work together for a generation.

During this time the Liberal Party and *laissez-faire* liberal ideas dominated British politics. The key figure, who held the party together was William Gladstone who, despite being an Anglican landowner and former Tory (a Peelite), was the darling of the commercial classes and the nonconformists for his commitment to free trade, to reform and to moral causes. However, despite the strong theoretical belief in *laissez-faire*, liberal governments nonetheless felt obliged, even in the days of highest prosperity, to engage in interventionist policies to deal with social problems, such as public health, working conditions and education. As the century wore on, it was increasingly apparent that the simple belief that things would get better and better and all problems would be solved without government was simplistic. Liberal theorists began to diverge as they came to terms with this reality. The divergence is clear in the writings of two of the leading thinkers of the period: Herbert Spencer and J. S. Mill.

Liberalism and progress

In the eighteenth century, the idea of progress developed among Enlightenment thinkers; but during the nineteenth century it became commonplace. It is famously expressed in Tennyson's poem *Locksley Hall* written in the

1830s (and published in 1842): 'Not in vain the distance beacons. Forward, forward let us range, Let the great world spin for ever down the ringing grooves of change.' These lines express the contemporary belief in technological progress, while the following looked to the ultimate benefit of free trade: 'Till war-drum throbbed no longer, and the battle-flags were furled In the parliament of man, the Federation of the world.' Though in the Victorian period everyone believed in progress, with the mounting social problems of the second half of the century different liberal theorists began to respond in different ways, exemplified in the writings of Herbert Spencer (1820–1903) and John Stuart Mill (1806–73).

Herbert Spencer

Spencer linked laissez-faire liberalism to the theory of evolution as developed by Charles Darwin. That theory suggested that species evolved in circumstances of competition for food and other necessities of existence. Those individuals and types best adapted to their environment would tend to survive and increase at the expense of the less well adapted. It did not follow from this that the 'best adapted' were either necessarily the strongest, or were 'superior' to the less well adapted. But these were precisely the conclusions that Spencer drew, and which he applied to society.

Spencer's ideal society was one characterised by maximum competition and the 'survival of the fittest' (Spencer's phrase, not Darwin's), by which he meant the strongest and the best. The result was progress, seen in terms of ever greater social complexity and integration, and an ever diminishing role for the state. Spencer systematically and actively opposed any extension of government, and particularly any policies to deal with social problems such as poverty or the exploitation of women and children in factories and mines. That the weak should go to the wall was part of the natural evolutionary process, and so helping the poor and exploited merely interfered with the proper order of things and held back progress.

Spencer was influential in late Victorian Britain although his views became increasingly out of step with the main trend of liberal thinking. His ideas seemed to reflect the harsher, more competitive and aggressive world of the late nineteenth century when, in both America (where Spencer was especially admired) and Europe, the political right took up Darwinism to justify elitism and aggressive capitalism in terms of the right of the strong dominate. Curiously, Spencer himself was a man of delicate constitution and claimed that he never read views contrary to his own because that made him physically ill. He died in 1903 not having changed his ideas for half a century.

John Stuart Mill

J. S. Mill was Spencer's contemporary. He was the son of James Mill and had been groomed by his father from an early age to be the philosopher of the Philosophical Radicals. However, his narrowly academic education (reminiscent of Mr Gradgrind in Dickens' novel *Hard Times*) seems to have induced some kind of mental breakdown in John Stuart's early twenties. As a result, he came to the conclusion that utilitarianism had thus far neglected the spiritual, aesthetic and emotional side of the human being. He was influenced by the notions of individuality of the Romantic movement, which saw each human being as a complex whole, and each precious in their uniqueness (in contrast to the selfish pleasure/pain machine of Benthamite utilitarianism).

In working out the political implications of this new sense of individuality, Mill was influenced by two writers. The first was the German Romantic thinker, Wilhelm von Humboldt, who believed that the state was intrinsically inimical to the flourishing of individuality, and that people needed freedom to fully develop their individuality. This view lies behind Mill's difficult distinction between 'self-regarding' and 'other-regarding' actions. He argued that: 'the only purpose for which power can be rightfully exercised over any member of a civilised community against his will is to prevent harm to others' (*On Liberty* [1859] (1910). Only where an individual's actions affect the lives of others – that is, other-regarding actions – can there be a case for state regulation in order to prevent harm. Where an individual's actions are self-regarding, that is, affecting no-one but themselves, then the state has no right to interfere.

Mill went on to defend more specific freedoms of speech and thought, all on the grounds that they are conducive to progress. In open competition, he believed, truth will always drive out falsity. But he was particularly interested in individual beliefs and life-styles which must be allowed to flourish since they are the source of creativity and therefore also conducive to progress.

The other influence on Mill was *Democracy in America* [1840], (1968) by the French aristocrat, Alexis de Tocqueville (1805–59). Its picture of American democratic culture, with its tendency to elevate public opinion as some kind of authority, resulting in strong social pressure to conform, horrified Mill and created something of a dilemma in his attitude to democratic government. He thought in general that the coming of democracy was inevitable and right, and yet he feared what he called the 'tyranny of the majority' (a view that would have been incomprehensible to Bentham or his father, James Mill, who saw nothing wrong with social pressure or conformity). Liberals had long fought against the tyranny of priest and king, but none dreamed before that if everyone were free of these there could still be any problems.

J. S. Mill was, in consequence, a somewhat reluctant democrat. He believed in representative democracy as an educative force, since participation would, he thought, make for responsible citizenship and therefore was progressive. On the other hand, his whiggish fear of democracy led him to all kinds of devices to prevent government expressing the direct will of the majority. Thus, he argued that while every adult should vote, those with education should have more votes. Again, while parliament should represent all the people and have a final say on legislation, it should be drawn up by a legislative commission of intellectuals. In ways such as these, Mill sought to protect the individualistic, creative intellectual he so much admired and upon whom future progress, he believed, ultimately depended.

However, while passionate in his belief in individualism, Mill was among the first liberal thinkers to advocate state intervention, in areas such as education, factory acts, and so forth. In some of his writings, Mill even questioned the superiority of capitalism and the desirability of a society based upon economic competition that produced such wide divergences of poverty and wealth. Mill's thinking is not always entirely consistent, and he sometimes advocated contrary things in different writings. On the one hand, he looks backwards to the classical liberal demand for the maximum possible freedom and the minimum of state interference; on the other, he is unhappy if this leads to evil social consequences, such as poverty and ignorance, and is prepared to countenance state intervention to deal with them. His thought can be seen as moving towards a new version of liberalism, social liberalism, which developed in response to the changing world of the late nineteenth century, and which will be considered more fully in the next chapter.

A changing world

The mid-nineteenth century was the golden age of free market liberalism in Britain. From the late 1840s to the mid-1870s there was continuous economic growth and ever-increasing prosperity. Many thought this would go on indefinitely, since the secret of unending progress, free market liberalism, had been discovered. The Liberal Party, which was the principal political expression of these ideals, was the party of the hour.

The recession of the mid-1870s did not shake confidence unduly, but the much more severe recession of the mid-1880s did. There was widespread distress and the social problems that had been allowed to accumulate in the years of prosperity now seemed intractable. The optimism of the years of prosperity that a new age was about to dawn when all would be prosperous and independent, looked facile. The vast poverty and squalor of the many stood beside the vast wealth of the few. For many in the last quarter of the nineteenth century, society was sick and new ideas were needed.

The mood of disillusionment is caught in Tennyson's poem *Locksley Hall Sixty Years After* (1885), in which the central character of the earlier poem reflects in old age upon the hopes of progress of his youth. The end of war seems as far away as ever. There were new and terrible weapons and the age was full of menace. As to science and social progress he writes:

> Is it well that while we range with science, glorying in the Time,
> City children soak and blacken soul and sense in city slime?
> There among the glooming alleys Progress halts on palsied feet,
> Crime and hunger cast our maidens by the thousand on the street.
> There the master scrimps his haggard sempstress of her daily bread,
> There a single sordid attic holds the living and the dead.
> There the smouldering fire of fever creeps across the rotted floor,
> And the crowded couch of incest in the warrens of the poor.

But there is little faith that anything will be solved by increased equality and democracy. We should, give up shallow talk of progress:

> 'Forward' rang the voices then, and of the many mine was one.
> Let us hush this cry of 'Forward' till ten thousand years have gone.

Needless to say most people at the time still believed in progress, but not with the same total confidence as in the middle years of the century.

The last quarter of the nineteenth century was the period when the working class began to make an impact on politics and demand answers to social problems. The Liberal Party, whose principal appeal had been to the commercial middle classes, and as the party of reform, was the natural home of the working classes who wanted social problems tackled (trade union leaders for example were, at this time, all Liberals.) The fragile unity of the Liberal Party, however, split over Irish Home Rule in 1886, when most of the aristocratic Whig element and some radicals left the Liberal Party and went over to the Conservatives. But this was just one of many internal tensions. The age of the party's dominance was over and it had to look to new ideas to deal with a new world.

A new version of liberalism developed which in time captured the party. *Laissez-faire* liberalism declined, although it was to enjoy something of a renaissance in the 1980s it was a doctrine associated with the Conservative Party and not with the Liberals. Mainstream thinking had in the meanwhile moved elsewhere; and this is the subject of the next chapter.

5

New Liberals to Liberal Democrats

The Tories dominated British politics in the first quarter of the nineteenth century and Burkean conservatism was the dominant ideology. But the next fifty years were the age of classical liberalism and in this period the Whigs and Liberals enjoyed the lion's share of power. For most of the period, there was continuously growing economic prosperity, for many the living proof of the efficacy and truth of *laissez-faire* principles. But the long Victorian boom eventually came to an end and the final quarter of the century had a very different character economically and politically. What had appeared self-evident in the days of seemingly endless prosperity began to be questioned, new problems had to be tackled and new ideas were needed to provide a rationale. Mainstream liberal thinking began to shift its course away from individualism and towards a more collectivist stance. A new version of liberalism developed which at the time became known as New Liberalism, although it is now more often called 'welfare liberalism' or 'social liberalism'. Eventually, this new version replaced *laissez-faire* liberalism as official doctrine and has remained the central inspiration of the Liberal Party to the present day.

New Liberalism

The industrialisation of Britain and the rapid urbanisation that went with it created enormous social problems. By the 1830s all governments were recognising the necessity to intervene in areas like public health, factory conditions, education and provision for the poor. Increasingly therefore, Liberal government practice was not in line with theory, especially in respect of the minimal state. There were those, like Spencer, who railed against the growing collectivism on theoretical grounds; others deplored the interference with the free market that government intervention involved; but most could see the necessity. There was also the spur of a working-class electorate after

1867 and, towards the end of the century, the growth of socialist ideas and organisations.

Furthermore, the society of free, independent, prosperous individuals promised by *laissez-faire* theories was not being fulfilled. A stream of government inquiries detailed appalling conditions and exploitation in mines and factories, while ignorance and disease were common. Free market economics was still a central belief, but total *laissez-faire* as a social as well as an economic policy, which implied government should do as little as possible, began to be questioned. Governments were intervening, although in a small way, and so was local government, in the provision of facilities and services, such as baths, washhouses, libraries, parks and a host of other things.

By the 1880s the Liberal Party possessed a radical wing which was prepared to advocate a drastic extension of public intervention. In fact the doyen of this radical liberalism was initially Joseph Chamberlain, the Birmingham radical who had been at the forefront of municipal provision. He became a Liberal cabinet minister and was a strong advocate of further state collectivist measures. However, he left the party over Irish Home Rule and effectively joined the Conservatives, where he advocated collectivist measures. There were other liberals, though, who remained in the party and sought to push it in a collectivist direction for both moral and political reasons, believing the party had to appeal to the working class.

Initially all this was way ahead of current theory, but in due course theory began to shift. John Stuart Mill had already been prepared to sanction limited state intervention and even questioned economic laissez-faire, yet this did not sit well with the strong individualist thrust of the bulk of his writings. The first liberal theorist to strike out wholeheartedly in a new direction was T. H. Green.

T. H. Green

Thomas Hill Green (1836–82) was a young Oxford philosophy don, and also a local city councillor. He was influenced by German philosophers Kant and Hegel. Rejecting the conception of man as a pleasure/pain machine or merely as a being in perpetual pursuit of self-interest, Green offered an alternative conception based upon seeing human motivation in terms of self-realisation. He believed that we each have a complex nature that will unfold through time; one that is self-developed through our choices and how we fulfil ourselves in and through the moral community of which we are a part. Values and principles pervade the practices and institutions and communities in which we participate, including family, friendship, membership of organisations and citizenship. Participation involves moral obligations, which through fulfilling we fulfil ourselves, even when this involves self-sacrifice.

That we do feel these obligations and act accordingly is common human experience, despite the *laissez-faire* claim that self-interest is our only motivation. It is the ultimate purpose of society and its institutions, Green argued, to develop the moral character of its citizens, to develop their will and reason so that they may fulfil themselves as human beings. Indeed, history can be understood as the progressive self-realisation of mankind, through which man achieves his full moral stature expressed in social institutions and activities that progressively achieve the good life, with all contributing to the common good.

Green insisted that it was not laws that made people moral. The most the state may do is to create the conditions in which all citizens have the opportunity to genuinely exercise their will and reason; that is, have the opportunity for genuine choice. Thus, Green saw the role of the state as removing disabilities from people's capacity for choice. Such a view justifies state intervention in such areas as education, public health and factory acts. In respect of education, for example, he wrote that if denied it: 'the individual in modern society is as effectively crippled as by the loss of a limb'.

In terms of practical proposals, Green was advocating little more than what Liberal governments were already doing. He was sufficiently steeped in mid-Victorian liberalism to insist upon the virtues of economic independence, and see the salvation of the poorer classes in terms of acquiring middle-class virtues. He regarded aristocratic privilege as the great obstacle to progress and the fulfilment of mankind in the context of industrial capitalism. Like the most liberals of the time, he believed that industrial capitalism was the essential material base for a good society, and it was a question of allowing the poor and excluded the means to participate. Why Green was so important and influential (in fact much more influential than the better-known John Stuart Mill) was that he gave liberal thought a new way of understanding things, and a new vocabulary to go with it. The new way was to see society not as a collection of selfish individuals, but more of an organic whole, where we all have a duty of concern for, and to promote, the common good.

L. T. Hobhouse and J. H. Hobson

Between Green's early death in 1882 and the end of the century, a string of liberal intellectuals – writers, thinkers and rising young politicians – articulated similar ideas, while going increasingly beyond Green in their proposals. They all favoured greater state intervention in society and the economy in the name of removing the obstacles to full development. In these years liberal theory moved close to some forms of socialism which was currently undergoing an extensive revival. This was particularly true of the thought of two of the most radical and innovative of the new liberal thinkers, Leonard Hobhouse (1864–1929) and John Hobson (1858–1940).

Hobhouse was a distinguished academic sociologist and also a journalist. He saw the development of society in terms of evolutionary theory; but, unlike Spencer and other *laissez-faire* thinkers, he did not see competition as the mechanism of progress, weeding out the inadequate and 'unfit'. Social progress was achieved rather through ever greater co-operation. *Laissez-faire* belonged to an earlier and lower stage of human social and moral development. Good citizenship, concern for others and co-operation for the common good were the marks of a higher stage of social evolution. Ultimately, the ideal society would be based upon co-operation and harmony and not competition.

Following his friend, John Hobson, Hobhouse did not see capitalism as an inherently good system within which the poor needed to be helped to compete. Capitalism, on the contrary, was an inherently flawed system that produced poverty, exploitation, squalor and other social ills as side-effects, that the state needed to step in and correct. High taxes were necessary and could be justified by the fact that no-one could produce a fortune through free enterprise on their own; society was needed, and society was consequently entitled to its share of the wealth created.

Hobhouse believed that the state should not only provide an extensive system of welfare, but should also guarantee a decent standard of living for every citizen; although beyond this, guaranteed minimum incomes should vary to take account of differences of energy and talent. To the charge that this was not liberalism but socialism, Hobhouse argued, in his *Liberalism* [1911] (1964) that his conception of a better society was a fulfilment of liberal ideals and not a denial of them.

John Hobson was an economist who argued that capitalism, far from creating an optimal distribution of goods as classical economics taught, inevitably tended to create a situation of vast wealth for the few and poverty for the many. This was not only immoral, and a denial of the necessary role of society in the creation of wealth, but was in fact bad for the economy. With a more equitable distribution of wealth there would be more demand for goods and more prosperity all round. Capitalists would not then have the same compulsion to exploit the colonial world in search of profits which Hobson saw as the major source of imperialism and international conflict.

Hobson was prepared to see extensive state intervention in the economy, including nationalisation, and a considerable degree of redistribution of wealth through the taxation system. After the First World War he joined the Labour Party, although he remained at heart a social liberal. Before then, however, New Liberalism had inspired a remarkable era of social reform, which laid the foundations of the modern welfare state.

New Liberalism and the liberal tradition

Laissez-faire liberals protested that the new 'social liberal' thinking and the new policies were a betrayal of liberalism. And these sentiments were echoed by Thatcherite 'neo-liberals' in the late twentieth century. However, those who were developing New Liberalism, as it was called at the time, did not see it as a betrayal but rather as a fulfilment of liberal ideals.

The critical departure of the New Liberals from the *laissez-faire* tradition was their rejection of the ideal of the minimal state and the general suspicion of the state as a necessary evil, which should legislate and tax as little as possible. New Liberals argued that the state may have been the enemy of liberty in the past, but that was when it was under aristocratic control. As the state became more democratic and bureaucratised it automatically became more benign and might be trusted to use its power to alleviate the social evils attendant upon industrial capitalism. Good legislation and efficient administration, the argument went, could promote freedom, as could higher taxation if put to good use. The policies of state intervention to provide welfare and prevent exploitation may have had much in common with socialism, yet remained distinctly liberal because individual liberty was still the central ideal.

The argument was that people are not free to develop themselves and participate fully in society if they are forced to live in squalid conditions, are overworked for starvation wages or have no opportunity for education. The state must therefore intervene to make up for the deficiencies of the free enterprise system by taxing the well-off to pay for welfare for the worst off. Thus, collectivist state intervention was justified in terms of removing obstacles to free individual development and extending equality of opportunity.

Human nature and freedom

Behind this New Liberal conception of the good society lies a different conception of human nature from that which animated the *laissez-faire* view. It is a conception that goes back to the Romantic movement in Germany, and was introduced into British thinking by J. S. Mill. It is the view that we are all unique individuals, with our own unique array of characteristics and talents. The purpose of life is to fully develop and express our individuality. The purpose of the good society is to provide the optimum conditions in which individuals can fully develop themselves in a rich diversity of human life. Mill argued that it is only through society's encouragement of such diversity that there can be human progress. In the opening of *On Liberty* [1859] (1910) Mill quotes the German Romantic thinker and educationalist Wilhelm von Humboldt: 'The grand, leading principle, towards which every argument unfolded in these pages directly converges, is the absolute and essential importance of human development in its richest diversity'.

This is a view of human nature very different from the *laissez-faire* liberal view of individuals as selfish egoists in pursuit of their own interests, still less the pleasure/pain machine of Benthamism. This is the Romantic view that human beings are not all basically the same with the same motives and drives, but each is unique and special. The whole point of freedom in this view is not to pursue self interest but to fulfil each individual's unique nature. This suggests a quite different role of government, as one where it seeks to create the conditions for everyone to fulfil themselves, which may mean intervening to remove the obstacles to them doing this. Such obstacles might be ignorance or exploitation or squalid conditions.

Along with this new view of human nature, as compared with the *laissez-faire* view, went a new view of freedom. Freedom was not simply doing as one wished or pursuing one's selfish concerns. That was merely negative freedom. Genuine freedom, it was argued, was 'positive freedom', when people had the opportunity to fulfil themselves. Green argued that people were truly free when they overcame their selfish concerns and co-operated for the common good.

Triumph and decline

The impact of New Liberal thinking was far from immediate. In the 1890s especially after the resignation of Gladstone, the Liberal Party was weak and divided. It had split in 1886 over Irish Home Rule, losing many traditional Whigs and some radicals. There was also the loss of some middle-class business support, that continued to gravitate to the Conservative Party, especially as the party tried to court the working class more and more.

More than any other single influence it was religious nonconformity that was the social base of the party by this time, together with many single issue constituencies. There was little unity. Around the turn of the century the chief whip of the time complained that the party was 'plagued by obstinate faddists' whom the leadership could not control. These were groups preoccupied with one issue, such as disestablishment, temperance, land reform and so on, at the expense of the party as a whole. Gladstone's obsession with Irish Home Rule had, perhaps, set the tone. The voice of New Liberalism, the radical progressive wing of the party, was growing in influence, but not at the higher levels of the party.

Welfare reform

Despite the disunity of the party, the Liberals won a landslide victory in January 1906, largely as a result of the Conservatives' massive unpopularity. Campbell-Bannerman, the new Liberal prime minister, had little interest in social reform which had played little part in the party's election programme. It was only after Herbert Asquith became prime minister in 1908, and Lloyd George and Winston Churchill were promoted to the cabinet, that New Liberalism became the inspiration of the government. After 1908 the government introduced a series of New Liberal measures which were the first beginnings of the modern welfare state; they included old age pensions, school meals, the beginnings of medical and unemployment insurance for some workers, and labour exchanges. All were paid for by progressive taxation and therefore involved a modest redistribution of wealth.

There might have been more along the same lines, but the First World War intervened. During the war the Liberal Party split and began a steep decline. There were Liberals in the Labour coalition governments of 1924 and 1929–31, and the subsequent National government, but there would not be a Liberal government again. In the 1930s the party split once more, with free trade Liberals, protectionist Liberals and Lloyd-George's own group. The party nearly died.

It might be wondered why a party that has contributed so much to British politics for so long, both practically and theoretically, and indeed still had important ideas to contribute, should suffer such a catastrophic decline.

Liberal splits and the rise of Labour

The Liberal Party, much more so than the Conservative Party, was a coalition of sometimes conflicting views and interests. It was thus prone to internal divisions and splits. One such was over Home Rule for Ireland, splitting the party in 1886. Another source of division came from working-class supporters of the party who were dissatisfied with the party's programme which they felt should be more collectivist. Progress in this direction was prevented by middle-class businessmen still committed to *laissez-faire*. Furthermore, middle-class Liberal constituency associations were often unwilling to select able working-class candidates. This led to a certain amount of frustration among the working class supporters of the party.

In due course, despite that fact that many trade union leaders were committed Liberals, the Labour Party was formed largely at the instigation of the unions, as a party that would promote and protect the interests of the working-class. The Liberal Party and the Liberal government after 1906 co-operated a good deal with the new Labour Party. But when the Liberal Party split during the First World War between the supporters of Asquith and Lloyd George, the Labour Party was poised to replace it as the country's second party of government.

Deeper causes of decline

However, there is more to the Liberal Party's decline than the accidents of personalities and events. For one thing, similar parties in other countries suffered a similar fate. Liberal parties in other European countries (such as the Free Democrats in Germany) are usually small centre parties as the Liberal Party in Britain became. This suggests, therefore a more general explanation that applies in other countries.

As was suggested above (Chapter 2), the last decades of the nineteenth century saw the beginning of a general realignment of politics along class lines, with the main line-up between the propertied and the propertyless.

Those with different kinds of property had hitherto supported different parties. Those with landed wealth the tended to support the Conservatives, while the commercial and industrial classes tended to support the Liberals. But with the advent of the working class in politics, thanks to the extension of the franchise, those with substantial property of any kind increasingly felt that they had more in common with each other than either had with those without property. The Liberal Party might have moved decisively to capture the working-class vote, but to do so would have meant changing its nature completely, and there were too many other interests represented in the party for that to be realistic.

Nevertheless, the party won a massive electoral victory in 1906, which seemed to suggest it was in good health. The Conservatives were split over protectionism and were deeply unpopular, and the Liberals still had the support of one of their biggest constituencies, the Nonconformist vote. However, religion was about to decline rapidly, leaving the Liberals without any secure electoral base. The Conservatives had the propertied classes and the financial support of business, while the Labour Party had the working classes and the financial support of trade unions. The Liberals struggled to find a place in between.

The continued development of New Liberal thinking

Despite the political decline of the Liberal Party in the years after 1918, liberal theorists continued to contribute new and important ideas to the political debate. Indeed, it may well be argued that it was the Liberals whose response to the economic troubles and social distress of the inter-war years was the most creative, and provided principles and policies central to late twentieth century politics.

The Yellow Book

After the end of the First World War there was continuous recession in Europe for a decade, followed by even worse recession after the American economy collapsed in 1929. Nobody knew what to do. Conservatives, following orthodox economic theory, insisted on doing nothing; and while the Labour Party had a vision of a new society with no more capitalism, they had no distinctive solutions for the immediate crisis, and stuck to orthodox economics as well. Beyond Britain, communism and fascism were developing in Europe, each of them arguing (with some plausibility in the circumstances) that capitalism and liberal democracy had both failed, and that their doctrines were the answer to the world's problems. Both attracted some support in Britain, simply because they seemed to have answers and to be getting things done.

The Liberals sought a middle way between fascism and communism, between conservatism and socialism, indeed between collectivism and individualism; a way that would appeal to and benefit both sides, while addressing the current problems. Their aim was to develop a humane capitalism that provided welfare and employment, yet was also efficient.

The most important document the party produced from intensive work on these problems was *Britain's Industrial Future* (1928), otherwise known as the 'Yellow Book', to which a number of the leading New Liberal thinkers, such as Hobhouse and Hobson, as well as younger figures, like J. M. Keynes contributed. The Yellow Book advocated extensive public works, political control of investment and credit as well as a publicly accountable Bank of England, plans for a public body to channel investment of capital into deprived areas, a minimum wage for each industry, measures to encourage workers' participation and share ownership, among other policies. The overall aim, beyond tackling the problems of the hour, was a modernised version of the old liberal vision of a one-class society of independent, self-reliant individuals, who worked yet owned property.

John Maynard Keynes

The key figure in the development of Liberal economic thinking was J. M. Keynes (1883–1946). He was a great economist and one of the most brilliant minds of his age. His main economic ideas are discussed in Chapter 3; what is important here is their connection with political ideas.

In advocating a government-managed economy, Keynes was seeking to save capitalism from itself. To many in the 1930s its demise was only a matter of time. Uncontrolled capitalism had produced prolonged and worldwide economic disaster that mankind could not tolerate and so it would have to be replaced with some other system. But Keynes believed that capitalism could be domesticated and managed by a benign government in such a way as to work for the community as a whole. Unlike the socialists he did not believe it needed to be abolished in order to create a fairer society; nor like the Conservatives, now increasingly the home of economic *laissez-faire*, that the economy should be left alone. Capitalism still provided the best environment for freedom, variety, initiative and opportunity, but only if it was controlled and its destructive potential neutralised. The alternative was economic distress leading to social disorder, and perhaps to totalitarianism, as was happening in Germany.

William Beveridge

William Beveridge (1879–1963), though an active Liberal, was not part of the group of intellectuals who produced the Yellow Book, since at that stage he disagreed with Keynes' economic ideas. But he had changed his mind by the time he was asked by the wartime government to produce a report on standardising the current, very limited, welfare provision. He largely ignored this brief and produced a report in 1942 entitled *Social Insurance and Allied Services* (better known as the 'Beveridge Report') which envisaged a comprehensive welfare state, far in advance of anything currently advocated let alone provided. It was not a plan for harmonising arrangements existing at the time or before the war, but rather was a plan for what might be possible given the adoption and success of Keynesian economic policies; that is, full employment and steady economic growth.

Against this background, Beveridge outlined a system of social security 'from the cradle to the grave' where poverty would be eliminated along with its attendant evils of idleness, squalor, ignorance and unnecessary disease. It sounds socialist and it was a socialist government that subsequently implemented it, but it was fully in line with New Liberal thinking, and was inspired by some distinctly liberal notions. Crucially, it was not to be system of payments to the poor, according to need and financed out of general taxation, but one based on the principle of insurance, upon payment during employment in order to cover periods of unemployment and ultimately old age.

This was deliberately designed to preserve the notion of self-reliant individuals making provision for themselves (albeit in a scheme run by the state); and indeed the principle of universality, with the same payments, benefits and services for all whether rich or poor, was inspired again by the traditional liberal ideal of a single-class society of such independent individuals. There was to be a system for the very poor who had not made sufficient national insurance contributions, but this was meant to be a fall-back for what was expected to be a small and dwindling minority, and to be paid at a level clearly lower than the benefits paid to contributors to the national insurance scheme. Beveridge meant his welfare state to be a distinctly liberal one.

Post-war liberalism

Keynes and Beveridge made a huge contribution to the post-war consensus policies which dominated British politics for a generation. Yet their enormous success did nothing to help the fortunes of the Liberal Party of which they were both members. The party continued to produce ideas and policies that were influential and subsequently adopted by other parties. Both Conservative and Labour came to adopt the Liberal policy of Britain's membership of the European Community; and both parties came to adopt environmental policies pioneered by the Liberals. Even the Labour government elected in 1997 has been implementing some of the constitutional reforms Liberals have been advocating, in consultation with the Liberal Party. A development indicating a considerable recovery in Liberal fortunes since the 1950s.

The Alliance and the Liberal Democrats

In the post-war period the fortunes of the Liberal Party itself reached their nadir, when it faced extinction as a serious political party.

Electoral fortunes

In 1951 the Liberal Party reached an all-time low of 2.5 per cent of votes and six seats in parliament. But thereafter a new generation, led initially by Joe Grimond, began a long slow recovery, with periodic by-election victories, new policies and a new strategy as a centre-left radical party seeking a general realignment of the left and centre of British politics.

The most significant leap forward came in the two general elections of 1974, when support for the two main parties slipped while that of third parties surged. The Liberals gained nearly 20 per cent of the vote, although thanks to the workings of the electoral system, which tends to penalise small parties, they won only fourteen and then thirteen seats. After decades of consensus politics the two main parties were moving apart to the right and left respectively. It was an opportunity for centre parties to flourish. Furthermore, Labour's move to the left after 1979 eventually led to a split, when much of its right wing departed to form the Social Democratic Party (SDP).

The SDP and the Alliance

No sooner was the SDP formed in 1981 than it formed an Alliance with the Liberals. In broad ideological terms, the Social Democratic Party were (with some additions) as much the heirs of social liberalism as the Liberals, and they were natural allies. Furthermore, in electoral terms, they would be fighting for the same centre-ground votes, and would thereby cancel each other out if in direct competition. A formal alliance was thus negotiated to divide the constituencies up between them and agree a range of policies.

At first this was enormously popular. A Gallup poll of January 1982 gave the Liberal–SDP Alliance 50 per cent of the vote, and the other two parties a mere 23 per cent each, suggesting the Alliance would win a general election with a landslide. However, other factors intervened, most notably the Falklands War, which massively boosted the government's popularity. Even so, in the general election of 1983 the Alliance gained just over a quarter of all the votes cast (26 per cent), and nearly as many as Labour (28 per cent), but while the Labour Party won 209 seats, the Alliance won a mere 23. The two-party system had been saved by the electoral system and the Liberals were denied a role in politics commensurate with the level of their support.

The election of 1987 had a similar result, but following it, the Liberal leader suggested a merger between the Liberals and the SDP, which most members of both parties wanted, but the SDP leader, David Owen, did not.

A ballot was held producing a majority in favour of merger to form the Liberal Democratic party but David Owen and some of his fellow SDP MPs refused to accept it. The bitterness and rancour that followed was in sharp contrast to the earlier talk of partnership and parties working together to form new politics. Opinion poll support plummeted and in the 1989 European elections they came fourth behind the Green Party. For the third time since the 1930s the Liberals suffered a near-death experience. From its low point in the late 1980s the party began a slow recovery. David Owen's SDP faded away and the new Liberal Democratic Party did moderately well in the 1992 election under Paddy Ashdown. The subsequent unpopularity of the Conservative government helped all opposition parties including the Liberal Democrats, and in the 1997 General election the party won 46 seats, twice the number of any previous election since the 1930s.

Liberal Democrat thought and prospects

After 1945 the Liberals had the task of rethinking their ideas, constructing a new strategy and carving out a distinctive position and programme. This was substantially achieved, although a major revival of Liberal fortunes has been elusive. Nevertheless, a degree of electoral success in the late 1990s offers the best prospects for major advances in fifty years.

A new strategy

Late twentieth-century Liberals are social liberals. They are the heirs of Edwardian New Liberalism and its culmination in the thought of Keynes and Beveridge. But by the 1950s so too were the two main parties who accepted the post-war consensus based on the New Liberal ideas of Keynes and Beveridge. These two parties had implemented Liberal ideas and took the credit for their success because they were supported by massive class voting. Since the two main parties were so close together in policies the Liberal Party faced the problem of providing a distinctive outlook and policies.

The revival of the party under the leadership of Joe Grimond in the late 1950s included a redefinition of the party's stance. It henceforth defined itself as a left-of-centre, radical, non-socialist alternative to Conservatism. Along with this went a strategy of working towards a 'realignment of the left', based upon the Labour Party splitting into two parties. The traditional socialists would be in one party and the social democrats in another; the latter, in due course, joining in some form of permanent alliance with the Liberals. This possibility has been a persistent theme of liberal thinking ever since.

Decentralisation and Europe

The key policy theme of the revived Liberal Party, within the broader context of managed, welfare capitalism, was decentralisation. That is, the diffusion of power downwards to the people. This has remained central a part of liberal thinking. The implementation of the ideas of Keynes and Beveridge massively increased the power of the state to influence people's lives, reinforcing a pre-existing trend. Liberals insist upon the need to counteract these developments by devolving and decentralising power, through pluralism and participation, so that people are involved as much as possible in decisions that effect their lives. Liberals believe that this is something that should not be left to the Labour or Conservative parties, who are much too statist and ultimately authoritarian in their outlook.

The theme is an old one. Ever since the formation of the Whigs, the party, in its various manifestations, has been the party of constitutionalism: constitutional monarchy, greater democracy, devolution and decentralisation and other reforms according to the needs of the time. This persistent constitutional theme manifests itself today in the Liberal calls not merely for greater decentralisation, but for both national and regional devolution, federalism, a written constitution, a bill of rights, electoral reform, freedom of information and other matters. Electoral reform would be of vast benefit to the Liberal Party, but it is fully in line with Liberal principles and traditions.

Belief in institutions has traditionally extended to the international level, combined with a belief in the virtues of international co-operation for the sake of peace, a belief that was a feature of Gladstonian liberalism. The Liberals have been long-standing supporters of the United Nations and other international bodies for the promotion of peace and the establishment of a constitutional order in world affairs. The Liberals were also the first significant party to embrace the European Community and advocate British membership. Other parties eventually followed suit, but today the Liberal Democrats are still the most ardent Europeans, and the only party to be unequivocally in favour of a European currency.

Community, individualism and the SDP

The Liberal Party has been consistently portrayed as a centre party; Liberals do not see themselves in this light, but rather as a radical left-of-centre party whose major themes do not fit easily into the left–right spectrum at all. This is true of Liberal demands for constitutional reform and decentralisation and of the Liberal commitment to European integration and internationalism, but also applies to a variety of other issues, such as the environment, and to its concern for community. It is especially true of Liberals' opposition to class politics generally, represented by the two-party system, and the industrial system. Liberals are long-time supporters of industrial democracy, with workers as shareholders and directors. Again there is the theme here of people being involved in the decisions that affect their lives. Another theme is concern for the community.

In the 1960s Liberals claimed to be developing a new style of politics known as 'community politics', where local people are encouraged to work together to solve local problems and campaign on local issues. This proved a means for local Liberals to build support in areas where local Conservative and Labour parties were moribund and taking their constituents' votes for granted (Liverpool, for example). It helped to build Liberal grass-roots support but was also fully in line with the Liberal ideal of a more participatory society and a more active citizenship where individuals and communities take greater control of the own affairs.

The stress on community does not necessarily detract from the party's traditional emphasis on individualism. The party has always had the reputation of being a party of individualists and the natural home of those sometimes regarded as cranks and eccentrics: vegetarians, naturists and those who want to live differently from the majority. It was J. S. Mill, the great Victorian liberal thinker, who famously defended and celebrated such choices. The party's reputation in this respect is the source of both embarrassment and pride.

One of the drawbacks of a party of individualists is that it tends to be difficult to control, a difficulty reinforced by the party's belief in grass-roots democracy. The Tory tradition of strong leadership and discipline from the top was not for the Liberals. This was reflected in party structure, which was federal, with a great deal of local autonomy. party conferences could be as unruly as the Labour Party's, and often overturned the leadership's policies. The Liberal Party was the first to adopt full democracy in the election of their leader (David Steel) in 1976.

The Social Democrats came from a different tradition. Although sharing many of the policies and principles of the Liberals, they tended to be more centrist and less suspicious of the state, reflecting the Fabian inheritance. Nevertheless, they did share many important ideas which were part of a common tradition of social liberalism. What the SDP did bring with them was a notion of a more professionally managed, more centralised and disciplined party than the Liberals had had before.

The doctrine of the Liberal Democratic Party in the 1990s has arguably stronger roots in its past than any of the other major parties. It is in line with traditional liberal ideas going back to seventeenth century: including constitutionalism, tolerance and equality of rights, but modified by a later conception of human nature and the role of society in fostering individual self-development.

Future prospects

Between the general elections of 1992 and 1997 the Liberal Democrats made considerable progress. They won their first seats in the European Parliament and overtook the Conservatives as the second party of local government in Britain after Labour. Furthermore, they collaborated with the Labour Party on a number of constitutional issues such as Scottish devolution.

The election of 1997, despite a Labour landslide, opened up a host of opportunities for Liberals: devolution, limited proportional representation, and shared Labour/Liberal views on a number of other constitutional questions. Prior co-operation with the Labour Party on constitutional issues earned the party a seat on the cabinet committee dealing with these matters. Proportional representation, the party's 'holy grail', has been secured for European elections and for devolved parliaments in Scotland and Wales, while a commission was set up to study the possibility of proportional representation for Westminster elections. These developments together give the Liberal Democrats their best prospects for more than sixty years.

A realignment of the left is a possibility with proportional representation and the two left-of-centre parties working together to the exclusion of the Conservatives. The two parties are close on many issues. Indeed, it now seems that in their promises on higher taxes and public expenditure the Liberals are somewhere to the left of the Labour Party. In the wake of the 1997 election and subsequent co-operation, some have argued that a long-term arrangement or even merger of the two parties are realistic possibilities for the future. Some Liberals have voiced concerns that the Liberal Party may become an adjunct of Labour and lose its identity. But then as a distinct organisational and ideological entity, the Liberals have shown extraordinary powers of survival since their last days of real power at the beginning of the twentieth century.

6

Traditional conservatism

The Conservative Party has undergone profound changes in its outlook and beliefs. Traditional conservatism has been largely displaced by Thatcherite conservatism as the party's main ideological stance. However, this older conservatism dominated Conservative thinking before the advent of Thatcherism and will, some believe, dominate it long after Thatcherism has gone away. Others disagree and insist that traditional conservatism is dead and cannot be revived as a complete ideology. Yet some of the attitudes and themes of traditional conservatism are perennial and were expressed as far back as the ancient world; they were part of the outlook of the old Tory Party that emerged along with the Whigs in the 1670s.

Conservative ideas were not, however, put together as a coherent doctrine, a modern ideology, until the French Revolution, when the kind of values conservatism stood for, hitherto largely taken for granted, came under threat. This doctrine was first set out by Edmund Burke (1729–97), a writer who was not an English Tory, but who was an Irishman and a Whig.

Tories, Whigs and Edmund Burke

The Tories, along with the Whigs, were founded at the time of the 'exclusion crisis' in the 1670s when the great political issue was whether King Charles' Roman Catholic brother, James, should be excluded from the succession to the throne. The Tories supported James, but when he became king he sought to rule without parliament and return Britain to the Catholic fold. The Whig-led Glorious Revolution of 1688–9 ensured a Protestant succession and kept the Tories out of power for most of the next hundred years.

Toryism

The Tories, it might be said rather simplistically, were the heirs of the royalists of the Civil Wars. Above all they defended the authority of the king against those who upheld the privileges of parliament and thereby sought to limit the king's power. It was the Tories who upheld the doctrine of the divine right of kings and backed the Stuart kings in their assertion of it. They did this despite their concerns over James II's Catholicism. The Tories were also the great upholders of the Church of England against the dissenters who were supported by the Whigs.

Despite being shown little favour by the later Stuart monarchs and still less by the early Hanovarians, the Tories continued to stand by their assertion of the royal prerogative. Their conception was of a monarch with divine authority to rule, who would be advised by a parliament representing all the interests of the country; not as the Whigs would have it, as a partnership in ruling between king and parliament. The king was seen by the Tories, in somewhat medieval fashion, as the head of a God-ordained social hierarchy.

However, by the time the Tories were again in office these views were out of date. The divine right of kings was no longer taken seriously, while the notion of a God-given social hierarchy hardly made sense in a rapidly changing society. However, a few years after King George III brought the Tories back to power in 1784, the French Revolution began, which transformed British politics and occasioned Edmund Burke's fierce and brilliant attack on the French revolutionaries and all they stood for.

Burke was a Whig, but while many of his party were, initially at least, sympathetic to the French, and the Whigs continued to be the party of moderate reform, Burke passionately attacked the French for destroying an established way of life. He lauded the British constitution and gave a coherent defence of traditional values. In due course the Tories adopted Burke's ideas and they became the foundation of modern conservatism. His ideas need to be considered in some detail.

Burke's organic view of society

Burke's conservatism is most fully and eloquently set out in his *Reflections on the Revolution in France* of 1790 (1969), in which he fiercely attacked the revolutionaries of Paris for the mindless destruction of what they did not understand for the sake of an abstract theory which was for all practical purposes useless and dangerous. An extremely complex social organism was being obliterated in the name of some vague idea that human beings had certain natural rights whose existence nobody could prove. The result could only be bloodshed and chaos (Burke wrote before the deposing of the king and the Terror). These origins are significant. Traditional conservatism is, to put it very crudely, a defence of the status quo, of the established order of things, against radical or revolutionary change. It is a sophisticated defence that traditional Conservatives today still express in essentially Burkean terms.

Traditional Conservatives reject the idea that society is like some sort of machine that can be broken up and reassembled at will. Society, they insist, is much more like a living organism, which cannot just be cut up and rearranged to suit some theory. Society is infinitely complex and interconnected, so that changing one part of society affects every other part and may do so in any number of unforeseen ways, probably most of them bad. Sudden or radical change is therefore bound to lead to disaster and chaos because its consequences cannot be controlled. Conservatives are always suspicious of change, while at the same time recognising that changing things is occasionally necessary. Society must be always adapting to new circumstances; but the organism must be allowed to evolve at its own pace. The politician can assist this process of adaptation with reform, though this must always be piecemeal and pragmatic in order to minimise any bad effects.

A stable and well-organised society is the work of centuries. It is built out of institutions, such as the family, church, private property and local communities. It is through these institutions that individuals have rights, and also obligations, and are bound together in an established pattern of living that embodies long-held values and is sustained by custom and tradition. It is custom and tradition, and even prejudice, that are the best guide to action, since these represent the stored-up wisdom of the past. Relying on theory or 'pure reason' is a very poor guide.

Every established society is a unique achievement, and makes a unique contribution to civilisation. But this achievement is vulnerable to breakdown and destruction if subject to drastic change. Politics is the art of preserving what is best (i.e. conservation, hence 'conservatism') and adapting it to new circumstances. This cannot be done by following some blueprint or plan which gives a picture of the ideal society that can be achieved. Politics is a matter of experience and judgement, not the application of a doctrine as Jacobins, radicals, communists, fascists, and umpteen varieties of socialist have believed. Conservatives reject abstract theory in politics, which they call 'ideology', and claim to be non-ideological. Conservative principles, they argue, are pragmatic and derived from history and tradition, providing a guarantee of what does and does not work.

Inequality and order

The preservation of the established order implies preserving inequality. Traditional conservatives believe all should have the opportunity to better themselves, but the idea that everyone should be equal is anathema. People are unequal in talent and energy, and society has to reflect this. Besides, without differences of wealth and status there would be no incentive for people to work and strive. The fact there are different stations in life, and different social classes, is not something to be lamented; it is a functional necessity. Different people need to do different kinds of job, and be rewarded according to their contribution. Social class is essentially an integrative feature of society, not a divisive one as the socialists think. As with any living organism, all the parts must work together in harmony if the organism is to be healthy. The task of government is to maintain that harmony.

Conservatives place special value on order and stability, and the social hierarchy and discipline that these, in their view, necessitate: that is, some people need to be superior to others, and all should know their place. Property is vital to the maintenance of social hierarchy and is an essential bulwark of both order and liberty. They put little faith in unrestrained human nature or entertain much hope that it can be improved. Rational schemes to fundamentally improve the human condition, ideas for a better organised society that will solve all social problems, are viewed with suspicion. Greater faith is placed in established ways of doing things. Behind traditional conservatism is a conception of human nature as corruptible, flawed and imperfect. Theories that tell us that mankind can be perfected are dangerous illusions. There is a streak of evil that cannot be eradicated, and necessitates a firm framework of law and order. Hence authority, order and hierarchy, and the discipline that goes with them, are primary conservative values. They make civilised life possible, allow what is good in human nature to flourish, while minimising the effect of what is bad.

Patriotism is important to Conservatives, as is respect for authority and law, while good government and strong leadership are admired. Leadership is a key conservative concept; it is a skill which can be fostered and developed (for example in public schools) but resides most naturally in the traditional ruling elite who can command authority without engendering hostility.

Contrast with continental conservatism

British conservatism developed as a response to the French Revolution. This was also true in Europe where in France, Germany and elsewhere conservative ideas developed simultaneously. However, there are marked differences between the British and continental versions. In Britain there was a pre-existing and strong liberal tradition, which had become embodied in the constitution. Burke, it will be remembered, was a Whig and he articulated a Whig outlook, which meant he upheld traditional English liberties, constitutional monarchy and the Glorious Revolution of 1688.

In France and Germany, by contrast, liberalism was associated with the French Revolution. Their conservatism tended to be backward looking, advocating the restoration of a lost ideal. That is, a reactionary conservatism that not only wished to prevent all further changes but to turn the clock back. Such Conservatives have a picture of an ideal society, something which British Conservatives have tended to regard as unwise and unrealistic.

Later in the century, the European conservatism, although highly authoritarian and anti-democratic, developed a new populist appeal based on nationalism, militarism, and sometimes crude racism, and was thus still far removed from British conservatism. This harsh continental conservatism was associated in the twentieth century with fascism and was thereby discredited. It was not until the rise of Christian Democracy after the Second World War that Europe developed a form of moderate conservatism similar to that which existed in Britain.

Tories to Conservatives

For a period of almost fifty years, from 1783 to 1830, the Tories enjoyed a virtual monopoly of political power in Britain. The reason for this lay in the turbulence the French Revolution had brought, along with the wars and conflicts of its aftermath and the powerful forces of change they represented. The Tory commitment to keep everything as it is and resist all change was the general response of the ruling class, but also of a majority of the rest of the population.

This mood and outlook were caught and powerfully expressed by Burke in his *Reflections*. He gave Tories a sophisticated intellectual defence which revered tradition, exalted the British constitution and attacked on principle the use of abstract theory in human affairs. Burke did in fact allow for the possibility of cautious reform, but the Tories who adopted Burke's views tended to be more rigid. Change was regarded as the 'thin end of the wedge' and the whole idea of reform as 'revolution by instalments'. Coleridge, the great poet (who was himself a romantic and somewhat unorthodox Tory), described the Tory party at this time as a Cyclops with its one eye in the back of its head. The leader of the most hard-line Tories was Lord Eldon, the long-serving lord chancellor, who regarded any kind of change as wicked, even the abolition of slavery and hanging for petty offences.

Along with this attitude of resistance to change went a belief in the perfection of the British Constitution. The last old Tory leader, the Duke of Wellington, in one of his last speeches as prime minister said of the English parliament before reform, with all its rotten boroughs and other 'oddities':

> The English parliament answers all the good purposes of legislation, and this to a greater degree than any legislature has ever answered in any country whatever. It possesses the full and entire confidence of the people. I will go further. If at the present moment I had imposed upon me the duty of forming a legislature for any country, and particularly a country like this, in possession of great property of various descriptions, I do not mean to assert that I could form such a legislature as we possess now, for the nature of man is incapable of reaching such excellence at once, but my great endeavour would be to form some description of legislature which would produce the same results.

The British constitution was so perfect it could not possibly need changing. But while parliament may indeed have had 'the full and entire confidence of the people' during the Revolutionary or Napoleonic wars, by the time Wellington made this speech in 1830 there was widespread discontent. Furthermore, a generation was coming to the fore who were not obsessed by anti-Jacobinism.

Fear of Jacobinism had for a generation effectively put a stop to all reform, and all forms of working-class movements were repressed. Some cautious reforms occurred in the mid-1820s, but since then very powerful forces of change had been building up that, by 1830, could no longer be resisted. In 1830 there was a general election that finally brought the long period of Tory rule to an end. It was the new Whig government that forced through the Great Reform Act of 1832, and heralded an age of reform. The Whigs were the party of moderate reform. It was a party dominated by aristocrats, many of whom were unhappy with the reform of parliament, but recognised its inevitability. Radical ideas had by this time penetrated the wider ranks of the party, and even influenced some Tories.

In the early part of the nineteenth century the Tories had been little more than the party of the landed interest defending itself against change. It was Robert Peel (1788–1850) who first attempted to modernise the party, and lead it into coming to terms with the modern world of industry and urbanisation.

Robert Peel

Peel was successful in persuading the party to accept the 1832 Reform Act, and under him the party became known as the Conservative Party. He also sought to widen the party's support to include the new manufacturing class with their free market ideas. He thought the free market could be encouraged so long as it did not undermine existing institutions and social relations. Peel did not succeed, in that he split his party over the abolition of the Corn Laws in 1846. These had prevented the import of cheap food and kept agricultural prices high, and had been the great symbol of the power of the landed interest. After the split, some of Peel's followers joined the Whigs, and the surviving Conservative Party reverted to being a narrow class party of the landed interest. As such it had too narrow an appeal and remained out of real power for a generation.

Late Victorian conservatism

Liberal ideas and the Liberal Party dominated the middle years of the nineteenth century and the Conservatives had only a few brief years of shared power. But Conservative fortunes recovered after Benjamin Disraeli (1804–81) moved the party in a new direction.

Benjamin Disraeli

Disraeli gave the party a new vision as the party of national unity. This involved a care for the whole of society, including the problems of ordinary people, as well as those of high position who have a duty to rule. By the middle of the century most people felt that greater democracy was inevitable, probably through the efforts of the Liberals, as the Whigs were then called, to extend the franchise. Disraeli pre-empted this by persuading his reluctant party to pass an Act greatly extending democracy. This was the 1867 Reform Act which gave some working-class men the vote for the first time.

The idea was, in a sense, to form an alliance between the old ruling class and the working classes, against those who only saw virtue in free market principles, no matter what effect they had on the condition of the people. Conservative reforms to help alleviate social problems would be in sharp contrast to the destructiveness and divisiveness of *laissez-faire* capitalism, which was associated with the Liberals. This was Disraeli's conception of Tory democracy (although the phrase was not invented until shortly after his death in 1881). It is a concept of 'one nation' instead of the two nations of rich and poor that unbridled free enterprise was creating in his day. On this basis, Disraeli was able to claim that the Conservatives were the party of national unity and of the whole nation, unlike other parties who represented a single class.

One further dimension Disraeli added was that of empire. He depicted Britain, rather romantically, as having an imperial mission to bring peace and civilisation to distant lands. This was 'peace' through the assertion of national sovereignty, in contrast to the Liberals who sought international co-operation and tended to be hostile to notions of empire. Disraeli's imperialism was immensely popular, and along with concepts of Tory democracy and 'one nation' could appeal to all classes and conditions. It was a new and more populist conservatism that went beyond Burke, who had had little concern with the 'condition of the people' and still less with empire. It was a conservatism redolent with aristocratic paternalism and the values of the land-owning class, in sharp contrast with *laissez-faire* individualism, and yet designed for a new age of democracy, seeking a mass appeal.

Disraelian conservatism also represents the increasing influence of collectivist ideas in conservative, liberal and socialist thought in this period. 'One-nation conservatism' was designed to appeal to the newly enfranchised working class, over the heads of the middle class, and address 'the condition of the people' in the sense of tackling social problems. In his famous Crystal Palace speech of 1872 Disraeli said that the Tory party had three great objects: to maintain the institutions of the country; to uphold the empire; and elevate the condition of the people. On the last of these he said:

> The health of the people [is] the most important question for a statesman. It involves the state of the dwellings of the people, the moral consequences of which are not less considerable than the physical. It involves their enjoyment

of some of the chief elements of nature – air, light and water. It involves the regulation of their industry, the inspection of their toil. It involves that purity of their provisions... A leading member of the Liberal Party described this ... as 'the policy of sewage'. Well, it may be the 'policy of sewage' to a Liberal Member of Parliament. But to one of the labouring population ... it is not a 'policy of sewage' but a question of life and death ...

This collectivist dimension was an attractive contrast to the Liberal Party of the time with its preoccupation with the free market, and the needs of businessmen. Collectivist legislation usually meant interfering with somebody's property rights, as with slum clearance, to which the Liberals were opposed. The Conservatives thus developed the argument, maintained ever since, that they were the party of the whole country and not just one particular class as the Liberals were (and, later, the Labour Party). The aristocracy, Disraeli believed, were the proper rulers of the country, but it should be rule for the benefit of all.

Conservatism and capitalism

Disraeli did not embrace the free market in the way that Peel (and to some extent Burke) had done, yet by the end of the century the Conservatives were increasingly seen as the party of free enterprise. This was as much the result of what was happening in the Liberal Party as among the Conservatives. There was a split in the Liberal Party in 1886 over Gladstone's obsession with granting independence to Ireland. Joseph Chamberlain led the 'Liberal Unionists' out of the Liberal Party and joined with the Conservatives. Unionism has been a central tenet of Conservatism ever since. However, this change of allegiance was indicative of a more significant change, namely the move of the middle classes to the Conservative Party from the Liberals.

Hitherto, the Liberals had been the pre-eminent party of capitalism and business, but towards the end of the nineteenth century the Conservatives were taking over this role. This was partly a result of electoral reform and the growth of socialism, which revived and began to flourish from the 1880's onwards. With the recruitment of more middle-class members, especially from the world of business, the Conservatives increasingly adopted and defended classical liberal values and preached the virtues of free enterprise and individualism, and the horrors of state intervention and collectivism. The superiority of a capitalist society over a socialist one became a major theme. These free-market principles were, however, held within a framework of traditional conservative thinking.

There was, therefore, in the late nineteenth century a greater polarisation of politics based, one might say, upon a developing realignment which pitted defenders of property against those perceived to be its enemies, even though as yet the socialists had no representation in parliament. In such a realignment it was natural that the propertied, both landed and commercial wealth, should seek common cause in the same party. This was eventually to leave the Liberals stranded in the middle, trying to appeal to both sides with a more collectivist social liberalism.

The Conservative leader in the closing years of the nineteenth century, Lord Salisbury, was a partisan figure in this polarisation. He was in a sense, a class warrior: elitist, anti-democratic, defending property, trying to slow down any further extension of the franchise, and having little Disraelian concern for the 'condition of the people'. In consequence the Conservatives were a little closer to the continental right than they had been previously, or indeed have been since. This rather reactionary kind of conservatism dominated government until the party's massive defeat of 1906.

Tory democracy and tariff reform

During this period, Disraelian 'one-nation' conservatism was kept alive by a dissenting group within the party led by Lord Randolph Churchill. However, his notion of 'Tory democracy' seemed to mean little more than the deference and gratitude of the masses in return for some very moderate legislation on their behalf. The term was really more a rhetorical device, or 'demagogism', as Gladstone called it.

Joseph Chamberlain, or 'Radical Joe' as he was nicknamed, was a much more substantial figure. He helped to split the Liberal Party in 1886, and voted with the Conservatives on the issue of Irish Home Rule. His group was called the 'Liberal Unionists' and attached itself more and more to the Conservative Party. Chamberlain extracted a few minor concessions from Salisbury in return for his support. More importantly he became a cabinet minister responsible for the colonies. Unlike most radical liberals he was an ardent imperialist, but he also saw in imperialism the answer to Britain's economic and social problems.

Chamberlain argued that Britain was suffering because of increased international competition, and was too hamstrung to do anything about it because of a now inappropriate commitment to free trade. The result was economic decline, unemployment and social distress. The answer was to create an imperial economic system where a free trade partnership existed between Britain and her colonies which excluded the rest of the world. This would protect British industry and jobs and provide sources of raw materials and markets. This would mean the end of a general policy of free trade, with instead a policy known as 'tariff reform'. In 1903 Chamberlain was prepared to resign from the cabinet in order to conduct a crusade on behalf of tariff reform, a policy which split the party in two (as had abolition of the Corn Laws, essentially an issue of free trade, sixty years earlier). In this divided state, the party fought and lost the 1906 election. The party was subsequently captured by the tariff reformers, but the First World War intervened to eclipse the issue.

Return to moderate conservatism

Ten years out of office, the success of Liberal reforms and the coming of the First World War, all helped to restore conservative thinking to its 'one nation' tradition – a concern for the nation as a whole – and to dampen its antipathy to collectivism. In the inter-war years, extremisms of left and right (communism and fascism) made the Conservative Party again the party of national unity and moderate social reform, both in the figure of Stanley Baldwin, and in the young Harold Macmillan in *The Middle Way* (1938), and other writings. At the same time, the depression of the 1930s dragged the party (particularly as the senior partner of the National government) into ever greater state intervention, with national plans, regional aid, subsidies and protectionism. In due course these were to merge to form essential wartime measures for organising the economy and society for the purposes of survival and victory.

The Second World War and consensus

During the Second World War it was realised that there could be no postwar dismantling of government control, as had happened in 1918. There was all-party agreement on the need for intervention in the economy, policies to maintain full employment, and the development of a welfare state. However, Labour's victory in 1945 and subsequent adoption of social democratic policies, meant that the Conservative Party had to develop its own version of what became a common framework of social and economic policy, the post-war consensus.

The acceptance of the consensus policies could be justified in terms of traditional conservative thinking fairly easily. In the first place, they worked. They appeared to provide prosperity and full employment, and at least the alleviation, if not the elimination, of such social problems as poverty, squalor, disease and ignorance. They also appealed, therefore, to the paternalistic, 'one-nation' strand of conservatism. Furthermore, the acceptance of a modest degree of socialism seemed a small price to pay for the preservation of the free enterprise system. It involved a massive increase in the size of the state, but traditional conservatives have never been averse to the use of state power when they deemed it necessary.

Justifying the consensus in terms of party traditions was done for the Labour Party by Anthony Crosland, while for the Conservatives it was a group calling themselves the 'one nation' group of Conservatives, whose ideas were sometimes referred to as the 'new conservatism'. The leader of the group was R. A. Butler, and it included such figures as Iain Macleod and Edward Heath.

New conservatism

The basic idea of new conservatism was the interpretation of the consensus policies in terms of traditional conservative values and principles, in such a way as to make it distinct from, and more attractive than, the Croslandite socialism of the Labour Party. In social policy the theme was a rejection of universalism in favour of concentrating welfare on those in need, and giving the choice of public, private or voluntary provision to the rest. Economic policy rejected nationalisation and favoured free enterprise as the motor of prosperity, as well as the guarantor of freedom. Taxes should be as low as possible. People should be encouraged to pull themselves up and not become dependent on the state, with the reward of wealth and property for success. A property owning democracy was the ideal. Good education was the foundation of a meritocratic society of opportunity for all, allowing everyone to develop as far as their talent and energies would allow. The state had an important role in providing the economic infrastructure, but should not be excessively powerful or bureaucratic.

This new conservatism was pragmatic and realistic and yet in line with the tradition of Burke and the 'one nation' tradition of Disraeli, as well as the liberal inheritance. However, the consensus formula, whether interpreted through one nation toryism or Croslandite socialism, did depend upon the continuance of steady economic growth. Only growth could provide the resources for greater opportunity for all, and the room for some to 'make it' in a meritocratic way; that is, to make possible a process of 'levelling up'. No growth makes such an expansion of opportunity impossible, and the only way the to achieve greater equality is for there to be a process of 'levelling down', necessarily involving some kind of socialist redistribution of wealth. When, in the 1970s, the growth of the previous two decades ceased, and the economy was plagued by recession, unemployment and inflation, the consensus policies were undermined and new conservatism was undermined with them. It was this failure that opened the way for the 'Thatcher revolution'.

The Heath government 1970–74

In 1970 Edward Heath came to power convinced of the need for greater encouragement for market forces and less reliance on demand management. It was not that Keynesian economics (see Chapter 3) and the mixed economy were rejected, but that the balance was wrong. Britain's economic performance had been poor compared with international rivals, and this was put down to too much state intervention, planning, taxation, and high public expenditure, as well as too much trade union power. Consequently, there was to be no more incomes policy or, propping up of 'lame ducks' (large firms in financial difficulties). Instead, measures were needeed to help the free market work better, measures we would now describe as 'supply-side'. However, within two years there was mounting unemployment and the government reversed all its policies. It became known as the 'U-turn'. Incomes policy returned, and large subsidies for ailing industries were provided (even to the extent of nationalising Rolls-Royce and Upper Clyde Shipbuilders). There was also a massive injection of demand into the economy in a 'dash for growth'. In other words, there was a return to consensus policies. It did no good. Heath fell foul of another of his 'supply-side' measures, trade union reform. A miners' strike which led to a three day week, together with rising inflation, lost Heath both the 1974 elections and his job as party leader.

The Thatcher leadership

The Conservative Party voted for Margaret Thatcher because they wanted a new leader, not because they believed in what she stood for. She did indeed stand for something new: it was a new economics, a new social policy and an entirely new approach to politics that was very different from traditional conservatism. It was in fact much in line with Heath's original 1970 programme. That government was, from Thatcher's point of view, on the right track, but backed down when the going got tough. They were, in Thatcher's words, 'wet'. This is somewhat unfair on Heath and most of his cabinet, who were pragmatists in the best conservative tradition, believing that if something did not work, it was sensible to try something else. Thatcher, by contrast, was a true believer. She was convinced her free-market approach was not only practically sound but morally right, and the entire framework of consensus politics was dismissed with contempt.

When Margaret Thatcher won the 1979 general election, her views were still a minority in her party and even in her cabinet. But she persisted and, with determination and some good fortune, succeeded in turning her ideas into the majority view. Traditional conservatism, or 'one nation' conservatism as it was more often called, steadily lost ground and committed traditionalists or 'wets' gradually became a minority. Whether traditional conservatism may again dominate the party's thinking remains to be seen. But whether or not this may be, Margaret Thatcher undoubtedly brought about a revolution in the Conservative Party and in British politics generally.

Traditional conservatism versus Thatcherism

The advent of Thatcherism in the late 1970s seemed to call traditional conservative principles into question. This has given rise to a debate concerning the relationship between Thatcherism and the traditions of the party. Where some have argued that Thatcherite ideas are fully in line with at least some strands of past thinking, others have seen Thatcherism as a distinct and alien

ideology. The argument turns partly upon the place of free market capitalism in the party's traditional beliefs, and partly upon the extent to which
Margaret Thatcher rejected or ignored long-standing features of traditional
conservatism.

Free market principles and the conservative tradition

Until the final quarter of the nineteenth century, the Tory/Conservative
Party had been predominantly the party of the landed class, while free market principles were associated with the emerging commercial and industrial
classes and the Liberals. Nevertheless, there were Tories and Conservatives
who were influenced by *laissez-faire* ideas, including Robert Peel who wanted
to attract business people into the party. Peel's party followers were later to
join the Liberals. Disraeli emphasised the difference between traditional conservatism and the *laissez-faire* outlook of the Liberal Party. He saw *laissez-faire*
capitalism as destructive of community and tradition, which it was the duty
of a Conservative Party to uphold. He also pointed to the social effects of
laissez-faire in creating 'two nations' of rich and poor, which Conservatives
should overcome by social policies. Hence the origin of 'one nation' conservatism.

Nevertheless, in the closing decades of the nineteenth century more and
more business people moved from the Liberals into the Conservative Party,
which became the principal party of property. These business people took
their economic liberal ideals with them and in due course the Conservative
Party became the pre-eminent party of capitalism and free enterprise and the
natural home of those most passionate believers in *laissez-faire* liberalism.

From the end of the nineteenth century belief in free enterprise and the
capitalist system became central to the thinking of the Conservative Party.
However, these beliefs were held in place within a wider framework of traditional conservative thought. *Laissez-faire* ideas were largely confined to economic life, with notions of tradition and slow organic change applying to
institutions and social life. Despite the seeming failures of unregulated capitalism in the recessions and slump of the inter-war years, there were strong
opponents of any government interference in the free market who were Conservatives rather than Liberals. Writers such as Ernest Benn and A. M.
Ludovici were fierce in their condemnation of the collectivist trend. Some of
the most notable conservative thinkers of the post war world sought to
combine a strong commitment to traditional conservatism with a vigorous
defence of free enterprise. These writers included Michael Oakeshott
(1901–90) and Enoch Powell (1912–98).

Oakeshott was a distinguished academic philosopher who argued that the
role of theory in practical affairs was a false and distorting one, and that
practices such as politics are fundamentally misconceived when thought of
as putting some theory or programme or plan into practice (a very Burkean

point). Politics, Oakeshott maintained, is not going anywhere, not trying to achieve some ultimate destination, but is rather a matter of maintaining the civil association, which in its ideal form is a fairly fixed and predictable body of general rules which guarantee freedom for individuals to do as they please within the context of accepted and more or less permanent institutions. He was thus opposed to the welfare state and the managed economy, as these, he considered, were not the business of government. Controlling and shaping society by government could only end in confusion and loss of freedom.

Enoch Powell was a rising politician when he discovered monetarism long before anyone else in British politics. He began to advocate cuts in public expenditure and a withdrawal of government from direct control of demand and the vital importance of controlling inflation. He argued that there is a tendency in democracy towards inflation, because political parties compete to make promises to electorates in order to get elected, promises that inevitably involve higher public expenditure, which will cause inflation. But Powell combined his economic radicalism with a strong sense of nationalism and the maintenance of national sovereignty and cultural identity with all its traditional institutions and ways of life. It was his virulent crusade against immigration that made him notorious (and in some quarters very popular) as a politician. It also alienated him from many colleagues. His alienation was complete with his equally passionate opposition to Britain's membership of the EEC. He effectively resigned from the party in 1974 when he urged voters to vote Labour because they were the only party offering a referendum on Europe, and therefore an opportunity for Britain to withdraw.

Both Oakeshott and Powell combined a belief in the more or less unregulated (or certainly unmanaged in the Keynesian sense) free market; but both also believed in tradition, in the manner of Burke. Margaret Thatcher, however, was a self-confessed radical who wanted rapid change with little respect for people or institutions, however old, that might obstruct what she wanted to do. She saw the free market as the answer to all social ills, and the conquest of inflation as the overriding political objective, no matter what the cost in terms of the destruction of industries and unemployment. Traditional conservatives in her cabinet, such as Francis Pym, Jim Prior and Ian Gilmour, tended to call themselves 'one nation' conservatives to indicate their scepticism at the government allowing market forces free reign at the expense of jobs, instead of showing a Disraelean concern for the 'condition of the people'. These traditional or 'one nation' conservatives were characterised by Margaret Thatcher as 'wets' and steadily weeded out.

A group of traditional conservatives, of whom the most notable was the philosopher Roger Scruton, criticised the undue reliance on the free market. They believed that an ethos of competitive individualism undermined traditional values, practices and institutions, and the attitudes of responsibility and duty to the community upon which the state ultimately depends. Another critic, Ian Gilmour, has argued that with Thatcherism the Conservative Party became 'infected with ideology' and that unless it returned to its tradition of 'one-nation' conservatism was doomed to many years in the wilderness (Gilmour, 1997).

Theory, tradition and change

Traditional conservatives insist that their principles are practical and derived from experience. These are not self-evident truths or derived from some abstract theory about how society ought to be: what conservatives call 'ideology'. They are principles based upon what has been found to work over time and so embody the wisdom of previous generations. Hence the emphasis upon tradition, and the veneration of long-standing institutions and established ways of doing things. True politics is about the slow and gradual adaptation of society to changing circumstances; it is not about changing things to fit some theoretical ideal. Rapid change that goes along with ideology is unwise and potentially dangerous.

By contrast, Margaret Thatcher wanted change immediately. She had a picture of an ideal society based upon the theory of *laissez-faire* liberalism and she wanted it brought about as rapidly as possible. In traditional conservative terms Margaret Thatcher was an ideological politician doing precisely the opposite of what they believed to be true politics. Margaret Thatcher was notoriously impatient with arguments about tradition and gradual change, and had minimal respect for venerable institutions that stood in her way. The Conservative MP, Julian Critchley, once said of her that she could not see an institution without wishing to hit it with her handbag.

Thus, there is a strong case for arguing that Margaret Thatcher was not a conservative, at least not in a traditional Burkean sense. On the other hand, Margaret Thatcher did subscribe to certain values and attitudes associated with traditional conservatism, values and attitudes that nineteenth-century *laissez-faire* liberals did not share. These included nationalism and the willingness to assert national sovereignty, particularly marked in Thatcherite attitudes towards Europe. The maintenance of the Union of the United Kingdom has been another conservative theme to which Margaret Thatcher strongly adhered, as expressed, for example, in her hostility to devolution. Finally, while Margaret Thatcher talked of 'rolling back the state' in respect of the economy, she did believe that government ought to be strong to cope with its true tasks, as conservatives have traditionally thought.

Thatcherism constituted a new version of conservatism, a New Right conservatism, distinct from, yet related to, more traditional forms. It took those elements of *laissez-faire* liberalism that had been absorbed into conservative thinking from the late nineteenth century and elevated them to a dominant position in the doctrine. But it also combined them with more traditional elements and concerns, while being in conflict with others. It would not be accurate to say, as some have done, that Margaret Thatcher was not a conservative at all. On the other hand, those who maintain that Thatcherism is essentially an updated version of nineteenth century *laissez-faire* liberalism are not too far wide of the mark either.

7

Thatcherite conservatism

Margaret Thatcher was elected leader of the Conservative Party in 1975. She brought about an ideological revolution in her party, and yet she was not chosen on ideological grounds. Few Conservative MPs knew or cared about how her ideas differed from Edward Heath; they simply wanted a change of leadership. At this stage 'Thatcherism', as it came to be called, was still in embryonic form, and some aspects, such as privatisation, only really developed after she became prime minister in 1979. But from the beginning of its development as a political programme it was built upon an solid and elaborate body of theory, of which what is called 'neo-liberalism' was the central element.

Neo-liberalism

Thatcherite conservatism has been accurately described as 'neo-liberal' since it involves a revival of the basic ideas of *laissez-faire* liberalism of the nineteenth century. John Nott, one of Margaret Thatcher's senior ministers in the early 1980s, put the matter succinctly: 'I am a nineteenth century Liberal. So is Margaret Thatcher. That's what this government is all about' (*Guardian*, 13 September 1982).

A number of thinkers have contributed to this revival of early liberal ideas, including Friedrich von Hayek (1899–1992), an Austrian economist and social thinker who worked in Britain from the 1930s to the 1950s, and the American economist Milton Friedman, both much admired by Margaret Thatcher. This way of thinking had become fashionable in some quarters (especially in the USA) in the early 1970s. After the Conservatives' defeat in the 1974 elections, Sir Keith Joseph became interested in these ideas, and it was he who converted Margaret Thatcher shortly before she became Conservative leader in 1975.

Neo-liberal principles

Neo-liberalism is a complex set of ideas with many dimensions, but at the centre of them, and what links them with the classical liberalism of the past, is a passionate belief in three things:

- the free market
- the minimal state
- individual liberty and responsibility.

These ideas are believed to be closely interconnected. Free market capitalism is seen as an economic system uniquely capable of creating maximum wealth and prosperity, and at the same time as the only real guarantee of full human freedom. Both are only feasible if the government interferes as little as possible in the economy and in people's lives. From 1979 the Conservative government saw virtually all its policies as contributing to the encouragement of the free market, reducing the role of the state and extending individual liberty.

The benefits of the free market

The free market is thought to provide the best of all answers to an old problem. The human condition is such that human needs and desires are always far greater than the means of satisfying them. Given this situation of scarcity, what is the best means of sharing out the goods of the world: how is it decided who gets what? It is possible, for example, for the state to decide everything; or to have various kinds of controlled or managed markets. Neo-liberals claim that the free market alone can distribute the goods of the world with greatest fairness and efficiency.

They argue that the mechanism of supply and demand is the most efficient means of distributing goods so that the greatest number of people get the greatest amount of satisfaction. A good quality product of low price will always outsell an expensive poor quality product. Makers of the latter will have to improve quality and cut costs and price to compete. Thus, competition ensures the best quality at the lowest prices, and maximum efficiency among firms who must satisfy their customers or go out of business. There are always opportunities for the entrepreneur to prosper by finding out what the consumer wants and providing it. Consequently there is an opportunity for all to benefit, and the system ensures maximum prosperity for society as a whole. The system at the same time ensures the greatest possible freedom of choice and freedom of opportunity. Furthermore, the benefits of the free market apply in the international sphere. Free trade provides the most efficient distribution of wealth among nations, and a higher level of general prosperity than any controlled system could provide.

These benefits, it is argued, are possible only in conditions of maximum freedom. And this does not just mean economic freedom but social freedom as well. The free market system is, for example, inconsistent with feudalism, if only because a free labour market where all can sell their labour to whoever pays best is an essential part of the free market. Everything depends upon everyone being free to make economic choices. Above all consumer choice between competing suppliers drives the system; it determines prices which tell producers what to produce and investors what to invest in, as no other system can.

Adam Smith's 'invisible hand'

The free market, and the free society which it implies, presumes everyone does what they want within the law. It used to be assumed that social life could not exist unless the majority of people were subject to discipline and control within an ordered hierarchical society. Surely, it was thought, everyone pursuing their own selfish interests can only result in chaos. It was Adam Smith, the founder of classical economics, who first argued that chaos would not be the consequence, but ever greater prosperity. In his *The Wealth of Nations* of 1776 (1970) he wrote that the individual who:

> intends only his own gain is led by an invisible hand to promote an end which was no part of his intention. Nor is it always the worse for society that it was no part of it. By pursuing his own interest he frequently promotes that of the society more effectively than when he really intends to promote it.

Thinkers today prefer not to speak in quite such mystical terms but rather of the spontaneous order that tends to arise from free human exchange. Hayek in particular argues for the superiority of such an order in terms of freedom and prosperity from which all benefit, as compared to any kind of imposed order.

Inevitably in free competition some will succeed and others will fail, and there will be great inequalities of rich and poor. But all will partake to some degree in the general prosperity, so that the worst off will still be in a better position in a prosperous society than they would be in a poor one. It might be pointed out that the Victorian Poor Law was exceptionally harsh on those who failed. But at least for most neo-liberals, there would still be a welfare-state 'safety net' for the few; and even in the USA there is welfare or 'workfare'. The more extreme neo-liberals would have no welfare and rely entirely on charity. They would contend that if people, who are free and responsible for their own actions, fail and 'go to the wall' then so be it; it is not the business of government to make everyone happy and contented.

Against socialism

Whatever the disadvantages of the free market are seen to be, they cannot, neo-liberals claim, be compared with the state controlled systems that are advocated by various kinds of socialism.

Communism and social democracy

Communism is the most extreme example of a state controlled system. Quite apart from the oppression and violation of human rights, it has been an economic disaster. We have seen in the twentieth century how communist governments have decided what is produced, at what price, the levels of wages and salaries and so on; and we have also seen how the economic performance of such systems has been uniformly dismal to the point of collapse.

Free-market capitalism has been the main alternative to this, and it is beyond doubt that the free market has been the more productive and prosperous. But since the Second World War there have been two versions of free-market capitalism. First, there is leaving everything to the market; but this was discredited for a time (wrongly in the neo-liberal view), because of the Great Depression of the 1930s. The alternative of controlled capitalism, with governments pursuing the consensus policies of the mixed and managed economy and the welfare state, was pursued by most Western governments after 1945. Neo-liberals insist that this was a great mistake; that it was just a watered-down version of East European communism. This is why Margaret Thatcher spoke of eliminating socialism from Britain. The free market cannot work, it is insisted, if governments try to control or manage or plan it.

State intervention, along with inflation and monopoly, are thought to be among the main obstacles which prevent the free market working properly. Early nineteenth century liberals insisted that government should be confined to a very limited range of essential functions, such as law and order, foreign relations and defence, and maintaining a sound currency; everything else should be left to the free market. Modern society is far too complex for that to be possible. Nevertheless, latter day neo-liberals believe in reducing the role of the state to the absolute minimum, especially in relation to the economy.

Neo-liberalism is partly a reaction to the steady growth in state activity that has gone on throughout the twentieth century, and particularly since 1945. The greatest objection is to the dominating role of the state in the policies of the managed and mixed economy. These involved state ownership, state regulation, state economic planning, along with price control, incomes policy, regional policies and a variety of other forms of state intervention; all preventing the free market operating efficiently. Furthermore, state ownership meant state monopoly which, because of the absence of healthy competition, breeds inefficiency and neglect of consumer needs. Cushioned against failure, nationalised industries become increasingly dependent on state subsidy, wage increases cannot be effectively controlled because the unions know the government will not allow the industry to go out of business. This is also true of firms relying on state subsidy, whereas in a proper free market wage awards have to be within what the firm can afford or it goes bankrupt.

Planning and public services

Economic planning is also seen as inherently bad. The working of the free market depends upon prices being determined by millions of people making millions of decisions about what to buy or sell or invest or produce. Planning cuts across all this and implies that government knows better than all these millions of people. Interference can only distort the market and make it work less efficiently. Friedrich von Hayek has done most to develop this view of the market as a system of communication which deteriorates the more governments interfere. He is also largely responsible for the argument that planning forces people to do things they would not otherwise do, which is an infringement of their liberty. In his view all socialism, however mild, is incipient totalitarianism.

Neo-liberals also dislike public services. It might be argued that state-provided services are superior to privately provided ones because they derive from the motive of public service and not from that of profit. The neo-liberal answer to this is twofold, both a structural case, and a psychological case.

The structural case has been put succinctly by the Adam Smith Institute:

> The public sector is not exposed to the commercial pressures which generate an efficient operation within the private sector. For example a public operation which fails to satisfy its market does not risk bankruptcy in the same way that a private firm does. There is thus absent an important spur to efficiency. A public sector operation is usually protected by a complete or partial monopoly, and thus misses the impetus which the presence of competition provides. A private firm must constantly watch to keep its costs down and keep its output attractive, or it risks a competitor taking its market. A public monopoly knows few such pressures. Absent too, in the public sector is the impulse to innovate, to keep abreast of new technology, and to keep a watching brief on the newest cost-saving developments. Without rivals to take away its business, the public sector is insulated from these important pressures. (*Privatisation Worldwide*, 1986)

The psychological case goes by the name of 'public choice theory', and argues that public services are often inefficient and ineffective and invariably inferior to private provision because the people who work in them have no proper incentive to make it otherwise. This is because human behaviour is ruled by self-interest. In commercial organisations this is openly manifested as the pursuit of profit, whereas in public organisations other things are less openly pursued as a substitute for profit. Thus, politicians pursue votes, while officials pursue status, larger departments and budgets. This being so, public services, such as the National Health Service (NHS) or local authority services, tend to be run more for the benefit of the producers (officials, doctors and other professionals), rather than consumers (the patients). The point about commercial organisations is that those involved have an interest in providing what the customer wants, an incentive to provide the best. Both the structural case and public choice theory suggest to neo-liberals that there should be as few public services as possible, and as much as possible given over to private enterprise.

Government's role in the economy

For neo-liberals, the state has only a strictly limited, but nevertheless very important role to play in the economy. Most important is the control of inflation.

Inflation

Inflation is deemed to be among the greatest threats to the free market, and therefore to freedom generally. As just noted, the efficient working of that market is dependent on a multitude of individual decisions about buying and selling, borrowing and saving, what to invest in and what to produce. But inflation distorts the market, interferes with all these calculations and generally makes people reluctant to invest and save. Banks and other sources of investment finance will only lend at very high interest rates to ensure their return is not wiped out by rising prices. Inflation, therefore, causes stagnation and decline, and may completely ruin an economy, as happened in Germany in the 1920s.

There are, however, different theories about what causes inflation. The Keynesian view is that the major cause is 'cost-push', so that the cost of production rises, especially because of wage rises, which pushes up prices, causing higher wage demands, and so on. The remedy usually proposed by Keynesians is an incomes policy. The neo-liberal answer, developed by Milton Friedman, is called 'monetarism'. The argument is that inflation is caused by an excess of money (i.e. both cash and credit) in the economy; this is the result, more often than not, of excessive government expenditure financed by borrowing and printing money. Consensus policies, especially borrowing money to pump into the economy in a recession, are an especially important cause of excessive money. It is a primary duty of the state, the argument continues, to eliminate inflation and guarantee a stable value for money.

It should be noted that for Keynesians the great economic evil is unemployment, and a government's first economic duty is to maintain full employment. In contrast, monetarists see inflation as the greatest economic evil and government's most essential task is its elimination.

'Supply-side' measures

Neo-liberals believe in the absolute minimum of state interference in society, and especially the economy, that modern conditions will permit. That rules out economic planning, nationalised industries, government investment, prices and incomes policies, regional policy, and more. The government's proper role is not to interfere in the market, but to create the conditions in which the market can operate efficiently. This is done through what are sometimes called 'supply-side' policies. Controlling inflation is the most important, but they also include reducing public expenditure, cutting taxes, reducing the power of trade unions and, cutting down bureaucracy, together with various schemes to encourage small businesses. These will help the free market and encourage the 'enterprise culture', that sees the setting up of businesses and participating in the market as worthy and desirable activities.

Neo-liberalism and the New Right

Neo-liberalism is not merely an economic doctrine, but is equally a political one, concerned to promote particular political values, which are those of what is now well to the right of the mainstream political spectrum. Hence the term New Right, which most neo-liberals would readily accept.

Primacy of economic freedom

Neo-liberals pursue supply-side and monetarist economic policies not only to allow the free market to operate most efficiently and prosperously, but also, they argue, because it maximises human freedom. They believe that economic freedom is the most basic freedom, which makes other kinds, such as our civil liberties, possible. (The civil and religious liberties that the early liberals were so concerned about we now rather take for granted as part of our 'liberal democracy', and so the neo-liberals are more concerned with economic freedoms and being independent of government support.) State intervention, it is argued, leads to socialism in which freedom is denied, as we can see from the communist experience. In his book The *Road to Serfdom* of 1944, Hayek even goes so far as to argue that state welfare provision is an unwarranted interference in the free market and therefore a step on the road to a kind of slavery.

It should be noted that the only freedom that is accepted by neo-liberals is what is called 'negative' freedom. That is, an absence of legal or physical obstacles to what people want to do. It does not include giving people greater power to do things by providing welfare such social security, free health care or subsidised housing. That just makes people dependent, and also necessitates a redistribution of wealth that is deemed unfair.

Fairness and freedom of capitalism

Socialist arguments to the effect that the outcome of the capitalist system is always unfair are countered by the argument that capitalism rests upon the principle of contracts freely entered into. Individual transactions, where no dishonesty is involved, cannot in themselves be unfair, and consequently the system cannot be unfair. If in the end there are rich and poor then that is nobody's fault. It is interference with the system (for example, to redistribute wealth) which is unfair. So long as liberty and opportunity are not denied, that is sufficient for a good society.

Left alone, the free market will provide optimum prosperity with optimum opportunity for all and optimum freedom of choice for consumers. Everyone will have maximum freedom within the framework of law, within which all can enjoy equal rights and all have a chance to succeed, if they have the talent and energy to do so. This is the neo-liberal vision of the good society where everyone will be independent, self-reliant and believe in the virtues of the free-enterprise system.

Neo-liberalism and the wider right

The kind of ideas that Margaret Thatcher stood for were not unique to her; she was rather the leading British representative of a body of ideas that have also found favour in the USA, and to a lesser extent in Japan and Western Europe. Despite being a modern version of *laissez-faire* liberalism, in all cases these ideas are on the right of the political spectrum. This is because avowedly liberal parties are now normally parties of the centre which are committed to welfare policies and managed free markets. It is parties of the right that have become the parties of vigorous free enterprise and of the business class.

Thus, neo-liberal ideas have been found in association (sometimes rather incongruously) with the values, attitudes and policies of the traditional right, such as law and order, aggressive foreign policy and large defence budgets. For example, Margaret Thatcher and Ronald Reagan were fiercely anti-communist before the great collapse, with massive government spending on Trident missiles and 'Star Wars' defence systems. A clearer case of conflict was Margaret Thatcher's policy on broadcasting. On the one hand, she wanted market forces to be given free reign, while on the other she was determined to limit the amount of sex and violence on television.

Some of the more extreme neo-liberals (often called 'libertarians') who believe the state should do virtually nothing, find this relationship with the right rather uncomfortable. This is especially true in America where the various strands of the New Right include Christian fundamentalists of a distinctly authoritarian kind.

Thatcherism in practice

Margaret Thatcher came to power in 1979 with a set of policies based on her neo-liberal beliefs. Although there were some modifications and compromises on individual policies, the programme as a whole was pursued with remarkable consistency through the subsequent decade. The central theme of this programme was the reversal of Britain's post-war decline and the restoration of the country's prosperity and economic health. To begin with, this involved a wholesale rejection of the post-war consensus.

Analysing Britain's problems

The neo-liberal analysis of Britain's post-war failure put the blame on those consensus policies of the managed and mixed economy and the welfare state, that to most people at the time had seemed to give steadily growing prosperity combined with social progress. However, neo-liberal analysis maintained that consensus policies had also created massive government with high taxes, endless regulation, state ownership, state planning, state monopolies, state subsidies, incomes policy, regional policy and various other forms of state intervention. Nationalisation had directly diminished the private sector, putting in its place costly and inefficient state enterprises which were a burden on the taxpayer and soaked up investment funds that should have gone to private industry. At the same time, the free enterprise system was being strangled by bureaucracy, weighed down by excessive taxation, intimidated by over-powerful unions, and exploited by inefficient state monopolies.

Meanwhile, neo-liberals insisted, the independent spirit of the people was being undermined by too much state provision of everything: health, pensions, houses, jobs and whatever else people thought they needed. The welfare state had created a 'dependency culture' where growing numbers of people simply lived off the state and had no thought of doing anything else. It was a situation Margaret Thatcher called the 'nanny state'.

All this regulation and provision had necessitated a massive civil service and local government bureaucracy with a vested interest in maintaining consensus policies and making sure that nothing ever changed. Margaret Thatcher maintained that her favourite television programme was *Yes, Minister*, a comedy series in which wily civil servants ran rings around their supposed masters to make sure everything stayed as it was.

Furthermore, consensus policies created huge government borrowing, easy credit and printing of money in order to sustain demand and maintain high employment in accordance with Keynesian economics, despite wages being too high and industry being uncompetitive. All this generated inflation, which ruined savings and investment and was the great enemy of free enterprise. Thus, the argument concluded, Britain had declined economically and was sinking into a condition of dependence on the state for everything. To reverse these trends required an economic policy quite different from those pursued since 1945.

Economic policy

The overall aim of the Thatcher government's economic policies after 1979 was the restoration of the UK's prosperity by following the classical liberal principles of relying on the free market, minimal government interference, and maximum individual liberty, responsibility and independence. This meant that economic recovery could *only* be by means of a flourishing private sector. The government's economic strategy, therefore, was to create the conditions in which free enterprise might flourish by means of policies which can be broadly grouped into four closely related areas:

- the conquest of inflation
- reducing the size and cost of the state
- providing incentives for hard work and enterprise
- removing restrictions on the operation of the free market

Defeating inflation was the absolute priority, taking precedence over everything else, although the initial purely monetarist approach, involving the restriction of the amount of money in circulation by high interest rates and other measures, was abandoned after a couple of years. Great efforts were made to reduce government spending, although success really only amounted to slowing the rate of growth. The centre-piece of the incentives policy was a substantial reduction in income tax, although other taxes had to rise to compensate. Removing restrictions covered many things from reducing trade union power to the setting up of enterprise zones. (Local taxes and planning regulations were suspended in certain inner city zones to encourage small businesses.)

Giving the priority to inflation, rather than full employment as previous governments had done, required high interest rates which resulted in mounting unemployment. The belief was that merely reducing inflation would so stimulate the economy that it would grow and solve the unemployment problem that way. The trend in large firms was constantly to shed labour to reduce costs, but given the right conditions, entrepreneurs ('those wonderful people' as Margaret Thatcher called them) would create small businesses that would be labour intensive.

Government under Margaret Thatcher adhered to the belief that there was a 'free market solution' to virtually all problems from inner city decay to funding the arts and sport. Even parts of government itself, national and local, were made subject to a system of 'competitive tendering' where private firms were encouraged to compete with government departments to supply a wide range of public services.

But perhaps the most striking policy of the Thatcher revolution was privatisation in its various forms. For the neo-liberal it fulfilled all ideals virtually at a stroke: reducing the role of the state; expanding the free market; providing more consumer choice; and for those who bought their council houses or shares in privatised industries, greater freedom and responsibility. Whatever the criticisms of privatisation, it was the most characteristically neo-liberal and Thatcherite of all the policies.

Social policy

Of the three pillars of the post-war consensus, it is the welfare state that has proved to be the most durable. This is despite the fact that, for several reasons, it is anathema to hard line neo-liberals. They believe that welfare provision is not the proper business of government. People should be responsible for their own lives and look after their own welfare. Moreover, the welfare state is wasteful. Its universality is not targeted on those in need; thus the rich can benefit from free education, health care, pensions and other benefits which they can perfectly well afford. Finally, national and local government provision was not subject to commercial constraints: there was no consumer control and no market forces.

Despite neo-liberal hostility to both the idea and the practise of the welfare state, its popularity made it impossible, except on the margins, to seriously tamper with it. No significant part was abolished under Margaret Thatcher. There was nevertheless substantial neo-liberal influence on social policy, manifested in a number of ways. The crudest was cuts in public expenditure. There was also encouragement for private provision of education, health, pensions and other services. But more important were the attempts to subject areas of the welfare state to market forces, and the disciplines and opportunities of the private sector. This was particularly true of health and education, where the 'internal market' and greater parental choice were designed to make hospitals and schools behave more like private businesses.

The basic idea in education was to give parents free choice of school, and then to fund schools according to the numbers of pupils they could attract. This would make parents the consumers for whose custom the schools compete, and as in the marketplace those with the poorer 'product' must either improve or go out of business. The 'internal market' in the NHS was similarly designed to gain the benefits of market forces by creating a kind of simulated market. In this case the 'consumers' were health authorities and doctors' fund-holding practices, and the 'producers' were hospitals who had to compete for their contracts. An attempt was also made to make the provision of certain services (such as homes for the elderly) a matter of competition between local authorities and the private sector.

The success of Thatcherism

The question of just how successful the Thatcher revolution was in making Britain 'a better place' is a matter of fierce controversy. How people answer it depends a great deal on their political point of view and what they mean by 'a better place'.

It is widely argued that Thatcherism shook up Britain's economy and made it more competitive and prosperous. On the other hand, it is argued that the deep recession of the early 1980s, at least partly caused by monetarist policies, destroyed large parts of the British manufacturing industry from which it more than a decade to recover. Furthermore, while there was a brief boom in the late 1980s, unemployment was never reduced below 1979 levels, and in any case the boom led to another recession.

Many see the control of the trade unions as a plus, although it would not have been possible without massive unemployment, with its associated poverty and insecurity. It is widely felt that the welfare state declined under Thatcherism with poorer services trying to meet greater need. Whether Thatcherite policies have made people less dependent, or whether major organisational changes have improved health care, education or welfare services in general, remain open questions.

Overall, many feel that Thatcherism made Britain economically viable again, and raised its status in the world. Others feel that Britain became a meaner, less tolerant place where making money was seen as more important than anything else. In the end, it may be that it is a matter of opinion or personal values whether Thatcherism is seen as a good thing or bad.

What is certainly true is that Thatcherism changed the political landscape in Britain. Many policies, such as trade union reform and privatisation of major utilities, were almost inconceivable in 1979. Because many of these policies have been popular, Thatcherism was an electoral success. As a result, other parties have had to abandon old policies and come to terms with Thatcherism and change their ideas and policies accordingly. Good or bad, Thatcherism amounted to a revolution in British politics.

The Conservatives after Margaret Thatcher

Despite her successes, not least in elections, Margaret Thatcher was forced to resign in 1990 by the Conservative Party in parliament. John Major won the subsequent leadership election and became prime minister. He was clearly a very different kind of personality. More importantly, despite being Margaret Thatcher's chosen successor, it was not clear what his policies might be or whether he would take the party in a new direction

The Major style and early success

John Major was a more emollient and consensual figure than his predecessor, and it did seem that he had a very different approach to leadership. He was not an ideologue in the way Margaret Thatcher was, tending to follow the cabinet majority, instead of imposing his will upon it in the way that she had. He was more in the pragmatic mould of past Conservative prime ministers whose style was more in keeping with a traditional conservative outlook. The Thatcherite right, who felt Margaret Thatcher had been betrayed by her party, developed an open hostility to John Major for his lack of leadership qualities as compared to those of their heroine, and their suspicion grew that he intended to lead the party back to a more traditional moderate 'one-nation' conservatism, where, they felt, his true instincts lay. In his memoirs, Nigel Lawson, Margaret Thatcher's former chancellor, records that in 1990 Margaret Thatcher backed John Major as her successor because she was under the quite mistaken impression that he was a Thatcherite (Lawson, 1992).

John Major represented a more inclusive and less dogmatic style than the rather narrowly focused moral crusade of Margaret Thatcher. While he seemed Thatcherite on economic policy and continued with the Thatcherite themes of privatisation, together with pressure on inflation and bureaucracy, nevertheless Major gradually began to depart from Thatcherism in significant ways. Instead of Thatcherite hostility to the state, there was a new emphasis upon improving what the state did. Better services, citizens' charters, more parental control of schools, and the aspiration to improve schools and hospitals were new priorities. Even more significant for the Thatcherite right, Major shed Thatcher's ill-concealed hostility and suspicion of the European Union and insisted that Britain must be 'at the heart of Europe'.

Despite the growing disillusionment with his leadership, of Margaret Thatcher and her followers, John Major did enjoy a good deal of early success, including the Gulf War victory and the negotiations for the Maastricht Treaty. This culminated in the winning of the 1992 general election, which seemed to vindicate the Conservative Party in choosing a new leader in 1990 and John Major in particular. He had held the party together, despite growing disagreements between left and right and the country's economic difficulties, and did so sufficiently to deliver five more years of power.

Economic crisis

Although widely expected to lose the 1992 general election, John Major won it with a majority of twenty seats. This increased his authority since he was now prime minister by right of winning and not merely inheriting someone else's success. This in turn strengthened his hold on power and put him in a better position to choose his own cabinet and his own policies. However, the 1992 election victory was the high-point of John Major's premiership; thereafter things soon began to go wrong.

When he became premier, John Major had inherited an economic recession from his predecessor. There had been a boom in the late 1980s which had got out of hand and had allowed a resurgence of inflation. Since, in Thatcherite economics, inflation was the great enemy which had to be defeated at all costs, measures had to be taken to eliminate it, even if they brought the boom to an end, causing recession and unemployment. When he was chancellor of the exchequer, John Major had persuaded a very reluctant Margaret Thatcher that the best way of combating inflation was for Britain to join the European Exchange Rate Mechanism (ERM) which fixed the value of the pound sterling to other European currencies. Very high interest rates were needed to maintain the value of the pound in the ERM, which seemed to make the recession just go on and on.

However, in September 1992, a few months after the election success, on what came to be called 'Black Wednesday', there was a financial crisis. The pound sterling came under intense pressure, was forced out of the ERM and effectively devalued. Since devaluation tends to cause inflation in the long run, this was widely seen as a disaster, as well as a humiliation for the government whose economic strategy had been left in ruins. Yet many Thatcherites were happy since at least Britain was less tied to Europe on this issue (ERM was the first step to a single currency which they abominated) and Britain was again in charge of her own economic destiny.

The crisis in 1992 did two things. In the first place, the Conservatives lost their reputation for economic competence. After Black Wednesday their opinion poll rating plummeted and remained low thereafter, confirmed by heavy losses in subsequent European and local elections. Secondly, the crisis and its outcome greatly encouraged the Thatcherite right of the party, especially after the economy very gradually began to recover without inflation returning. They believed this demonstrated the folly of being a member of the ERM in the first place. The right were also confirmed in their low opinion of John Major's leadership.

Party divisions

The continuing unpopularity of the government over subsequent years, despite some degree of economic recovery, led to discontent within the party, which became progressively more divided. Left and right had different strategies for overcoming the party's deep unpopularity. The left wanted a move towards the centre with policies that showed a socially-concerned government, with more expenditure on areas such as health and education (in line with traditional, moderate, 'one-nation' conservatism), combined with a co-operative and non-confrontational attitude towards Europe. The right wanted to put what it called 'clear blue water' between the government and Labour, which required more right-wing policies and a continuation of the 'Thatcher revolution'. Such policies included, first, more radical cuts in public expenditure which would make cuts in taxation possible, and second, a much more aggressive stance towards Europe. The demand for expenditure cuts fitted with the Thatcherite commitment to minimal government, leaving more to the free market and encouraging people to stand on their own two feet. In a recession, government expenditure inevitably tends to rise because of increased demand for welfare payments, especially unemployment benefit. The right insisted that there must be other cuts in the welfare budget to make up for it. Substantial rises in taxation, as occurred in 1994–5, were anathema to them. They insisted that only tax cuts could restore popularity to the government.

The other great right-wing cause was Europe, where the minimum demand of the right was a firm commitment not to join a single currency, and an end to any extension of the powers of the central institutions of the European Union. By this time some significant figures, such as the former chancellor of the exchequer, Norman Lamont, were openly suggesting that the time may come when Britain might need to withdraw from the European Union altogether. Right-wing cabinet ministers, such as Peter Lilley and Michael Portillo, grew increasingly strident in their attacks on Europe, to the delight of the party conference.

The shift to the right

What these ministers had perceived was that the party as a whole was moving to the right, both among the activists in the constituencies and in parliament. The 1992 intake of new MPs made the party more Thatcherite than before, although it takes time for new members to find their feet and become vocal. The consequence was, that although at the beginning of the parliament it seemed clear that John Major's successor as prime minister would be on the left – either Michael Heseltine or Kenneth Clarke – as the party moved progressively rightward after 1992 they became increasingly isolated.

Thus while it seemed in 1990–2 that Thatcherism and the New Right had had their day, they returned with renewed vigour thereafter. The new wave of Thatcherites were more fierce and uncompromising in their New Right beliefs than Margaret Thatcher herself (who was in many ways a cautious politician). An example is Alan Duncan, who was one of the new Conservative MPs who gained their seats at the 1992 election.

Duncan has set out his views in a book, *Saturn's Children: How the State Devours Liberty, Prosperity and Virtue* (Duncan and Hobson, 1995) in which he seeks to demonstrate that the modern high-tax, high-spending state is the root cause of all the ills of society. He believes that despite fifteen years of Thatcherite government trying to reduce the monstrous size of the state in Britain, there still exists 'a despotism spawned by egalitarian democracy' which has encroached 'relentlessly but imperceptibly on the private lives, liberties and prosperity of the British people for over one hundred years'. He writes that 'As with syphilis, the last stages of such a despotism are worse than the first.' What he is trying to suggest by this extremely unpleasant analogy is that state involvement in society is like a disease that ends up corrupting everything. He clearly feels this corruption is in a very late stage. It is responsible, he believes, for ruining the British economy; 'devouring' personal freedom; crushing the originality, skill and energy of the people; creating poverty and insecurity; wrecking schools, hospitals, universities and local communities, undermining traditional values, and thereby inducing an epidemic of immorality, drug taking and crime. What is essential, Duncan argues, is to 'liquidate the state' which appears to mean a short-term programme of reducing state activity and expenditure by roughly half, and ultimately reducing the role of the state to little more than providing defence and law and order.

This is much further than anything Margaret Thatcher herself has proposed or would endorse publicly, although her sympathies with this way of thinking were apparent in a lecture she gave in January 1996 in memory of Sir Keith Joseph who had introduced her to many of the New Right ideas in the mid-1970s. In this very polemical address she claimed that the: 'very existence of the state, with its huge capacity for evil, is a potential threat to all the moral, cultural, social and economic benefits of freedom'. Margaret Thatcher went on to dismiss the suggestion that the Conservatives were unpopular (at that time they were forty points behind in the opinion polls) because of right wing policies, as 'baloney'. She went on to attack the left wing of her party, the traditional or 'one nation' conservatives (implying criticism of some members of the cabinet including John Major), especially over their pro-Europe views. 'Not One Nation', she said, 'but No Nation'. Despite such an outburst, the hostility of the right towards the 'one-nation' traditional conservatives is most clearly seen in some of the writings of Margaret Thatcher's admirers. One such is Simon Heffer, the *Daily Mail* journalist, who wrote a few days later:

> One Nationism is an anti-individualist creed that patronises, collectivises, and expropriates. It claims the State knows best when, as the last 50 years have shown us, the State knows very little. It also poisons national self-confidence, and lacks a truly global vision. It radiates defeatism, guilt and even cowardice ... It is about power for the sake of keeping power, not about power for the sake of extending the liberty and prosperity of the individuals. (*Observer*, 14 January 1996)

Needless to say, there are many Conservative MPs who regarded this as a travesty of the truth, proudly adhering to a traditional conservative outlook. Some have took an interest in new 'communitarian' ideas (that Tony Blair and others were also interested in – see Chapter 9) arguing that belief in communities has always been a part of traditional 'one-nation' conservative thinking. They argued that it was the right's undue emphasis on individualism that threatened to undermine communities. The right responded that it was the massive growth of the modern state, to which Conservative governments of a 'one-nation' persuasion have made a substantial contribution, that undermined communities by encouraging people to look to the state instead of their families and communities in times of difficulty. Thus the right tended to see traditional 'one-nation' conservatism as the discredited ideas of a previous age. 'One-nation' Conservatives who held such traditional views had a majority in the party, even when Margaret Thatcher was in power, but by the mid-1990s they were an increasingly beleaguered minority, regarded by the right with contempt.

There were calls for John Major's resignation and frequent rumours that he would be challenged. Things became so bad that in the summer of 1995 he resigned as party leader in order to fight again for the leadership of the Conservative Party. He won against the Eurosceptic John Redwood, but it was not an overwhelming victory. More than a third of Conservative MPs did not vote for him, and it was clear that many of those who *did* vote for him had done so only because they believed he was the one person who could hold the party together. Thereafter he was increasingly seen as a prisoner of the right wing of his party.

The hostility of the right, and its increasing power within the party, alarmed the left to such an extent that some MPs defected to other parties. In September 1995 a prominent backbench MP, Alan Howarth, joined the Labour Party, while in December another, Emma Nicholson, joined the Liberal Democrats, and a third, Peter Thurnham, a few weeks later gave up the whip to sit as an Independent. (Later still, George Gardiner left to join the Referendum Party, having been deselected by his local party.) They complained that the rightward shift of the party threatened to drown out the kind of ideas for which they had always stood. These defections decreased John Major's majority, putting the prime minister even more at the mercy of the right. He was especially vulnerable on European Union issues since the Eurosceptic right were much more prepared to vote against the government than left-wingers were on any issue, on the grounds of patriotism, of putting their country (which they see as threatened by Europe) above party demands. In April 1996 the *Sunday Express*, one of the most fiercely loyal of conservative newspapers, announced in a front page banner headline, 'TORIES SET TO SPLIT' (28 April 1996). The article reported the belief of a growing number of Conservative MPs that they would soon divide into two, possibly before the forthcoming election, but certainly afterwards. The Conservatives moved towards the 1997 general election as a manifestly divided party.

Defeat and taking stock

In May 1997 the Conservative Party suffered a catastrophic defeat, worse than the crushing defeats of 1906 and 1945; in fact, its worst election defeat since 1832. John Major had left the election to the last possible moment to allow the greatest possible time for the economy to recover from the early 1990s recession. The economy did indeed continue to recover, but it was to no avail. The Conservatives had lost their reputation for sound economic management on Black Wednesday in 1992 and had trailed in the opinion polls ever since. Furthermore, the party suffered from a series of financial and sexual scandals involving Conservative MPs and former ministers. But probably most damaging of all was that the party was deeply and very publicly split, or as many observers and Conservatives themselves would have it: in a state of civil war. In the previous year no less than four MPs had left the party. During the campaign John Major appeared to plead for unity among his candidates.

The immediate issue was Europe and whether Britain should rule out being a member of the single currency. However, the split was much deeper than Europe. It was essentially an ideological conflict between traditional conservatism and New Right conservatism. The traditional one-nation conservatives were a minority after 1992, but they continued to produce some of the most able people in the party, and have a considerable input into policy. The question was whether after the trauma of the 1997 election the two sides of the party could unite. The subsequent campaign to elect a new leader after John Major resigned seemed to suggest that, while a number of leading figures from both camps were prepared to work together, there was little prospect of unity among the MPs as a whole. Consultations with the party outside the Commons, showed a consistent majority among Lords, constituency associations and Euro-MPs for Kenneth Clarke as the most able man in the recent government, a successful Chancellor of the Exchequer, the most popular candidate in the opinion polls, and by all accounts the one leading Tory the Labour Party feared. Despite his qualifications, and support both inside and outside the party, the MPs chose to vote for William Hague, the youngest and least experienced of the cabinet and the candidate without any clear political stance. It was apparent that a considerable number of MPs could not stomach Clarke's one-nation conservatism and overt sympathy for Europe. Hague later indicated that he only wanted people in the shadow cabinet who were not prepared for Britain to join the single currency in the foreseeable future. This provoked resignations from the shadow cabinet, the loss of another MP and widespread discontent on the left of the party.

However, a divided parliamentary party was not the new leader's only problem. The party in the country, once regarded as the most formidable election fighting machine in Europe, was in an advanced stage of decay. Since 1979 the organisation had been neglected and by 1997 the consequences were clear. In 1979 the party had 1.5 million members but by 1997 membership was estimated at 300,000, with an average age of 62. As a result the party was in considerable financial difficulties and reliant upon foreign donations that are not declared. In 1979 the party had 12,100 local councillors, but by 1997 it was reduced to 4,400, with only control of a handful of councils in England and none at all in Scotland or Wales. The organisation of the Conservative Party was said to be in state of anarchic shambles.

A massive rebuilding faced the new leader if the party was to recover in the future. A new party, better organised (based on 'New Labour') and attractive to younger people was needed. Also needed, most commentators agreed, was a party with a more democratic structure. But perhaps most of all the party required a new ideological stance, rethought from scratch, that could unite and attract the support of the whole party. There is wide disagreement over whether this might be possible.

Future prospects

Two distinguished academic students of political ideas in Britain, Rodney Barker (Barker, 1997, Chapter 8) and John Gray (Gray and Willetts, 1997) have both declared conservatism to be dead. Gray argues that the Thatcherite preoccupation with free markets has so undermined people's economic security that they have rejected New Right conservatism in favour of a party that believes in community and the importance of public services. However, market forces, encouraged by Thatcherism, have also been destructive of communities and traditional institutions and practices to such a degree, Gray insists, that the Conservatives cannot go back to traditional conservatism either. Conservatism, therefore, is dead. David Willetts, on the other hand, sees conservatism as the doctrine to cope with the new economic and social world that it is developing because it advocates both free markets and communities.

In the 1997 general election the Conservatives, although badly defeated, still won nearly ten million votes, and the party has come back from devastating defeats before. Nevertheless, if the party becomes a narrow, right-wing, nationalist, anti-European, unregulated-free-market party, leaving the centre ground to Labour, then it may be in the wilderness for some time. But perhaps the greatest nightmare the Conservatives have to face, is that the Labour and Liberal Democrat parties will learn to co-operate to make the twenty-first century, in Tony Blair's words 'the radical century'. That could exclude the Conservatives from power for a very long time indeed, whatever their ideological stance.

8

British socialism
and the Labour movement

Britain has its own distinctive tradition of socialist thought. But the term 'socialism' is so broad and contested that before examining British variants, we need to consider the nature of socialism as such.

Classical and liberal socialism

Some people have seen the origins of socialism in the Bible, in Ancient Greek thought, in the medieval monastery, and of British socialism in Thomas More's *Utopia* [1516] (1991), along with the ideas of the Diggers and other radicals of the mid-seventeenth century. But none of these helps us to understand the nature of the doctrine in the modern world. As a modern ideology, socialism is best understood as a response to developments in the late eighteenth and early nineteenth centuries: in the French Revolution, and above all in the Industrial Revolution.

Types of socialism

Socialism comes in a multitude of forms, and a great variety of people have called themselves socialist from Joseph Stalin to Tony Blair. Some forms of socialism claim to be the only genuine socialism, while others claim that theirs is the only form suitable for the times. All deny that everyone who claims to be a socialist is one. Classifying the different kinds of socialism is difficult in that are many variants, and labels are used differently on different occasions, and even change their meaning completely. 'Social democracy' is a good example of this. However, all socialists are concerned with the nature and consequences of capitalism, and the different types of socialism may be distinguished by their relationship to capitalist society. Two divisions are particularly important. The first concerns means, or how the desired society might be brought about; while the second is to do with ends, or the kind of society for which socialists should strive.

For most of socialism's history the main division concerned means: either evolutionary or revolutionary. It is only since the Second World War that differences over ends have become the critical divide. Traditionally socialists, whether evolutionary or revolutionary, have seen capitalist society as something that needed to be replaced by a system based upon socialist principles, and it is convenient to call this kind of socialism 'classical socialism'. However, in the second half of the twentieth century many socialists have come to see virtue in capitalism as an economic system, and have sought to control, modify and domesticate it so that it serves society as a whole and not merely individual self interest. It will be convenient to call this version of socialism 'liberal socialism.' The present chapter concentrates on the tradition of classical socialism in Britain, while the next chapter will consider the varieties of liberal socialism that have prevailed since the 1940s.

The elements of classical socialism

Classical socialism developed as a response to early industrialisation, and the appalling conditions it created for the new class of industrial workers. Movements such as the Luddites attacked machines, while most workers in some way blamed greedy and ruthless factory owners for their condition. The authentic socialist note was struck when blame was attached, not to individual capitalists, but to the capitalist system itself, and when this in turn stimulated ideas of what a better society, without capitalism and its attendant evils, might be like.

Many types of socialism developed in the nineteenth century, but a general case against capitalism and the outline of a socialist alternative were common to most. Three broad categories of criticism were levelled against capitalism. It was first of all seen as inevitably creating a society with hostile divisions between classes of exploiters and exploited; a society where the few enjoyed wealth and privilege at the expense of the many who led poor and diminished lives, with most of what they had produced being taken by the capitalist for profit. Second, the system was seen as grossly inefficient. Competition was chaotic and wasteful, and led to periodic crises of over-production when people and machines were idle and useless because of the blind workings of an anarchic system. The capitalist system was seen as producing a plethora of goods that people do not need and were only induced to want by clever marketing, while the real needs of many were ignored. Finally, the system brought out the worst in human beings, making them greedy, ruthless and uncaring. Thus, capitalism was deemed a corrupt and evil system that causes or exacerbates exploitation, poverty, crime, violence, squalor and other preventable ills by which humanity is afflicted.

A socialist society, free of capitalism and based on equality and co-operation, would, it was said, have the opposite characteristics. It would be harmonious, with no exploitation or conflict; it would be productive, and provide amply for all; and it would bring out the best in human nature. Each individual could develop to their full potential and all could contribute to the common good.

This moral and practical contrast between the bad capitalist society and the good socialist one was the basis of the beliefs of most socialists up to the Second World War, as well as of many afterwards, and still some today. At least at this very general level such beliefs offer an attractive picture of a world free of the ills that have plagued mankind for most of its existence. However, it is a view that rests on certain assumptions that many find difficult to accept. For most socialists the assumption is that human nature is essentially good, and that it is only the system that makes them bad. Socialist theories also assume some kind of natural harmony would exist among people who were genuinely equal that would require no authoritarian regime to impose or retain. And finally, it is presumed that a socialist economy, without the waste of capitalism, would deliver abundance. There would be no scarcity, which is a by-product of the capitalist system. There would be plenty for all if everything was properly organised and planned along socialist lines.

What we have here is an ethical vision of a good society in which people will be naturally good and evil will be eliminated. As a vision it has a strong moral and emotional appeal. However, it is a rather vague picture and much depends on the details. For example, how free would people be in a socialist society? If they can start their own businesses and employ workers, then this will surely soon lead to the reinstatement of capitalism. Again, who would decide how free people will be; who would do what job; who would decide what the factories would produce? Who would be in charge and enforce these things? If 'everyone' is involved in all decisions would that not be chaotic? But if there is a government of the few, complete with bureaucracy, police force, and so forth, will that not inevitably produce inequalities of power and opportunity? Different kinds of socialism answer these problems and dilemmas in different ways within the same 'classical' framework.

Revolution versus evolution

Differences over these fundamentals has not in fact been the main source of division among classical socialists. Historically, the most important division has been over the more immediate, but essentially short-term, question of how socialism is to be achieved. Broadly there are two routes: the revolutionary and the evolutionary. Marx has long been the most important advocates of revolutionary means. He insisted that the ruling class – that is the capitalist class who have the bulk of all the wealth and power – will never voluntarily relinquish power and will use any means to cling on to it, including force, propaganda or making concessions. For example, in modern liberal democracies like Britain, the Marxists argue, the ruling class has bought off revolution by effectively bribing the workers with welfare state benefits and consumer goods. The only way to remove such a ruling class is by a revolutionary overthrow.

The alternative is the evolutionary, peaceful route to socialism. Persuasion, protest and trade union action were among the means of change suggested, until the franchise began to be extended to the working class, after which democratic and parliamentary means became the standard method of bringing socialism about. The argument here is that, since workers have had the vote, it has always been possible to persuade the electorate of the virtues of socialist measures, and by winning elections to introduce socialism gradually with full democratic support. Indeed, many who hold this view insist that unless socialism is introduced in this way it will not be a socialism worth having. Marxists accuse parliamentary socialists of helping to keep capitalism going, while parliamentary socialists accuse of Marxists of being totalitarian and enemies of human freedom.

Perhaps surprisingly, it is this question of the means of achieving socialism, rather than the seemingly more fundamental question of how a socialist society should actually be organised, that has always caused greatest conflict among socialists. Such conflicts have often been more bitter than those between socialists and non-socialists. In the British socialist tradition evolutionary socialism has always predominated, although the revolutionary strand has also been represented from time to time.

The birth, death and rebirth of socialism in Britain

Socialism as a modern ideology begins in the early nineteenth century as a response to the impact of industrial capitalism. Since Britain was the first industrial nation it might be expected that socialism developed first and most completely there, much as liberalism had done. But this was not so, partly because the growth of liberal ideas had been so strong. Early socialism developed simultaneously in Britain and France in the years after 1815. But while there was then a continuous development of continental socialism through various peaceful and revolutionary versions, in Britain after an early flourish it faltered and then died. Socialism in Britain had to be reinvented in the 1880s, and with a version quite distinct from what had become the European tradition.

Utopian socialism

The period following the end of the Napoleonic Wars saw the development of modern socialism as a mass movement, in Britain and France, based on the writings of a group of thinkers: Charles Fourier and Henri de Saint-Simon in France, and Robert Owen in Britain. Marx famously dismissed them collectively as 'utopian socialists'. This was meant to suggest they were naive, impractical dreamers, which was less than fair. What Marx was doing was seeking to discredit thinkers who at the time of writing (1848) had bodies of followers who were rivals.

All three of these thinkers saw that the old pre-revolutionary world was gone for good and a new one not yet born. After twenty-five years of turmoil, war and social unrest, a new world was needed that would recreate community in a way that the old social hierarchies could not. After the horrors of the immediate past, all three were hostile to revolutionary methods, but beyond that they differed in their approach. Only Saint-Simon embraced the new industrial civilisation, Owen and Fourier rejected it, and opted for a society of small communities. This was particularly surprising in the case of Owen, who was the leading figure in the early phase of British socialism.

Owenism

Robert Owen (1771–1858) was born in modest circumstances in North Wales, was apprenticed in the drapery business and eventually became involved in factory management. While still in his early twenties he and some friends purchased a cotton mill in Scotland with a community attached. Owen was to make it immensely profitable and very famous, by means of the novel strategy of treating his employees decently and educating their children. People came from far and wide to see his New Lanark Mill in operation. His fame was such that he was invited to join a government-appointed commission to study the serious unemployment created by the end of the Napoleonic Wars. His solution was 'villages of co-operation' where the unemployed and their families would be given land and houses and help to set up a self-sufficient communal economy in which all property would be owned in common and all production would be for the common good. Within these villages the poor would be re-educated, while for the rest of the country he advocated a national education system that would teach co-operation and help generate a national character that would be the foundation of a prosperous and harmonious nation.

His early ideas, set out in his best known works, *A New View of Society* [1814] (1969) and *Report to the County of Lanark* [1821] (1969), were ignored and the funding needed to set up such a system was not forthcoming. But he developed his ideas further and he came to the conclusion that his villages were the ideal environment for everyone to live in. Production would be based upon co-operation, and would consequently be more efficient and effective. The success of such methods would be an increasingly attractive alternative to capitalism, which it would eventually replace. He became increasingly disillusioned with the benefits of industrialisation and appalled at its social effects. Machinery put people out of work and so reduced the market for the goods produced. The free market was therefore a recipe for chaos. Production needed to be controlled and made to fit the needs of all the people.

Owen had a somewhat mechanical view of human society, (not unlike his contemporary, Jeremy Bentham – see Chapter 4). People's characters, he believed were shaped by the environment in which they were brought up and by their education. He thought it was up to society to choose what kind of character it wanted its people to have, and this could be engineered through the educational system and living conditions. All evil was the result of ignorance. Hostility between the classes was the result of environment and education. Change these and a happy, prosperous and harmonious society could result. The developing industrial system, and its attendent over-production, he believed was the result of false ideas. A false emphasis on individualism encouraged the illusion that people created their own characters and were responsible for their own fate. This idea, sanctified by false religious beliefs, only encouraged greed and the pursuit of wealth for its own sake. Poverty and unhappiness for the majority was the result.

Disillusioned with government indifference at home, Owen went to America and sank a large part of his considerable fortune into creating an ideal community he called 'New Harmony'. It was a failure and he came home to England after several years having lost all his investment. But on his return, Owen found himself at the centre of a movement. He had a substantial body of followers, some of whom were trying to establish ideal communities, and various kinds of co-operative ventures, as well as running Owenite journals and newspapers.

Although villages of co-operation and other ideal communities were his central idea, Owen threw himself into organising alternative activities involving working-class self-help, trade unions, friendly societies and producer and consumer co-operatives. It was a group of his followers who founded the Rochdale co-operative society which was to grow into the modern Co-operative movement. These activities culminated in the Grand National Consolidated Trades' Union (GNCTU). This was a sort of union of unions which adopted a policy of general strike (in the manner of the French syndicalists later in the century), although this was somewhat against Owen's better judgement, since he remained resolutely hostile to notions of class war. The government intervened, took severe action against some trade unionists – most famously the 'Tolpuddle Martyrs' transported to Australia – and the movement collapsed.

There were other socialist writers and organisers at the time, including a number developing the ideas of the liberal classical economist, David Ricardo. They adapted the Ricardian theory of the value of any object as being derived from the amount of labour that has gone into it, by arguing that the working class therefore create all the wealth, and the other classes expropriate it in an unjust and immoral manner. However, despite a lively discussion of socialist ideas at the time, no socialist writer or organiser had the stature of

Owen, who continued to write and lecture and organise up to his death. But with the collapse of the GNCTU many socialists joined the wider Chartist movement, devoted to parliamentary reform. When that collapsed in 1848 socialism as a significant political movement died in Britain and remained dead for more than thirty years.

The non-socialist Labour movement

The withering of the socialist movement had one overwhelming cause. This was the long Victorian boom, which began around the middle of the nineteenth century and continued with rapid economic growth, full employment and ever-rising prosperity. The new model unions based on highly skilled operatives, like engineers and toolmakers, were well placed to take advantage of the situation, and their members prospered. The union leaders, far from being attracted to socialism, were greatly in favour of the capitalist system, and the liberal outlook that underpinned it. Liberalism was the doctrine of the age and they embraced it with enthusiasm. Their outlook was 'labourist': that is, the workers created the wealth and it was the task of labour unions to make sure their members received their fair share of the rewards, although without challenging the system.

It was different in continental Europe, where socialism continued to develop, both in its peaceful and its revolutionary forms. Socialist anarchism also grew strongly in this period. But most important of all, Marxism grew and by the 1880s had become the dominant form of socialism in Europe. Despite the fact that both Marx and Engels spent most of their working lives in Britain, their ideas had little lasting impact there. The only new socialist thinking between 1848 and 1880 was a small group of intellectuals who founded the Christian Socialist movement. But they were mainly concerned with people working together in Christian harmony. They did not challenge the social order, and had very little political content in their ideas at all. By 1854 that, too, had died.

Politically, this period in general cemented a strong link between the Liberal Party, especially its radical wing, and the working class, a link that was not really broken until the First World War. Not even when the great boom began to falter in the mid-1870s was there any loss of working-class support; although after the Reform Act of 1867 gave the vote to working-class householders in the towns, the new voters were wooed by both Liberals and Conservatives. It was not until the recession turned into the disastrous slump of the mid-1880s that socialist ideas began to revive.

This was part of a much wider political sea change towards collectivism that affected the two major parties and political thinking in general. Society was widely perceived to be in serious difficulties, and *laissez-faire* liberalism was seen to have failed. New ideas began to circulate, with socialist ideas among them.

A very British Marxism

The revival of British socialism in the 1880s included Marxists, Fabians, ethical socialists and Christian socialists. There were also Owenite co-operative ideas, but mass industrial society had advanced to such an extent that his ideal communities no longer seemed viable. The first significant socialist grouping in the revival was Marxist, in the form of the Social Democratic Federation (SDF), founded and sustained by the eccentric figure of H. M. Hyndman (1841–1921). Hyndman was a rich, upper middle-class, Oxford-educated financier and talented amateur cricketer, with a passionate belief in Britain's greatness and the British Empire. He was originally a Tory, but came to see the existing political parties as incapable of solving Britain's severe social and economic problems. On a business trip he happened to read Marx's *Capital* in a French edition (it had yet to be translated into English), and became completely convinced by its economic arguments and conclusion that the advent of socialism was a historical necessity. Soon after, he wrote a history of England along Marxist lines, *The Textbook of Democracy: England For All* (1881), although he did not acknowledge Marx, who was furious, and neither Marx nor Engels would have anything further to do with Hyndman or his organisation.

Hyndman used Marx in fact to frighten the middle classes. Bloody revolution would be the unavoidable consequence unless the middle classes came to understand the inevitability of socialism and take the lead in establishing it peacefully and providing intellectual leadership. His ideal was a socialist British Empire continuing to lead the world.

Although the SDF saw itself as a political party which fought elections, it was never much more than a group of mainly middle-class intellectuals, with a handful of working-class members. It made little attempt to become a mass working-class party, in the manner of Marxist parties in Europe. Hyndman was in fact hardly interested in trade unions and strikes and the sort of issues that working people were interested in. He was far more interested in theoretical matters, and with everyone seeing the world correctly. Some have argued that Hyndman thereby failed to take advantage of a historic opportunity to create a mass Marxist party in Britain on the European model, although it might be doubted whether anyone could have done this.

William Morris

Morris (1834–96) was influenced by Marx, but could hardly be called a Marxist. He read *Capital* but candidly admitted that while he had enjoyed the historical bits, the economics left him befuddled. He saw socialism primarily in moral and aesthetic terms, and was as much influenced by the great Victorian critic, John Ruskin (1819–1900), as he was by Marx. Ruskin was an art critic who insisted that good art was the product of a good society, and bad art the product of a bad one. He railed against the ugliness and squalor of the new industrial age, and the moral degeneracy of *laissez-faire* liberalism that preached individual self-interest and the virtues of the free market. But although Ruskin's writings, especially his attacks upon capitalism, influenced many socialists, he was not a socialist himself. He was more a Tory traditionalist, believing in social hierarchy and the responsibilities of the higher orders for the welfare of the lower, and was firmly opposed to democracy. He looked to the late Middle Ages, when art and craftsmanship were at their height as the model of a well-ordered and healthy society.

Morris was greatly influenced by Ruskin long before he had even heard of socialism, and shared Ruskin's detestation of the new industrial, urban world of his own day. But his initial belief was that capitalism might be reformed in some way that involved a return to craftsmanship and good design. However, his discovery of socialism provided the key to his thinking about art and society. In fact he developed a theory not unlike Marx's theory of alienation (of which he could have had no knowledge). Human beings were creative, Morris thought, and the making of beautiful and useful things for oneself and one's fellows was deeply satisfying. Work of this kind was a natural human activity which combined pleasure and satisfaction. Exploitation, and the demeaning and degrading machine production, and cheap production for profit, destroyed that natural impulse to create and made the worker dissatisfied and unfulfilled. Only a socialist society could restore that natural relationship.

Once he had come to this conclusion, somewhat late in life, Morris threw himself into political organisation, which became added to all his other activities (great designer, conservationist, poet, social theorist, scholar and businessman). He helped to found and run the Socialist League, which had broken away from the Hyndman's SDF in 1884. Morris, in fact, despised party politics with its compromises and betrayals, and the League made no attempt to stand for elections or influence parliament. The central task was to convert people to socialist thinking. Although Morris was personally a peaceful and gentle man he believed that in the end only a revolution by the working class, defending themselves against excessive exploitation could change society for the better.

Morris, however, felt strongly that it was not enough to analyse and theorise and insist that socialism was inevitable or so much more efficient, as Marxists and Fabians tended to. People must be given a vision of the kind of society socialism would make possible; their hearts must be engaged and they must feel that a socialist society is something for which it was worth fighting and making sacrifices. This was the point of his writings like *A Dream of John Ball* (1886) and his most famous work, *News from Nowhere* [1890] (1993).

Oddly enough, the writing of *News from Nowhere* was occasioned by the publication of another utopian socialist novel whose picture of the future

Morris disapproved of. This was *Looking Backward* [1888] (1986) by Edward Bellamy, about a man who goes into a trance and wakes up in the year 2000 to find his home town of Boston has been transformed into a vast metropolis. It is a world of abundance, a veritable consumer paradise, with huge industries supplying all human wants. It is all rationally organised with industrial armies rather than military ones, and run by a massive centralised state. This vision of a socialist utopia appalled Morris so much that his alternative utopia is the very opposite of Bellamy's. The same device, of a sleeper awakening in the future to a world transformed, is used. But here the vast metropolis of London has been ruralised, and has become a series of villages set among trees. There is no industry and there are no disciplined industrial armies. People work as and when they want, and at what they want, and simply supply each other with goods and services without charge. Everything is charm and beauty, even the people are healthier and more beautiful than in the past. There is no central government (the Houses of Parliament have been turned into a dung store), but local communities settling their affairs by discussion and consensus. It is a tranquil, static, happy rural idyll.

The book provided inspiration for generations of socialists of different kinds and, like the ideas of Robert Owen, are part of a tradition of socialist writing that rejects the idea of a centralised socialist state. The people today closest to believing in Morris' vision might be 'green anarchists'.

Fabians, ethical socialists and British socialism

Morris' writings, especially *News from Nowhere*, had a considerable influence on the ethical socialists, who, together with the Fabians, were mainly responsible for the construction of a distinctively British socialism in the closing decade of the nineteenth century. The Fabians were established first.

The Fabians

Within a few months of the founding of Hyndman's SDF, a group of young people started to meet regularly to discuss the state of the country. Some were interested in 'moral regeneration' and soon left to create their own movement. Those interested in politics discussed radical liberal and socialist ideas and they formed the Fabian Society in 1884. It was not a political party, more a debating society of mostly young people with disparate views. They developed a general commitment to socialism, although they were still defining what that meant. There was also a commitment to a gradual non-violent means of change, which was the point of their original symbol, the tortoise, and of their name. They called themselves Fabians after the Roman general Fabius Maximus Cunctator, who fought Hannibal by delaying tactics and refusing open battle. It was not until their first publication, the

Fabian Essays in Socialism of 1889 (1911), that their ideas really crystallised. It was this publication that put the Society on the map as a significant source of new and interesting ideas. Branches began to spring up in many parts of the country. There was never a party line, but there was a broad approach that was mainly worked out by Sidney Webb and endorsed by the second most influential member of the Society, and editor of the *Essays*, George Bernard Shaw.

When the Fabian Society began, Marxist ideas were in the air and had inspired the rather Anglicised versions put forward by the SDF and the Socialist League. But after extensive study of Marx's ideas (especially by Shaw, Sidney Webb and Graham Wallas) they were rejected by the Fabians on two grounds, economic and political. They rejected Marxist economics in favour of the neoclassical ideas of Stanley Jevons and others, as a more satisfactory explanation of economic phenomena. They also developed a theory of rent, which meant that all the factors of production – land, capital and labour – had their proper rent. However, the system worked so that the many were systematically deprived of their due portion by the few. The lack of contribution from this few was emphasised by financial developments in recent decades which allowed ownership at a distance and a divorce between ownership and the entrepreneurial function. Thus, a large proportion of the wealth of the country was owned by people who did nothing, literally the idle rich.

The significance of this was that the Fabians did not see a fundamental and necessary conflict of interest between the bourgeoisie and the workers, as Marxists did, but rather a conflict of interest between the class who did not work and lived off the rent of their land or capital, and the rest of society who did work. Instead of the Marxist politics of class war leading to revolution, the Fabians offered the strategy of the permeation of existing institutions and parties with collectivist ideas for change, financed by progressive taxation on unearned income.

However, like the Marxists, Sidney Webb did insist upon historical inevitability, and did see socialism as in some sense 'scientific', although in different senses to the Marxist version. Webb was influenced by ideas of evolution, interpreted in a collectivist manner, which saw progress in terms of ever greater co-operation, instead of the Spencerian individualist interpretation which looked to ever more competition. Webb saw socialism as a natural evolution, an inevitable outcome of the Industrial and French Revolutions that led to modern industrial society and democracy. Indeed, Webb insisted that socialism was happening already all around us, without most people realising it, not even those opposed to socialism. In *Socialism in England* [1890] (1893) he wrote:

> The 'practical man', oblivious or contemptuous of any theory of Social Organism or general principles of social organisation, has been forced by the necessi-

ties of the time, into an ever deepening collectivist channel. Socialism, of course, he still rejects and despises. The Individualist Town Councillor will walk along the municipal pavement, lit by municipal gas and cleansed by municipal brooms with municipal water, and seeing by the municipal clock in the municipal market, that he is too early to meet his children from the municipal school, hard by the county lunatic asylum and the municipal hospital, will use the national telegraph system to tell them not to walk through the municipal park but to come by the municipal tramway to meet him in the municipal reading room, by the municipal art gallery, museum and library, where he intends to consult some of the national publications in order to prepare his next speech in the municipal town hall, in favour of the nationalisation of canals and the increase of the government control over the railway system. 'Socialism, sir,' he will say 'don't waste the time of a practical man by your fantastic absurdities. Self-help, sir, individual self-help, that's what's made our city what it is.'

Webb interpreted all collectivist institutions and policy (even the army and navy) as manifestations of socialism.

The scientific aspect of the Fabian outlook came from a conviction (particularly strong with Sidney Webb and his wife Beatrice) that social scientific research would demonstrate that any social problem could not be solved by the free market, and collectivist provision was the only rational solution. The Webbs were great researchers, and produced major studies of institutions and problems and contributed to Royal Commissions. Sidney was the key figure in the creation of the London School of Economics in 1895 (using a legacy left to the Fabians) believing that objective research would inevitably lead to the greater establishment of socialism.

Like the Marxists and the ethical socialists, the Fabians were morally outraged by the effects of capitalism, but what they particularly emphasised was capitalism's gross inefficiency. Economic activity and society itself were becoming so complex that a planned and organised economy was essential to replace the chaos of the free market. The necessity of a more controlled system under common ownership, the Fabians thought inevitable. A necessity that would be recognised by both the main parties. Hence the policy of permeation, rather than that of pursuing class war tactics of the creation of the mass party, strikes, demonstrations and other activities which may do more to delay the coming of socialism than hasten it.

The key instrument, for the Webbs, in the creation and maintenance of a socialist society was the civil service. That is, a body of dedicated and trained public servants with expertise who would understand society and how it can be best run efficiently and humanely in the interests of all. These civil servants would be supervised by an elected and fully democratic government. But it was the bureaucracy rather than the politicians in whom the Webbs believed in. This reflected their increasing impatience with party politics. However, it would be inaccurate to say that their conception of the ideal state was one where a central bureaucracy controlled every aspect of peoples' lives. Apart from insisting upon the necessity of democratic control, in fact the Webbs saw the majority of services undertaken and owned by local communities, as is clear from the quote from Sidney Webb above. They envisaged a massive extension of local government.

From the 1870s both Liberal and Conservative governments increasingly found themselves compelled to pursue collectivist policies. In a sense the Fabians simply projected this trend into the future and to its logical conclusion. The strategy of permeation made sense in the light of the belief that all parties would necessarily adopt ever more collectivist policies to deal with social and economic problems. The Webbs in particular strove to demonstrate by massive research that socialism was implicit in many institutions, policies and trends without people being aware of it. Their approach is summed up, rather curiously by Annie Besant in her contribution to *Fabian Essays on Socialism* (Shaw [1889] 1911) where she rejects utopian theorising in favour of a method that begins with the present, and 'seeks to discover the tendencies underlying it; to trace these tendencies to their natural out-working in institutions; and so to forecast, not the far-off future, but the next social stage'. The Webbs were anxious to demonstrate, first of all, that socialism was fully compatible with English institutions and traditions, and secondly that socialism was a natural evolution of liberalism.

Their central strategy of 'permeation' meant the influencing of existing parties with collectivist ideas based upon rigorous analysis and clear reasoning to demonstrate the superiority of a collectivist solution. The idea that the Liberal Party, still less the Conservative Party, might be converted to socialism may seem bizarre, but collectivist action was an established feature of all governments at that time, and the Conservatives were clearly capable of associating and absorbing radical collectivists as the case of Joseph Chamberlain demonstrated. Besides, the Fabians never attempted to produce a final vision of a socialist society, but to approach problems piecemeal and encourage the collectivist trend already apparent in what governments were doing.

There were some differences among Fabians as to the extent to which they should become involved in working-class politics. But the dominant view of the Webbs and Shaw was to concentrate on existing parties and not encourage the formation of a specifically working-class one. As a consequence they played no part in the formation of the Independent Labour Party in 1893 and participated in the creation of the Labour Party with reluctance in 1900. Only later did their attitude change.

The Fabian disdain for working-class politics meant that a socialist working-class party did not grow out of their work. It grew from a quite separate movement among those with a different outlook known as 'ethical socialism'.

Ethical socialism

The 1890s saw a rapid development of socialism among the working class. This was achieved by people inspired by socialism as a new creed that needed to be brought to the working classes as though it were a new religion, as a moral crusade. The result was a very emotional and utopian form of socialism, emphasising the cruelty, greed and squalor of the capitalism-created world, in contrast to the world of community, fellowship, happiness and beauty that socialism would provide. The vision was of a new world peopled by a transformed humanity. Many of the socialists of the period, including Fabians and Marxists as well as ethical socialists, were people who had lost their religious faith and socialism was a substitute. Some, such as Keir Hardie, saw socialism as simply an extension of their Christian belief. Some of the most dedicated, passionate and effective propagandists (pamphleteers and public speakers) were women. That is, mainly educated middle-class women who saw in the socialist movement an opportunity for women to advance and be recognised as equals, an equality denied them by society in general.

The ethical socialist vision was largely inspired by William Morris, reinforced by the writings of his non-socialist mentor, John Ruskin. But just as Morris had ignored Ruskin's politics, so the ethical socialists ignored the anarchist and revolutionary aspects of Morris. They saw a democratically elected working-class party using the state to end the horrors of capitalism and bring about socialism through the nationalisation of the means of production, distribution and exchange. Beyond this there was little theory. The ethical socialists were frankly as weak on analysis and practical proposals as they were strong on rhetoric and vision.

Morris' romantic utopianism appealed to poets and artists and several of the leading ethical socialist writers fall into this category. John Bruce Glasier (1859–1920) was a Scottish poet who joined the SDF at the beginning, but then followed Morris into the Socialist League. When that fell apart in the late 1880s he moved on to the Independent Labour Party. His best known book was written with his wife, Kate Glasier, and called *The Religion of Socialism* (1890) It portrayed socialism as a new kind of religion where supernatural belief is replaced by faith in the highest ideals of humanity. Like many socialists of the time, he had come from a religious background, but had lost his faith after reading Darwin and T. H. Huxley. Socialism became his new faith.

Robert Blatchford (1851–1943) was a working-class lad from Halifax who had turned himself into a brilliant popular journalist. In his Manchester-based journal *The Clarion*, he set out, in a series of articles in 1893, his vision of a socialist future. These were published the following year as a book, *Merrie England* [1894] (1976), which was a huge success. In a few years it sold two million copies, was described by G. D. H Cole, the distinguished historian of socialism, as the most effective piece of popular socialist propaganda ever written. The book is addressed to John Smith of Oldham, a shrewd, practical man with a plain English sense of fair play, for whom is painted a picture of industrial England where capitalism has created great cities of slums, vice, destitution and filth, in which huge sections of the population live in poverty and ill health trapped in a selfish and cruel society driven by greed. By contrast is a vision of England stripped of modern industry, where everyone lives in a healthy, planned agrarian society in which scientific agriculture would provide for all. The economy would be self-sufficient and there would be no trade. Blatchford was deeply patriotic and identified England with the working class. He had little interest in workers abroad. It is similar to William Morris' vision in *News from Nowhere*, although Blatchford did see the need for a central state to organise everything.

Keir Hardie (1856–1915) was the most important of these evangelists. He had little interest in abstract theory, but was a brilliant speaker and organiser. He came from a poor working-class background, but managed to be elected MP in 1892, as yet without a party. He had helped to create the Scottish Miners Union, and the Scottish Labour Party, and was convinced that what was needed was a united working-class movement dedicated to creating a better world. Crucially, he wanted a new socialist party created by and led by working-class people, and not one dominated by middle-class intellectuals. To this end, Hardie played a leading part in creating the Independent Labour Party (ILP) in 1893 which was formally committed to socialism, ethical socialism, and to the nationalisation of the means of production, distribution and exchange. However, the party was not a major success and Hardie realised that a working-class party had to be based on the trade unions.

The problem with the unions, however, was that they were largely led by those hostile to socialism; they were mostly supporters of the Liberal Party and opposed to notions of wholesale nationalisation. Hardie, in order to facilitate the creation of the Labour Party, therefore moved to a position that was labourist and radical democrat rather than socialist in the sense of abolishing capitalism. However, the ILP remained an independent body affiliated to the Labour Party. The ILP also remained committed to socialism of an ethical and somewhat emotional sort, that had little theoretical content. When ethical socialists thought in terms of specific policies they tended to look to others, usually Fabians.

Keir Hardie had understood the need for a mass party and that only the trade unions could provide the masses. Hence Hardie's alliance with the trade unions, whose outlook can be described as 'labourist': that is, labour creates the wealth and should be entitled to the greatest share, to be fought for through trade union action. Adding 'labourism' to the mix of Fabian and ethical socialism produced a distinctive brand of socialism that might reasonably be called 'British socialism'. Initially, however, the Labour Party had no official commitment to socialism at all.

The distinctiveness of British socialism

This amalgam of Fabianism, ethical socialism and labourism – to which we might add the co-operative tradition of Owenism – formed a version of socialism, although a rather loose one, that was very different from the standard orthodox Marxist socialism that prevailed in Europe at the time. Comparing the two helps to show how British socialism was distinctive.

First, in relation to theory, orthodox Marxism is a highly theoretical system, and among Marxists generally great stress tends to be put upon correct theoretical analysis. By contrast, British socialism is distinctly untheoretical. There is indeed a distaste, and even hostility against theory in the British labour movement generally. Whether this is a matter of national temperament, the empirical tradition or something else is difficult to say. But it may help to explain why Marxism had virtually no impact upon the British socialist and labour movements.

It could be said that the extent of this disinclination to theorise varies among Fabians and ethical socialists. The Fabians were more inclined to theory, though not in the sense of explaining everything as Marxists seek to do; and not even in the sense of a having a very clear picture of where the whole process was leading. They theorised about the next step.

Ethical socialism, especially of the late nineteenth century, is notoriously atheoretical. It is essentially a moral condemnation of capitalism, and a highly utopian picture of socialism offered as an alternative. There is very little serious theoretical analysis, and few detailed policies.

Second, in relation to class conflict, orthodox Marxism taught class war between the two classes of capitalist society, bourgeoisie and proletariat. Society, they believed, would increasingly polarise between these two classes, and that could only end in violent overthrow of the exploiters by the exploited; an outcome determined by the inevitable course of capitalist development.

British socialism has never been revolutionary (only William Morris, who might be said to straddle the two sides, suggested some kind of final violent conflict of a not very severe sort). Ethical and Fabian socialism both thought in evolutionary terms. Marxist economics was not accepted; what was preferred was the more up-to-date neoclassical economics and the Fabian theory of rent. This gave a role to the capitalist entrepreneur and to the factory manager. They real conflict was more between those who worked and those who were too rich to need to. The unproductive idle rich were deemed an offence, with so much poverty and distress around, but they could be dealt with by taxation. The Fabians hoped for class co-operation, which is implicit in their policy of permeation.

Both Fabians and ethical socialists saw the transition to socialism in terms of democratic and parliamentary action, activity which the orthodox Marxists saw merely in terms of keeping the workers movement active until the time was right for revolution.

British socialists saw socialism as the inevitable outcome of social evolution, on grounds that in the end people would see the rationality and moral superiority of it, compared with capitalism. But there was no questioning of free will, and none of the rigid determinism of orthodox Marxism.

A third basic difference is in attitudes towards the state. The Marxists saw the state purely as an instrument of class oppression. They regarded it and all its works with the deepest suspicion, even when it seemed to bring benefits to the working class (for example, through legislation). British socialists saw the state as neutral, or potentially so. The state may now be in the wrong hands, and too much influenced by those with wealth and social position, but in the hands of a benign, democratically-elected socialist government it would be the instrument of increasing social justice and social progress. The British socialists were partly influenced by the Hegelian Idealist thinking of liberals such as T. H. Green who saw the state as the expression and instrument of the common good. However, not all British socialists had so favourable view of the state. William Morris's ideal was to have no state at all, but this was unusual.

Fourth, while orthodox Marxism saw liberalism as the enemy, the ideology of the bourgeoisie, and so part of the system of class oppression, British socialists saw liberalism in a different light. Liberal ideals were seen as intrinsically good, but capitalism was seen as the wrong vehicle for their achievement. Liberal ideals, in their radical formulation, of liberty, equality and fraternity could only be achieved under socialism. They argued that capitalist competition created inequality, even in the minimal liberal senses of equality of opportunity and equality before the law, there can be no genuine liberty in a grossly unequal society. Fraternity and community were also seen as incompatible with the selfish individualism of the free market. Liberalism, it was widely believed among socialists, would inevitably evolve into socialism if it was to be true to itself, and this fitted in with the socialist commitment to liberal democracy.

Fifth, where Marxists tended to put greatest emphasis upon historical inevitability, British socialism tended to stress different values and attractions of socialism. Fabians put greatest emphasis upon the contrast between the inefficiencies and wastefulness of capitalism as compared with what they saw as the rational organisation and national efficiency of socialism. The ethical socialists, on the other hand, saw socialism as above all a moral crusade. They stressed what they saw as the evils of capitalism, portrayed as an immoral system based upon greed and exploitation and producing vast wealth for the few and poverty and squalor for the many.

Finally, Marxism is strongly internationalist, with Marx insisting that 'the worker has no nation'. Nationalism was associated in Marxist eyes with liberalism. British socialism, on the other hand, tended to be patriotic. Even the British Marxist Hyndman was a passionate upholder of the British Empire.

The rise of the Labour Party

The development of socialist thinking and working-class political organisations in the nineteenth century culminated in the creation of the Labour Party in 1900. Although not at first an avowedly socialist party, it did become so. But it began as, and remained, a party to represent the interests of the working class, and certainly up to the 1980s could also be fairly described as a party representing the trade unions. Over a period of forty-five years the party rose from nothing to be a government with a massive majority able to implement a socialist agenda.

The creation of the Labour Party

The failure of the ILP to become a national mass party convinced Keir Hardie that the only way to create such a party was through the trade unions. Some trade union leaders had come to see the need for working-class representation in parliament, to protect the interests of the working class in general and the unions in particular, but other parties at constituency level were reluctant to adopt working-class candidates. Towards the turn of the century the time seemed increasingly ripe. There was, however, a snag in that most union leaders had little or no interest in socialism. Most were Liberals and some were Conservatives. The only doctrine that united them was labourism. The consequence was that when the Labour Party was created in 1900 it did not have any commitment to socialism or any other ideology. The Labour Party in its early years, therefore, devoted itself to furthering the interests of the working class without a wholesale commitment to any political doctrine.

The new party was originally known as the Labour Representation Committee (LRC), set up under the auspices of the Trades Union Congress (TUC). It consisted of the representatives of a handful of unions, the co-operative societies, the ILP, the Fabians and the SDF. When it was clear that the new party would definitely not adopt a socialist programme, Hyndman withdrew the SDF. Within a year of the formation, the Taff Vale judgement, which made unions subject to claims for damages by employers for the consequences of strike action, posed a considerable threat to trade union activity and many more unions became affiliated to the new party.

A secret alliance with the Liberals allowed the new party to make steady electoral gains. The election of 1900 produced two seats, but that of 1906 produced thirty. By 1914 there were forty-two members and the party had become a major force, but it was the First World War that decided its fate. The Liberal Party split and gave the Labour Party the prospect of becoming the second party of the country. The election of 1918 gave the party sixty-three seats, but this was against the wartime coalition. By the 1922 election normal party battle prevailed. Labour won 142 seats, while in the election the following year they won 193 seats and were able to form a government with Liberal support.

Party constitution

With the prospect of power, the party gave itself a new constitution in 1918, which allowed individuals to join the party directly for the first time, instead of via some affiliated organisation. It also confirmed the basic structure of the party which vested sovereignty in the annual conference. Unlike the other two parties, Labour was created outside parliament. Its conference was seen as a kind of parliament of the working class, with representatives of trade unions, co-operative societies, socialist societies and other affiliated organisations being represented. The party organisation was run by a national executive committee (NEC), mostly elected by conference to which it was responsible. It was conference alone which had the right to make policy, and the Parliamentary Labour Party (PLP) was there to do conference's bidding and had only a residual right to establish priorities between policies. This was in striking contrast to the Conservatives and Liberals, which had already existed as parties in parliament long before creating national organisations; a fact reflected in the right of their parliamentary parties to make policy.

However, although in principle the PLP has always been subordinate to conference, the Labour Party has always tended to be dominated by its parliamentary leadership (elected by MPs alone until 1981). Labour's policies have tended to prevail against those of the normally more left-wing constituency representatives because the leadership could usually rely on the massive block votes of the trade unions who could outvote everyone else at conference. Later, in the 1950s and after, when the party was more radically split between left and right, the issue of who runs the party – conference or the PLP – was to become a bitterly contested one.

The commitment to socialism

It was not until 1918, when Labour was on the brink of displacing the Liberals as the country's second major party, that socialism was firmly entrenched as the party's official doctrine. Socialism was embodied in the constitution in the famous 'Clause IV', which reads:

> To secure for the worker by hand or by brain the full fruits of their industry and the most equitable distribution thereof that may be possible upon the basis of the common ownership of the means of production, distribution and exchange, and the best obtainable system of popular administration and control of each industry or service.

This does not actually mention socialism, but it is there none the less. It is implicit in the phrase 'common ownership', but also in the phrase 'the full fruits of their labour'. This is because behind the clause is the labour theory of value which insists that all the value of a product comes from the amount of labour that has gone into its production. If the workers did indeed receive the full fruit of their industry, then there would be no profit; without profit there would be no capitalism, no class system, no exploitation, and none of the ills that were thought to flow from these.

However, beyond this Clause IV commitment to socialism there was a good deal of vagueness about what form of socialism the party supported, and by exactly what peaceful means it might be attained. For many in the party, including, James Ramsay Macdonald (1866–1937) who became Labour Party leader after Keir Hardie's death in 1915, a socialist society was a very long-term aim. Macdonald had been an early member of the Fabians and the ILP and was also influenced by the New Liberal thinkers (see Chapter 5). He dismissed Marxism as an unscientific, pre-Darwinian theory. Society, he argued in *The Socialist Movement* (1911) and other works, was a living organism that naturally evolved towards ever greater integration and co-ordination. This natural evolution was, however, disrupted and distorted by capitalism. It was the task of government to ensure that all parts of society worked together for the sake of the social whole, and this meant those representing labour, land and capital should work together for the sake of the economy. It was the advent of political democracy that had made this possible. Capital was as important as labour, although labour had yet to receive its fair share. Ultimately socialism would evolve, but in the shorter term what was important to Macdonald was social unity rather than class unity.

Macdonald's rather vague and hopeful socialism tended to prevail in the Labour Party at this time, although other socialist ideas were in the air. These included syndicalism, guild socialism and the ideas of R. H. Tawney.

Syndicalism and guild socialism

Syndicalism was a powerful anarchist movement in continental Europe in the years before the First World War, and similar ideas seemed to offer a way forward for some British socialists in that period. The movement was based on trade unions (*syndicat* is the French for trade union) and saw them, rather than the political party, as the instrument for gaining power and developing socialism. Tom Mann, one of the trade union leaders associated with these ideas in Britain, insisted that Labour MPs (only a handful at that time) could do little more than make a nuisance of themselves, whereas industrial action could change what was actually important to working peoples' lives.

If the trade unions were to be effective in changing things then small craft unions would not be the means, but rather the big industrial unions. This thinking lay behind some of the amalgamations and moves towards single-industry unions during the period.

Guild socialism drew some of its inspiration from syndicalism, but was essentially an intellectual movement whose leading figure was G. D. H.Cole (1889–1959). He envisaged a socialist economy based on self-governing industrial guilds. They would operate democratically on the basis of work-shop committees; there would be competition between factories in respect of quality rather than price; rewards for effort would be in the form of shorter hours instead of more pay. A national 'commune' would be needed to co-ordinate the activities of the guilds and would take the place of the state.

It was the failure of the general strike of 1926 that fatally undermined the idea of industrial action for political ends, and syndicalism and related ideas tended to fade away in the 1930s. More important in the longer term were the ideas of R. H. Tawney, whose ideas need to be examined in more detail.

R. H. Tawney

Richard Henry Tawney (1880–1962) came from an upper middle-class background and was educated at public school and Oxford, where he came under the Idealist influence of followers of T. H. Green (see Chapter 5). This helped to turn his strong Christianity towards social questions. He worked for a time among the poor in the East End of London, and this turned him decisively to socialism. He became a professional academic and eventually professor of economic history at the London School of Economics. But throughout his career he retained a commitment to educating the working class, and was a staunch supporter of the Worker's Educational Association (WEA).

Tawney's socialism grew directly out of his Christianity. He sought to demonstrate that socialism was a direct and logical expression of Christian belief, and that capitalism and its consequences were a departure from Christian teaching both theoretically and empirically. His major historical works, above all his *Religion and the Rise of Capitalism* [1926] (1938), were concerned with how capitalism grew up within a Christian society, and was able to emancipate itself from that society's moral control of economic activity. His chief polemical works are *The Acquisitive Society* [1921] (1964), which contains his condemnation of capitalism, and *Equality* [1931] (1964), where he attacks the class system and describes his alternative socialist society. With these works, Tawney gave ethical socialism a theoretical foundation and an intellectual coherence that it had hitherto lacked.

By the time of the Reformation, Tawney argued, capitalism had managed to free itself from Christian teaching in the pursuit of material wealth. What came to be emphasised, for example by John Locke (see Chapter 4), was the rights of the individual, while neglecting any talk of duties. There was no reference to the responsibility that the individual had to society; rights were divorced from social purpose. In the medieval Christian outlook wealth had to have a social purpose and had to be justified in relation to the needs of society, which imposed duties and responsibilities on those who possessed it.

But with capitalism free of this outlook, Tawney believed, those duties and responsibilities were ignored resulting in a society based on functionless wealth, a society which was greedy and heartless and exploited others in the pursuit of self-interest. Poverty in the modern world was not just the mark of an inefficient system, but a symptom of a much deeper disordering of social values. Tawney calls capitalist society the 'acquisitive society' because its central feature was the acquisition of wealth. He maintained that people were encouraged to accumulate wealth without any reference to morality or duty to the community or responsibility to employees or fellow citizens.

Tawney's alternative is what he called the 'functional society', a society based upon the performance of duties rather than the assertion of rights, and upon the priority of social purpose over personal gain. He wanted a society based on community and co-operation instead of division and conflict. Tawney did not, however, wish to see the abolition of private property. For one thing, such property *could* be socially functional. But he did wish to eliminate a situation where some people could enjoy wealthy lives without ever doing any work or making any contribution to society.

What Tawney wanted to see was a society where labour would be accorded its proper dignity. This involved a new conception of commerce and industry as not just geared to profit, but understood as providing a public service, namely the provision of the material conditions for everyone to live the good life, in the sense of the good *social* life. He wanted industry and commerce to be perceived as professions with an acknowledged social purpose and appropriate code of conduct, just as medicine and education are professions with an explicit social purpose. He believed they should be self-regulating professions run on democratic lines, so that all contributed to the running, the efficiency and the maintenance of quality in the profession, instead of all being absorbed in the battle between employers and employees.

In his ideas on the nature of industry and commerce as a profession Tawney was influenced by the ideas of the guild socialists. Later in his life, perhaps in tune with the climate of the times, he put more emphasis upon nationalisation, while in the 1950s he endorsed social democracy. But Tawney was much less interested in the general organisation of society than in the moral quality of the life lived therein.

Tawney did not, in fact, subscribe to the traditional socialist view of human nature, that human beings are essentially good and that it is the system that corrupts them and is ultimately responsible for the evil in the world. In fact Tawney had a rather bleak view of human nature, not greatly different from that of traditional conservatism. In Tawney's case, as with some conservatives, the root of the bad was sin. However, whereas such conservatives saw capitalism and social hierarchy as a remedy for sin, in providing ways of channelling and disciplining otherwise harmful impulses, Tawney saw them purely as a consequence of sin, and as part of the problem.

Tawney was the most significant British socialist thinker of the period and has since been admired by many socialists of different kinds, from Tony Benn to Tony Blair.

Labour in power

In general the inter-war years were dominated by economic recession. At the same time it was a period of advance and consolidation for Labour, but also of setback. The 1918 general election left Labour as the second party, and within a few years came their first brief taste of government. The second chance came a few years later, but was hit by the misfortune of the great depression. Socialists in government and out struggled with the problems of understanding and coping with an economic disaster all over the Western world, against a backdrop of the rise of communism and fascism in Europe offering dramatic solutions. Some in the Labour Party were attracted to communism, just as some on the right were attracted to fascism, but neither had much effect on Labour or Conservative policies.

The leader of the Labour Party and first Labour prime minister was Ramsay Macdonald, who was also a distinguished socialist theorist. Macdonald was essentially a Fabian who believed, like the Webbs, that capitalist society would necessarily evolve into socialist society over time, without a great deal of deliberate state intervention. His theoretical writings were principally concerned with linking social evolution with natural evolution, thereby making the Fabian view of social evolution 'scientific'. In the meantime his policy proposals were in terms of improving the lot of the working class, the vast majority of the population.

However, such an outlook, or that of any of the other socialist theorists of the time, was little use in dealing with the immediate problems of government. Such theory was not up to analysing the economic situation or offering solutions. Besides, in both periods of government, Macdonald and his chancellor of the exchequer, Philip Snowden, were determined to show that Labour could govern responsibly, and this they believed was most effectively achieved by the government maintaining the strictest financial orthodoxy, and pursuing the same policies as a Conservative government would have done. This meant cutting public expenditure to balance the books. When cuts extended to reducing the meagre benefits paid to some of the unemployed, most Labour ministers resigned. When the king asked Macdonald to lead a coalition National Government his party abandoned him and henceforth regarded him as having betrayed his party and his class.

The failure of Labour to join the National Government cost them dearly in the 1931 general election when their parliamentary representation fell from 288 to a mere fifty-two MPs. The party's leadership was decimated and Clement Attlee was elected as a stopgap until the established leadership could return to parliament. However, from this nadir in the Labour Party's fortunes it began to recover. In 1935, 154 MPs were elected, while at the same time the party began to construct a more realistic, pragmatic socialism capable of sustaining a programme of government. This, together with the ministerial experience of the Second World War years, prepared Labour for its most successful period of office which began in 1945.

9

Social democracy
to New Labour

The varieties of socialism that developed in Britain and elsewhere in the nineteenth and early twentieth centuries could all come under the general classification of 'classical socialism'. This is the view that, however long it might take (and for some it was a very long time), capitalism would eventually be replaced by socialism. The post-war Labour government could be said to be the practical culmination of this view of socialism in Britain. At the same time its programme included elements which looked towards the development of what might be called 'liberal socialism', a classification that embraces those socialisms that do not require the abolition of capitalism for their fulfilment. In this sense, the post-war Labour government was both an end and a beginning.

Much of the late twentieth century has been an age of liberal socialism, mainly in the form known as social democracy, which dominated political thinking in Britain, and much of the Western world, for a generation. Its main features were Keynesian economic management, the mixed economy and the welfare state, but it was Keynesian economics that was the key element (see Chapter 3). However, after the failure of Keynesian economic policies in the 1970s, and an electorally disastrous flirtation with a revived classical socialism in the early 1980s, the Labour Party slowly and painfully came to terms with Thatcherism. The result was a gradual emergence of a new form of liberal socialism in the mid-1990s, this time one based on supply-side economics. The attempted reconciliation of socialist values with Thatcherite political economy is the socialism of New Labour. Socialists of a traditional sort may look upon this 'supply-side socialism' with suspicion and think it is trying to reconcile the irreconcilable, but it nonetheless helped the party to a huge electoral victory in 1997, giving it at least the opportunity to develop into a more complete doctrine.

Before looking in detail at these two main strands of liberal socialism, social democracy and Blairite supply-side socialism, it is important to understand how the transition was effected from classical socialism in the post-war years.

Classical to liberal socialism

The first two Labour governments (1924 and 1929–31) were minority governments, relying on the support of the Liberals. They were, in consequence, in no position to introduce socialist measures. Between 1940 and 1945 Labour was in government, but only as the junior partner in the wartime coalition, although that was extremely valuable experience. It was not until 1945 that Labour became the government in its own right, backed by a large majority in parliament. It was in a position for the first time to put its socialist beliefs into practice.

The 1945–51 Labour government

The Labour Party won the 1945 general election by a landslide. The Labour government not only had a massive parliamentary majority, but also experience of office and a national mood in tune with what it wanted to do. Furthermore, unlike previous Labour governments, it had a coherent programme.

This programme involved the welfare state, to which all parties were committed following the Beveridge Report of 1942, it also included socialist planning and nationalisation as the first major steps to the creation of a socialist economy, and therefore a socialist society. It was a government of extraordinary energy in the very difficult circumstances of the aftermath of war, when the country was bankrupt. Creating the NHS alone would have been enough for most governments, as would the social security system, or the nationalisation programme. The post-war Labour government did all these things and more: including creating the Arts Council, a comprehensive planning system, the green belt and new towns policies, and the national parks.

The programme had been put together in the wake of the disaster of the National Government in the 1930s. It was not a theory-driven programme but a pragmatic one, although it is sometimes termed 'corporate socialism'. It took something of Fabian statism and something from labourism, but also something from managed capitalism too. There were five main elements: first of all, nationalisation of key industries, especially utilities. Second, there was economic planning. Third, a greater role for trade unions. Fourth, there was Keynesian demand management. Finally, the introduction of a welfare state, originally based on the Fabian conception of a 'national minimum' but superseded in 1942 by the Beveridge Report.

The experience of Labour ministers in the wartime coalition, combined with the experience and success of wartime controls, and the widespread national feeling that there must be no going back to the conditions of the 1930s, all gave the Labour government the confidence to see its programme through. It was a pragmatic programme designed to deal with the problems of the age, rather than the outcome of a theoretical analysis. As such it was a programme that satisfied all concerned, but it was complete in itself and did not necessarily point in one direction or another. Some could see it as a step towards full socialism, while for others it constituted in itself the framework for a good society. The overriding question was which way to go next. And upon this question the party quarrelled and split.

The emergence of social democracy

Major steps had been taken towards socialism. Nevertheless, before the Attlee government had left office in 1951, there had been a marked shift of opinion within the Labour Party. Some on the right of the party had begun to question both the necessity and the desirability of pursuing the ultimate aim of the elimination of capitalism and its replacement by a fully socialist society. There were many reasons for this questioning. One was the advent of the Cold War. After 1945, the Soviet Union rapidly became regarded as the great enemy of peace and freedom, a brutal tyranny bent on world domination and the suppression of democracy. The Soviet Union claimed to be a socialist state (communism was the ultimate goal) which had abolished capitalism and had everything run by the workers. But people began to question whether, if this was socialism, they really wanted to be working towards it. However much Labour's committed socialists insisted that the Soviet system was an aberration, and that the socialism they aimed for would be totally different because it would be achieved democratically and run democratically, the Soviet example still put many people off the whole idea. Capitalism, whatever its faults, did represent some kind of freedom.

Apart from the unfortunate East European model, there was also the fact of an alternative. Labour had come to power in 1945 committed to state economic planning of a basic kind: so many tons of *this* would be produced, so many tons of *that*. But the planning system never worked very well, and increasingly the government adopted Keynesian policies of demand management (see Chapter 3). After the loss of power in 1951 the right wing of the party argued that the managed and mixed economy was in fact the best kind of economy to achieve both freedom and equality. Further nationalisation was not only highly unpopular, it was unnecessary to realise Labour's ideals. The result was a growing gulf between left and right, between, as they called themselves, 'democratic socialists' and 'social democrats'. The party had been largely united when in government but divided into hostile camps in the 1950s, and this helped to keep Labour out of power for thirteen years between 1951 and 1964.

The social democratic analysis

The chief theorist of the social democratic view was C. A. R. (Anthony) Crosland (1918–77) as set out in his book *The Future of Socialism* [1956]

(1964), in which he argued that the socialist ideal of owning the economy was no longer necessary. The nationalisations of the post-war Labour government plus Keynesian economic management were sufficient to ensure that a socialist government could control the economy, maintain full employment, and make capitalism work for the people. As a consequence capitalism was no longer the blindly destructive force it had been in the past and free enterprise could now be the basis of a fair society.

Capitalism, Crosland argued, had changed its nature from the early days of ruthless *laissez-faire* and maximum profit at all cost. Classical Victorian capitalism was dead and Britain was no longer a capitalist society. For one thing, there had been a divorce between ownership and control among large firms. Owners were now for the most part passive shareholders, while control was in the hands of professional managers who were concerned less with maximum profit above all else, than an efficiently run business with long-term stability. This produced a more socially responsible capitalism, no longer existing to serve the exclusive interests of an owning class. Besides, Crosland argued, in a situation of permanent full employment, capitalism no longer had the power to exploit as in the past, since workers could always find another job.

Crosland also rejected the traditional socialist objection to profit. Moderate profit in an efficiently run business was healthy and a necessary source of investment, leading to higher living standards and better jobs. He pointed out that nationalised industries had not in fact proved to be more efficient than private ones, while their monopoly situation tended to restrict consumer choice.

Socialism, Crosland believed, should not be defined in terms of ownership or class, but in terms of values. With the wealth that the free enterprise system generated, society could be improved with social services and ever greater equality. It was equality, and not common ownership, that was the great socialist value, and this could be achieved through good education for all, and through the eradication of unemployment, poverty, squalor, avoidable ill-health and other avoidable obstacles to a decent life for everyone. Furthermore, with the continuous economic growth replacing the booms and slumps of the past, which Keynesian economics seemed to guarantee, there could be redistribution of wealth through steeply graduated income tax and high public spending. Common ownership for its own sake has no point if socialist ideals can be achieved more effectively by some other means.

Social democrats versus democratic socialists

These ideas led to severe internal conflict within the Labour Party in the 1950s, when the right adopted social democracy. The left rejected it as a betrayal of socialism, since it did not involve the replacement of capitalist society by a socialist one, as in genuine democratic socialism. The resulting conflict is sometimes referred to as the 'revisionist debate', a reference to a similar period of conflict within the German Social Democratic party in the 1890s. The issues then were different, but they too were about what the party stood for and whether it should 'revise' (i.e. abandon) its traditional doctrine.

The social democratic right was led by Hugh Gaitskell, Attlee's successor as party leader, while the democratic socialist left was led by Aneurin Bevan. Gaitskell wanted the party to 'modernise' itself by dropping Clause IV of the party constitution. The left were outraged and a fierce battle ensued. The constitution was not changed, but Gaitskell won the battle over policy. Apart from the steel industry (which was part of the original Attlee government programme), nationalisation was dropped from party manifestos until the mid-1970s. Another source of left/right conflict was unilateral nuclear disarmament. This was the heyday of the Campaign for Nuclear Disarmament (CND), which had captured Labour's left for its cause. The Labour conference of 1960 passed the policy, a decision Gaitskell famously refused to accept, but it was reversed the following year.

The Labour Party returned to power in 1964 under a new leader, Harold Wilson, who had a reputation as a left-winger but whose policies were more in line with those of Gaitskell. The 1960s saw a considerable revival of Marxist thought in the west, especially among the young, in a movement known as the New Left. It influenced many on the left of the Labour Party, which had high hopes of Wilson's leadership. But by the end of the 1960s the left had become thoroughly disillusioned with Wilson's right-wing policies, and when he lost the 1970 general election internal conflict broke out in the party again.

While in opposition, the left wing of the party grew increasingly hostile to social democratic policies and demanded more fully socialist ones to deal with the country's mounting economic difficulties. The result was a 1974 election manifesto which was the most left wing since 1945 with more nationalisation promised. However, despite the implementation of some further nationalisation, the 1974–9 Labour government did not live up to the left's expectations, and after the 1979 defeat the party erupted into bitter conflict.

Crosland's vision of a good society had depended heavily on continuing economic growth, which Keynesian economic management had seemed to promise indefinitely. With growth there could be a fairer distribution of wealth to the less well off through higher wages, social welfare and better education, without taking anything from the better off. Crosland believed that such 'levelling up' was the only way to a fairer distribution of wealth in a democratic society. With economic recession in the 1970s, involving unemployment and cuts in public expenditure, such levelling up was no longer possible. When in the 1970s Keynesian remedies no longer appeared to work, the left argued that a social democratic programme had been a mistake all along, and that the party must return to its true self, working for the end of capitalism and its replacement by a genuinely Socialist society.

The resurgence of classical socialism

The revival of classical socialist ideas in the 1970s was also a rejection of what was seen as the failures and disappointments of the Wilson years, when high hopes of a better society were disappointed, especially for the young influenced by the New Left thinking of the 1960s (see Chapter 12). A new version of classical socialism developed in the 1970s that was to divide the party for more than a decade.

Bennite socialism

The most prominent and influential left-wing figure in this period was Tony Benn. He rejected the compromise of the consensus years, years which he saw as having brought the country into crisis. A clear radical programme, he believed, was the only solution to the country's problems. For him, this meant a return to the Labour Party's traditional Clause IV socialism, but also a return to the earlier roots of socialism and radical democracy in Britain. His ideas were set out in two books, *Arguments for Socialism* (1980) and *Arguments for Democracy* (1981).

Benn emphasised his debt to Christianity. He pointed out that Christ's belief in equality and fellowship was revolutionary when it first appeared. It became lost once the church became institutionalised and part of the power structure. He also acknowledged a debt to the Levellers and Diggers of the English Civil War period, who called for equality, the sovereignty of a popularly elected parliament and state schools and hospitals as early as the seventeenth century. Benn also drew inspiration from the Chartists, whose declaration of 1842 stated that the worker:

> feels his cottage is empty, his back thinly clad, his children breadless, himself hopeless, his mind harassed and his body punished, that undue riches, luxury and gorgeous plenty might be heaped in the palaces of the task-masters and flooded into the granaries of the oppressor. Nature, God and Reason have condemned this inequality and in the thunder of the people's voice it must perish forever.

Benn also acknowledged Marx, pointing out that other leading British socialists of the past (including those on the right) had learnt from him. He stressed, however, that Marx had not been a major influence on British socialism. He also condemned absolutely the East European suppression of freedom in the name of Marx. British socialism, Benn insisted, was home grown. It lay in the Clause IV commitment to the common ownership of the means of production, distribution and exchange; in the policy-making role of Labour's party conference; and in the traditions of British radical dissent.

Tony Benn's socialism was distinctive in the importance he attached to combining socialism with radical democracy. For him it was an essential moral principle that people should be involved in decisions that affect them. This was not only right and just, but also conducive to greater commitment and efficiency. He had great faith in the curative powers of democracy applied to all levels of social and economic activity.

Benn believed that the advance of democratic power had reached the point where it was dislocating capitalism. It followed that a new economic system was necessary. In order to fulfil legitimate popular demands for better public services, capitalism needed to be taxed to such a degree that it reduced its capacity to create wealth. This 'log jam' effect was part of the crisis of capitalism. When Labour governments come to power they were faced with either implementing their manifesto, or trying to run capitalism in a humane and efficient way. What happened, Benn argued, was that they began with the first and ended up trying, unsuccessfully, to achieve the second. The only alternative was to progress towards a socialist economy which would be able to meet the demands of the people.

Furthermore, monopoly capitalism and multi-national companies had come to represent dangerous concentrations of economic power which were almost completely unaccountable to the people whose lives they so deeply affected. For example, in 1923 the top 100 companies produced 15 per cent of the country's manufacturing output, but by 1970 this had become 50 per cent. Only governments, Benn insisted, could deal with this concentration of power. He went on to assert that unemployment was endemic in capitalism, producing the situation in which unemployed builders live next door to dilapidated houses, with no means of bringing their energies and talents to bear.

Benn believed that neither the monetarism of the Conservatives, with its mass unemployment, nor the old consensus policies, with their growing undemocratic corporatism (leaders of government, industry and the unions settling things between them) could solve the economic crisis. This could only be done by a democratic socialist programme, involving a 'fundamental and irreversible shift in the balance of power and wealth in favour of working people and their families'. Together with further nationalisation and policies for full employment, Benn favoured policies for the re-equipment of British industry protected by import controls, industrial democracy at all levels; a return to 'self-government' (by which he meant withdrawal from the European Community and NATO); unilateral nuclear disarmament; a fairer society, with reductions of inequalities of income, wealth and opportunity, and more open government and access to communications.

Benn recognised that nationalisation had been a disappointment, but with more varied forms of public ownership and greater internal democracy they could be greatly improved. All of this could be financed through savings on defence and unemployment benefit, and greater productivity resulting from full employment and the directing of pension funds into productive invest-ment.

Benn also believed that our national institutions – including government, parliament, the civil service, the BBC, etc. – were inevitably biased in favour of the ruling elite. The House of Lords should be abolished; the immense power of the prime minister should be severely curtailed; the civil service sub-ject to firmer political control and to freedom of information laws; while the press and broadcasting ought to be subject to wider influence. The first can-didate for democratisation was the Labour Party itself. The leadership must be placed under greater control from the grassroots, as represented by con-ference, to ensure that a Labour government really does carry out its social-ist promises.

Renewed party conflict: 1973–83

The ideas of Tony Benn and other left-wingers influenced the 1974 election manifestos. There were to be new nationalisations of industries (shipbuilding and aerospace), and new forms of nationalisation, such as owning individual firms within an industry (the British National Oil Corporation), and taking shares in private firms needing investment through the National Enterprise Board. There was to be a 'social contract' with the unions on the economy and social policy; a strengthening of union rights; an expansion of social ser-vices; national planning agreements with agreed objectives for industry; and a wealth tax on the top 1 per cent of tax payers.

Although some of this was put into effect, economic difficulties forced much of the programme to be abandoned. Public expenditure had to be dras-tically cut to satisfy the International Monetary Fund's requirements for a large loan. The left was furious, and after the 1979 defeat sought not merely to make Labour's policies more socialist, but also to make the Parliamentary Labour Party accountable to the party at large so as to make sure that a future Labour government would not renege on its socialist promises.

At the 1979 party conference the leadership was publicly vilified for its failures, and there was much talk of betrayal. Left/right antipathy was, if anything, even more intense than in the 1950s. The left became determined to change the party constitution to make future 'betrayals' far more difficult. The problem, as the left saw it was the Labour MPs, the PLP, which was too moderate, too independent, and not committed to a socialist society. The left proposed, first of all, that the leader should be elected by the whole party instead of just the PLP; second, that the party manifesto should be written by the National Executive committee (elected by conference); and third, that a compulsory selection procedure was put in place for every MP before every election, making it much easier to remove a sitting MP.

The major breakthrough for the hard left came when the 1980 conference adopted the compulsory reselection of MPs and voted for a change in the method of electing the leader and deputy leader. The actual method was decided at a special conference in January 1981, and consisted of an electoral college that gave 30 per cent of the vote to the PLP, 30 per cent to the constituency parties and 40 per cent to the trade unions.

At this point a substantial number of right-wingers left to set up the Social Democratic Party. The new system also provoked Tony Benn to challenge the right-wing Dennis Healey for the deputy leadership (from which he would probably have been able to dominate the party and be the natural successor of the new leader, Michael Foot who was of an older generation and unlikely to remain leader for long). Healey won very narrowly at the 1981 conference in October; but the contest had been bitter and divisive because a number of MPs had been threatened with deselection if they did not vote for Benn.

The 1983 disaster

The 1983 Labour Party manifesto was much more left-wing even than that of 1974. It committed a Labour government to immediately take back into state ownership assets privatised by the Thatcher government, with only limited compensation. In addition, it promised the taking of a public stake in a range of important industries, including pharmaceuticals, electronics and building materials. There was to be immediate withdrawal from the Common Market, unilateralism and the end of American military bases in the UK, the abolition of the House of Lords and much else besides. None of this was very popular; the party had an unconvincing leader; the campaign was disorganised and leading figures ended up publicly disagreeing with each; and after four years of internal conflict the party was demoralised and in disarray. As a result, the 1983 election was a disaster. It was probably the worst election result in the party's history. Since the left was widely blamed for the defeat, its influence thereafter began to decline.

Labour under Kinnock

The disaster of 1983 was followed by a further fourteen years in the wilderness in which the Labour Party tried to come to terms with the 'sea change' represented by Thatcherism. The process was a long and slow one, but began with the election of Neil Kinnock a few months after the defeat.

The decline of the left

The 'far left', who dominated the party from 1979 to 1983, believed that a genuine socialist programme, promoted with vigour and commitment, would win the day. They also argued that given the Conservatives' overwhelming majority in the Commons, it was essential to carry the fight to the government outside parliament, through strikes and local government defiance. This would help to rally a new 'coalition of the oppressed' (the poor, women, gays, racial minorities, peace groups, etc.) with potentially sufficient support to win an election.

However, the majority in the Labour Party regarded such a strategy as suicidal (including some prominent 'hard left' figures), and united around Neil Kinnock in trying to develop a programme that would win back the traditional working-class votes that had been lost. This involved a repudiation of the hard left's tactics of confrontation. Kinnock was notably lukewarm in his support of Arthur Scargill and the miners' strike of 1984–5. And he also moved against the Trotskyite Militant Tendency in Liverpool, expelling the leadership from the Labour Party, and supporting other expulsions around the country (though most Militant supporters remained in the party, including two MPs).

These moves were popular among the majority of Labour supporters in the country, and rather isolated the hard left, especially in the PLP, such as Tony Benn, Eric Heffer and Dennis Skinner. More importantly, there was a steady movement away from the left-wing policies of the 1983 manifesto. Withdrawal from the EEC and extensive import controls was quietly dropped, while extending nationalisation, reversing Conservative trade union legislation and other controversial proposals were played down. The party was careful to reassure the City that it was not going to be financially irresponsible in government, by excessive public expenditure that would cause fresh inflation, or compulsory repatriation of foreign investment, or too much heavy-handed planning. Most importantly, the hard line commitment to nationalisation of 1983 was considerably watered down.

There was also a deliberate attempt to update the party's image, with the strident red flag being replaced by a thornless rose in soft pastel shades (and without the clenched fist holding it, as in the continental version). Advertising agencies were consulted to advise on 'more professionally packaged' party political broadcasts and party literature. Much of this offended left-wingers almost as much as the policy shift to the right.

The popularity of Thatcherism

Despite all these changes, Labour failed to gain in popularity. It had not been enough to return to the traditional moderate Labour policies of before 1979; and this may have been because Margaret Thatcher had shifted the centre ground of British politics to the right. In other words, policies thought too extreme to be realistic in 1979 (e.g. privatisation of major public companies) were now accepted; while things accepted in 1979 (such as the great power of trade unions) were now no longer acceptable.

In more general terms, it could be said that Thatcherism represented a general disillusionment with the omnicompetent state. Thatcher's determination to 'roll back the frontiers of the state', in the sense of reducing the extent of state control, state regulation, and state ownership in favour of the free market, along with greater stress on independence and democracy (in areas such as trade unions) had certainly been popular. Her professed desire to eliminate socialism in Britain – meaning all forms of state ownership, state planning and state control – would have sounded absurd in 1979, but by the mid-1980s this was no longer the case. The mixed and managed economy as Britons had come to know it had almost been dismantled, while the universal welfare state had at least been trimmed and private provision encouraged.

An increasingly important aspect of the social democratic post-war consensus was the trend towards a corporate state (i.e. unions, employer representatives and the government running the economy between them), and this too Thatcher had ended. In all this she seemed to catch a popular mood of disillusionment with the power of the state and what it can or should provide. More interestingly, she seemed to catch an international mood. Privatisation was becoming an international phenomenon, and in fact many foreign governments sent delegations to Britain to learn from British privatising experience. Indeed, the new faith in the free market become a universal phenomenon. The collapse of communist regimes in Eastern Europe in 1989, followed by the virtual collapse of the Soviet economy resulted in these countries embracing the free-market ideal. Even China was gradually liberalising its economy. State control was on the defensive everywhere.

All this boded ill for Labour. Labour was traditionally the party of the state. It always tended to see the solution to problems in terms of state provision and state control: a national system of social security for all, a National Health Service for all and a state education system for all, irrespective of wealth or status; state ownership of key industries; state economic planning; public provision for housing; state subsidies for problem industries, for the poorer regions, for the arts, for scientific research, for the inner cities, and so on. Part of the problem for Labour was that it saw all this government action as the community doing things, as the majority of citizens acting together; but the general public (encouraged by the Thatcherites) had became increasingly less inclined to see things this way. The state was increasingly seen as a vast bureaucratic and alien organisation that imposes things on people. In this situation Labour had a problem of establishing what it stood for and where it was going, and in a way that was attractive to the public at large.

Rethinking values

A great number of books and articles addressed this problem, but perhaps the most interesting trend was the attempt to respond to the current mood by elevating 'freedom' rather than 'equality' as the great socialist value, and by emphasising that markets have an important role in society (hence the label 'market socialism'). This was not entirely new. Back in the 1950s the dominant right wing of the party effectively abandoned the traditional goals of eliminating capitalism and replacing it with a fully socialist society, in favour of the social democratic compromise of a mixed and managed economy and the welfare state. Part of the justification for this change (bitterly opposed by the left) was that freedom was also an important value alongside equality, and that in a society where the state controls everything people's freedom is diminished. Roy Hattersley, in *Choose Freedom: The Future for Democratic Socialism* (1987) took this line further by insisting that it is in fact freedom which is the central value of socialism, and that the point of pursuing equality is to give more people greater freedom. He also saw a role for free markets, not just in the sense of giving people economic freedom, but also in promoting efficiency, consumer choice and making state provision more sensitive to public demand. Other Labour figures offered a similar analysis.

To the far left, however, this was not socialism at all. For them socialism meant the elimination of capitalism, and they still saw state provision, ownership and control as the alternative and as the answer to particular problems. The Labour MP, Eric Heffer, wrote a book with the significant title *Labour's Future: Socialist or SDP Mark 2?* (1986), which argued that, for example, the problem of achieving full employment: 'means socialist planning, and a development of public ownership. To suggest unemployment can be dealt with in any other way is a sham, (p. xii). But such views were increasingly in the minority.

However, despite major changes in policy, Labour failed to win the 1987 election. It fought a better organised and more attractive campaign than in 1983, but still lost badly. This might have signalled a fresh outbreak of conflict between left and right within the party, but this did not happen. Instead the party set about rethinking all its policies. The most crucial change was the final abandonment of Keynesianism and the commitment to full employment, which many on the left saw as a final abandonment of socialism. Instead there was a 'supply-side' commitment to conquer inflation.

However, despite a programme of significant change concerning its image, organisation and policy, Labour lost the election again in 1992. The conservative majority fell to twenty-one seats, but for Labour to fail again, and in the middle of a severe recession, was a serious blow. The party was in better shape than it had been when Kinnock became leader, he had made it more electable, but was unable to take it to victory. In the aftermath of defeat Kinnock resigned. His successor, John Smith, did not change the party's stance in any significant way and died suddenly in 1994. He was succeeded by Tony Blair.

The Blair revolution

After becoming its leader in the summer of 1994, Tony Blair began to bring about dramatic changes in the Labour Party. Whether this 'Blair revolution' represents little more than 'Thatcherism with a human face' as some left-wing critics suggest, or is a new kind of socialism that adapts basic principles to a new age, as others argue, remains a matter of argument. What nobody doubts is that a transformation has taken place in the party's thinking and organisation, and is still continuing.

After the disastrous defeat of 1983 the party made many policy and other changes in the hope of electoral success, but it became increasingly apparent to some, including Tony Blair, that much more radical changes in the party's outlook, programme and organisation were needed if the party was again to be a serious contender for government. The world was changing and the Labour Party had to change with it.

The Blair inheritance

The Kinnock era of the Labour Party's history was characterised by the movement of policies away from the left. Policies of renationalisation and unilateralism were progressively watered down and then dropped. But this was not enough, and while the party regained electoral credibility, it nonetheless lost the election in 1987 and again in 1992. Kinnock had begun as a left-winger and moved steadily to the right. His successor, John Smith, was a long-standing right-winger but made no attempt to move the party any further rightward in terms of policy. Instead, he sought to preserve the delicate left-right balance that he had inherited from Kinnock. His only controversial policy concerned the party's internal workings. This was OMOV (one member one vote) in the selection of candidates which tended to shift power in the constituencies away from the activists, who were traditionally more left wing, and towards the general membership, who were traditionally more moderate and more representative of the electorate as a whole.

The 'modernisers' on the right (Tony Blair and Gordon Brown) wanted to go further, but Smith adopted the cautious strategy, widely characterised as 'one more heave': that is, the party's policies and ideological stance were broadly correct, it was just a question of further convincing the public that Labour was a party to be trusted with power. Smith's policy was often seen as simply 'masterly inactivity', just letting the Conservatives self-destruct. Some felt this to be a high-risk strategy, that relied too much on disillusionment among voters rather than their voting for Labour for positive reasons. The wisdom of the policy was never put to the test since Smith died of a sudden heart attack in May 1994.

Modernisers and traditionalists

The real departure came with the new leader, Tony Blair, in the sense that he symbolised, and consciously encouraged the perception of, a decisive break, a radical change from old Labour to New Labour. Much of the policy changes, and especially the adoption of supply-side economics, had already come about under Kinnock and Smith. What Blairism particularly represented was a break with the traditional mass collectivism symbolised by Clause IV: that is, mass welfare, mass housing, mass health care, mass trade unions, labour-intensive industries and monolithic bureaucracies, all presided over by a benign, omnicompetent state. This was essentially a politics of class war, in which the working class had only one advantage, that of numbers, and hence mass action, as against the economic and social power of the City, big business and the establishment, who were deemed to be the enemy.

This mass socialism, Blair believed, was dead. He looked back to earlier conceptions of the socialist ideal that are ethical and Christian, in the hope of recasting the idea of socialism in a more modern form. It could be said that after 1983, what Labour leaderships essentially did was to pick among the wreckage of post-war British socialism, attempting to assemble from bits of the debris an electorally pleasing pattern. But Blair was something new. He was not just part of the Foot, Kinnock, Smith drift to the right in pursuit of votes, juggling the two wings of the party in the process (or, as some have put it, the two parties occupying the same organisation). Blair wanted to abandon the wreckage altogether. His revolution is summed up and symbolised in the new version of Clause IV that the party has adopted, and more succinctly in the phrase 'New Labour'.

Blair wanted to slough off old Labour, and he was young enough not to be carrying any ideological baggage. Given his age, his background and his circumstances, Blair had far greater freedom to reinvent the Labour Party than any of his predecessors. Both Kinnock and Smith were steeped in Labour tradition. Blair did not even have connections with the previous Labour government, which left office four years before he became an MP in 1983. His own father had been a prominent local Conservative likely to have had a distinguished career in national politics, had not illness intervened.

By the time he became leader, Blair had become the leading moderniser in the party. The terms 'moderniser' and 'traditionalist' had come into use during the party's policy rethink in the late 1980s. The modernisers were those who wanted a new kind of party. Traditionally the Labour Party was the party of the working class dedicated to promoting social justice on behalf of that class. The modernisers felt that such a party was no longer viable, since a changing world had rendered it out of date.

A changing world

Blair's break with the past was made possible, and necessitated, by two factors. The first was the Labour Party's chronic electoral failure since 1979 and its consequent desperation to end the sequence of defeats. The second was the fact that the world had changed since Labour was last in power, both internationally and within Britain.

In the late 1970s and 1980s, the economic programme of Bennite socialism was for Britain to withdraw from Europe and retreat behind a tariff wall enabling it to rebuild the British economy through nationalisation and state planning. But economic self-sufficiency, or even sovereignty, was somewhat unrealistic, given Britain's inevitable role as a trading nation a role that locked her into the international economy more than most. And if the left's economic isolationism was implausible at the time, it had become many times more so since. The most important economic development of the last quarter of the twentieth century was the globalisation of the world economy: particularly in finance, communications and industry. As a result, workers in Britain were competing directly with workers in every part of the world. Britain had to have a competitive economy or die, and socialists of whatever stripe could no longer deny that a free market economy, in some form, was the most efficient and competitive form of economy available. The traditional socialist belief that a state planned and controlled economy would be infinitely more efficient than a free market one is no longer plausible.

The implications of globalisation are manifold and complex. It is not enough for the economy to be predominantly free market and free of excessive external state regulation and planning. There are also implications for interest rates, exchange rates, taxation and public expenditure. To take one example, a low tax economy is more cost-efficient and competitive than a high tax economy. This has enormous implications for public expenditure, and therefore for policies on welfare and a host of other things. Thus, whatever the desirabilities (and the demands of the left) to increase pensions, solve unemployment, introduce a minimum wage, etc., these are necessarily problematic. In this situation, not only do the traditional socialist economics of state control and planning look out of date, but so do Keynesian economics.

One of the problems with Keynesian economic management is that it presumes that a national economy can be managed as a single unit, when the power of global markets makes this no longer feasible. It was the power of international finance – a loss of confidence in the international money markets – that undermined the 1974–9 Labour government; a fact that the left could not accept. The lesson was repeated on 'Black Wednesday' in 1992, when the international money markets forced the British government into a humiliating withdrawal from the European Exchange Rate Mechanism. Economic sovereignty in the global economy has become something of a myth.

The global markets exercise a continuous influence in that if a state is deemed to be following wrong-headed policies it will suffer through confidence in its currency and other factors that will be economically damaging. And from economic policy the implications spread to other areas of policy. High levels of taxation and welfare spending, for example, can have deleterious economic consequences if international markets see these as impairing that country's economic efficiency and thus lose confidence in it.

This is the harsh reality of the modern world that Labour's left are often accused of not facing up to. They argue that that it is possible to counter these influences, and sometimes point to France, which has a much larger public sector, higher taxes and welfare spending than Britain, and yet is more prosperous. On the other hand, it is argued that France has growing economic problems and will be gradually forced into line.

A changing society

British society had also changed since 1979. For one thing, the post-war shift from manual to non-manual employment had continued even more strongly. This had undermined Labour's traditional working-class constituency: council house tenants, trade unionists, public sector workers in mass industries, and so on. Continuing also had been the decline of labour-intensive heavy industries, often state-owned and heavily unionised, such as steel, coal, ship-building and the docks. While in other manufacturing industries, such as car-making, automation and shedding labour had been the way for these industries to modernise. On the other hand, there had been a massive growth of white-collar – particularly office – jobs, involving a shift from working-class to middle-class employment, with a corresponding decline in Labour support. It might be said that while in the late nineteenth century it was apparent that the Conservatives had to capture a substantial part of the working-class vote or die, so now the Labour Party had to capture a substantial part of the middle-class vote or die.

However, the skilled working class, sometimes known as 'C2s', (according to the classification used in the Census) were still the biggest single voting group (about 28 per cent of the electorate). They used to be overwhelmingly Labour in their electoral support, but no longer. Since 1979 they had become a major source of Conservative support and a vital factor in the success of Thatcherism. The reason was that the skilled working class were increasingly developing a middle-class lifestyle, with middle-class aspirations: car owning, house owning, share holding, and were actively consumerist. Margaret Thatcher's conservatism spoke to their aspirations with policies such as council house sales, tax cuts and privatised utility shares, while Labour did not. In fact this group had become increasingly disillusioned with Labour's combination of high taxes and wage restraint. Margaret Thatcher's free market strategy without wage restraint (workers would be left to price themselves out of their jobs if they wished), together with low taxes, was much more attractive.

The Blair revolution might be said to be about the abandonment of Labour's traditional role as principally the party of the working class, ignoring the left wing Bennite strategy of a coalition of the disaffected (bringing women, immigrants, gays and others disadvantaged by the system to offset the loss of working-class support). Becoming instead a much more middle-class party, that speaks to the aspirations and the fears of the comfortably off, as well as seeking social justice for the least well-off.

One-nation socialism

After the 1992 general election defeat, a post-mortem report prepared for the party's National Executive Committee observed that 'The Labour Party is seen as a Party of the past, as one which holds back aspirations and tends to turn the clock back.' (Quoted in Sopel (1995), p. 138). It was this perception that Blair set out to totally reverse, with a crusade to 'modernise' the party. That is, to create a new left-of-centre party of social responsibility that appealed to all classes on the model of many continental social democratic parties.

Blair has used the phrase 'one-nation socialism' to emphasise the idea of Labour being the party of the whole people and not just one class. He is also sought to score a point in the party battle. 'One-nation socialism' was obviously, and purposely, an echo of the old traditional conservative label 'one-nation conservatism', used by the Conservatives to emphasise their appeal to all classes in contrast to Labour. By using 'one-nation socialism' Blair was seeking to suggest that the situation had reversed and that it was now the Conservatives who represented a narrow class interest, while new Labour was now the party for everybody.

American influence

In reshaping his party, Blair was influenced by the example of Bill Clinton. Clinton sought to revive the Democratic party in America which until 1992 had not won a presidential election since 1974. He claimed to be a 'New Democrat', one that was not tied to traditional supporters of the Democratic Party, immigrants, trade unions, the 'liberal establishment', the poor. The failure of the Democrats in previous elections was partly perceived as the result of the voters identifying the party with certain interest groups that had a vested interest in 'big government', such as welfare programmes, federal subsidies to industries; and also with liberal attitudes, such as being 'soft' on crime. In the 1992 election Clinton sought to present himself as a Democrat not beholden to traditional interest groups, and prepared to be tough on crime, and also on welfare, where traditionally Democrats had been seen as 'soft'. This enabled him to attract voters across the spectrum, but especially those who had been traditional Democrat supporters but had been seduced away by the more right-wing populist message of Reagan. Recapturing these 'Reagan Democrats' was the key to Clinton's victory.

There were many parallels here with the Labour Party of which the modernisers were fully aware. The Labour Party's association with special interests had been part of its problem: trade unions, the poor, civil libertarians and others, who had in the past influenced Labour's policies in ways that had often been unpopular with the party's traditional supporters, let alone the rest of the electorate. One of Blair's aims was to create a new party free of such vested interests, especially the trade unions. That is, for New Labour to be seen as the party of the whole population and not just some sections of it (and indeed minority sections), a party that was committed to prosperity, peace and order as much as to social justice.

The end of Clause IV

Blair saw that central to modernisation was the question of ideology, of what the party stood for. First the party had to break with the past, and overhaul its ideological stance. The key move in this respect, that which was seen as making everything else possible, was the changing of Clause IV of the party's constitution.

A mere two months after his election in 1992, at his first annual party conference as party leader, Blair astonished everybody by announcing his intention of pursuing the reform of the party's constitution. It was clear that he meant Clause IV, which embodied the Labour Party's historic commitment to socialism. It caused astonishment because the last time such a change had been attempted (by Hugh Gaitskell in the late 1950s) it had been a miserable failure. Many leaders since then had wanted to change the clause, but had not dared to even suggest that it might be discussed.

Clause IV had been part of the party's constitution of 1918, and although it embodies socialist ideas, the word 'socialism' is not in fact used. The clause reads:

> To secure for the workers by hand or by brain the full fruits of their industry and the most equitable distribution thereof that may be possible upon the basis of the common ownership of the means of production, distribution and exchange and the best obtainable system of popular administration and control of each industry or service.

The commitment to the 'common ownership of the means of production distribution and exchange' clearly means a fully socialist economy with no room for capitalism at all. By the 1950s the majority of people in the Labour Party no longer believed in the complete abolition of capitalism, but attempts to remove the clause failed because it remained as a symbol of a commitment to nationalisation and state planning, which the left of the party was determined to retain.

In 1983 the left of the party, led by Tony Benn, was dominant and the party's general election manifesto of that year promised a massive extension of nationalisation and state planning, as a result the party suffered its worst election disaster of modern times. Subsequently, the commitment to nationalisation was greatly watered down. But after the defeat of 1992 some felt that further change was essential. These were the 'modernisers', while those still believing in nationalisation were called 'traditionalists'. With the election of Blair, the modernisers were in control.

Nevertheless, his decision to seek to change Clause IV was a considerable risk. This was clear when on the next day of the annual conference a vote was passed to keep Clause IV. Many felt that Tony Blair would fail. Or at least fail among the constituency parties (dominated by activists who were traditionally more left wing that the party in parliament) and would need the votes of the big unions to force the changes through.

The outcome was in fact quite different. After Tony Blair toured the country in an energetic campaign the constituencies massively supported the change where all members were consulted. It was the unions (who controlled 70 per cent of conference votes) that were the problem. The two biggest unions – the Transport and General Workers and Unison – both voted against change at the special party conference to decide the issue in April 1995. But this did not stop the new version of Clause IV being adopted by a margin of two to one.

The new Clause IV reads as follows:

1. The Labour Party is a democratic socialist party. It believes that by the strength of our common endeavour we achieve more than we achieve alone, so as to create for each of us the means to realise our true potential and for all of us a community in which power, wealth and opportunity are in the hands of the many not the few, where the rights we enjoy reflect the duties we owe, and where we live together, freely, in a spirit of solidarity, tolerance and respect.

2. To these ends we work for:
   - a dynamic economy, serving the public interest, in which the enterprise of the market and the rigour of competition are joined with the forces of partnership and co-operation to produce the wealth the nation needs and the opportunity for all to work and prosper, with a thriving private sector and high quality public services, where those undertakings essential to the common good are either owned by the public or accountable to them;
   - a just society, which judges its strength by the condition of the weak as much as the strong, provides security against fear, and justice at work; which nurtures families, promotes equality of opportunity and delivers people from the tyranny of poverty, prejudice and the abuse of power;
   - an open democracy, in which government is held to account by the people; decisions are taken as far as practicable by the communities they affect; and where fundamental human rights are guaranteed;

- a healthy environment, which we protect, enhance and hold in trust for future generations.
3. Labour is committed to the defence and security of the British people, and to co-operating in European institutions, the United Nations, the Commonwealth and other international bodies to secure peace, freedom, democracy, economic security and environmental protection for all.
4. Labour will work in pursuit of these aims with trade unions, co-operative societies and other affiliated organisations, and also with voluntary organisations, consumer groups and other representative bodies.
5. On the basis of these principles, Labour seeks the trust of the people to govern.

Some feel that the new clause is bland and meaningless, but others say it expresses a genuinely modern socialism, and what most Labour supporters believe in. Either way, it reflects the main themes of the new Blair outlook.

New Labour principles and policies

Two features of the new Clause IV particularly reflect the Blairist outlook. One is the prominence given to enterprise, competition and the free market; the second is the moral dimension, with references to personal responsibility, the family and our duty to care for each other. These reflect two broad streams of influence on Blair's thinking. One of these, perhaps surprisingly, is Thatcherism, while the other is a mixture of old and new and is responsible for the moral side of Blair's thinking. On this moral side there are, on the one hand, the old traditions of ethical and Christian socialism; on the other are the more recent developments in political ideas known as 'communitarianism' and the 'stakeholder society'.

Admiration for Margaret Thatcher

Blair is prepared to say, as few of his colleagues in the wider party are, that Margaret Thatcher got some things right (although one must bear in mind here the fact that Labour needed to attract former voters for Margaret Thatcher in order to win the 1997 election and Blair had an interest in presenting himself as, in some sense, her heir). One thing he admired was her economic realism. She understood that Britain had to compete in a global economy without any of the old protections afforded by state intervention. The economy had to be dynamic and competitive, and enterprise must be encouraged and rewarded. He found Thatcherism particularly important in destroying prejudices and vested interests. Margaret Thatcher was a radical rather than a Tory, and her attack on the establishment was to be welcomed. However, Blair believed that Thatcherism had, in the end, been an economic failure, and an even bigger social failure.

The economic failures were at least partly due to a lack of understanding of the proper role of state, under the illusion that the free market can solve everything. One result was a lack of investment in infrastructure, such as transport, training and environment. This is not, in Blair's opinion, a mistake a left-of-centre party is liable to make. But a further obstacle to prosperity is lack of consumer confidence, which in turn is related to job insecurity, a problem that has progressively worsened. Again, this is a problem which a left-of-centre party, with its traditional commitment to social justice, is in a better position to solve.

However, the insecurity that afflicts contemporary society in the new globally competitive world is far more than just economic. The greatest failure of Thatcherism, Blair believes, was the failure to spot the disintegration of society that Conservative policies were causing, manifested in crime, drug abuse, family breakdown and the weakening of communities. The key to success in these areas, Blair sees in terms of moral regeneration, which in turn creates stronger communities, better able to cope with a world of change. Again, it is left-of-centre parties, with their beliefs in society and social solidarity that are seen as best placed to provide the vision and the policies to tackle the problems.

Ethical and Christian socialism

Tony Blair proudly calls himself a socialist, but many, especially on the left of the Labour Party, question whether he is any kind of socialist at all. It is certainly true that Blair is not a socialist in the traditional Clause IV sense. But there are other and older socialist traditions that Blair draws upon. These are ethical socialism and Christian socialism which have a long and often intertwined history in the Labour movement. Christian socialism, the idea that the Christian virtues of caring for one's fellow human beings are best expressed in the desire for a better society in which all be treated with respect and can live a decent life, first appeared in the late 1840s and was a major factor in the spread of socialism among the working classes in the 1890s. Many of the leaders of the socialist movement at this time, such as Keir Hardie, were Christian socialists. The notion of ethical socialism is a wider and more general one that embraces Christian socialism and is essentially the idea that a capitalist society, based on competition and greed, is a morally deficient one, and that a society based upon co-operation and fellowship is the kind of morally good society that we need to create.

These two strands unite most influentially in the work of R. H. Tawney. But in fact, although influenced by Tawney, Blair was much more influenced by Tawney's contemporary, the Scottish philosopher John Macmurray (1891–1976). Macmurray was prominent in the 1930s, when he was a popular writer and broadcaster on philosophical subjects, but he became ignored and forgotten after the war when philosophical fashion moved in a different direction. Yet Macmurray was curiously prescient in at least two ways. In the first place, he was one of the first students and translators of Marx's early writings, which only came to light in the inter-war years. He was influenced by Marx's early ideas to do with alienation and liberation, while rejecting his later ones bound up with economic determinism and historical inevitability; a view which parallels the Marxism of the New Left of the 1960s.

More importantly for our purposes, Macmurray developed his own version of ethical socialism that was influenced by the founder of conservative thought, Edmund Burke. Consequently, Macmurray put much more stress upon tradition, traditional institutions and traditional communities, than Tawney and other better-known socialists did. He emphasised the bonds of family and community and tradition against the claims of reason and individualism. In this he anticipated an important philosophical movement of the late twentieth century which has also influenced Blair, and is known as 'communitarianism'.

Communitarianism is a line of argument developed by such thinkers as Michael Sandel, Charles Taylor and Alistair McIntyre, but whose chief publicist is Amitai Etzioni. Communitarian theory is in conscious opposition to prevailing liberal (especially New Right) notions of individualism. It puts the stress upon the community, the family and personal responsibility. Its ideas are very general and in some respects non-political, claiming to be a middle way between socialism and capitalism. It has its attractions to those on the right, left and centre. In *Persons in Relation* (1961) and other works, John Macmurray anticipated many of its arguments and conclusions.

Macmurray was critical of the general tendency of the philosophy of his day to begin with the individual: how the individual perceives the world; how the individual thinks, and so on. In politics the equivalent tendency was for liberal theory to begin with individual rights and individual needs. The picture is of the isolated individual who chooses what relationships he/she enters into and is free to do anything provided he/she does no harm to others. But Macmurray insisted that the isolated individual was a false starting point in every way. People do not exist in a vacuum; in fact, they *only* exist in relation to others. The completely autonomous self of liberal theory is a myth. People's personalities are created in their relationships with others, in the family and the wider community. By pursuing the interests of society as a whole we benefit individuals, including ourselves.

Macmurray believed that the noblest form of human relationship was friendship and that ideally society should be based on some form of fellowship and community where we all have a care for one another. It should not be based upon some kind of social contract or exchange of benefits. The model of society should be the family not a business or other voluntary association. Macmurray's combination of Christian socialism and a conservative critique of liberalism is shared by Blair and makes his political philosophy distinctive.

Policy implications

Blair's sympathy for such ideas is apparent in a number of ways. It is clear, for example, in the new Clause IV, with its stress on social responsibility and common purpose. But also in a number of policy changes that he introduced while in opposition. These reflected changes of attitude, very different from those associated with traditional Labour.

What is different about Blair is his emphasis upon the concept of responsibility. Like those in the communitarian movement he believes that people should start rebuilding communities by taking responsibility, and that, more generally, people should be responsible for their actions. There must be duties and obligations to match freedoms and rights. There must be a greater spirit of self-help and civic duty and a renewed emphasis upon the family. All this sounds conservative to some and certainly clashes with some of Labour's traditional thinking.

An early example of Blair's new approach was apparent in the tougher policies on crime, which Blair developed as shadow home secretary, and which were summed up in the slogan 'tough on crime: tough on the causes of crime'. This was meant to change the public perception that the Conservative Party was strong on law and order and the Labour Party 'soft'. But it also reflected Tony Blair's belief in people being held responsible for what they do. This is also reflected in his comments on one-parent families, insisting that while he in no way condemns anybody, he insists that the traditional monogamous, heterosexual, two-parent family is the ideal. Blair has also expressed condemnation (albeit obliquely) of parents of persistent school truants, and people who are aggressive and disruptive neighbours. Legislation on these matters began to be introduced after the election victory of 1997.

This kind of talk is more associated with conservatives. It is at odds with traditional Labour culture and offends the party's sense of political correctness. Traditionally, Labour's attitude to such people is that they are victims of 'the system' and that it is often unfair to apportion blame. People do not choose to be unemployed, poor, disadvantaged or ill-educated. Give people decent living conditions, education and opportunities to work and they would behave decently. Criminals must be condemned and punished, yet they too may be victims of circumstances and often in need of help more than harsh treatment. As to atypical families, such as those with one parent, their situation may be because of circumstances beyond their control or out of choice; in either case there is no reason to condemn then, even obliquely, by suggesting something else is the ideal. Much of this outlook derives from a traditional socialist view (although not one that has been held by all socialists) that human nature is essentially good, and that it is the system that is responsible for the bad in people.

But Tony Blair will have none of this. He insists that people must be responsible for their own actions, and sees this as fully in line with his own version of socialism. To the left, Blair is seen as pandering to middle-class Tory prejudice. There is no doubt, however, that Blair's ideas strike a chord among many who are conservatives, and indeed among many who are traditional Labour supporters.

The stakeholder society

On a trip to the Far East in early 1996, Tony Blair startled the political community (not least his own party) by suddenly talking about the 'stakeholder economy'. Few had heard Blair use the phrase before, although it had appeared the previous year in Will Hutton's book, *The State We're In*, and there was much discussion as to what he meant by it. (Partly because it is often wrongly assumed that Blair's idea of stakeholding is the same as Will Hutton's, but this is not so, if only because Hutton's ideas are connected with his Keynesian beliefs, beliefs that Blair and Gordon Brown, his future chancellor, did not share.)

The original source of the stakeholder concept is management theory, where the idea has been put forward that a firm's obligations are not just to the shareholders to maximise the company's profits. It has obligations to others who have a stake in the enterprise: to employees, customers, suppliers and to the community it serves. Ultimately, it would be better for firms, for the economy and for society (the theory goes) if firms were run with the interests of all its stakeholders in mind, instead of just the few who own shares. From this comes the idea of a 'stakeholder capitalism' that is socially responsible.

The stakeholder society is a further extension. It suggests a society where everyone has a stake and nobody is excluded. It also comes from the perception that the heavy emphasis upon the free market by Conservative governments since 1979 has created a society with a widening gap between rich and poor, of consequent social division, of a growing sense of exclusion among those who are deprived or who are insecure.

The new Clause IV of the Labour Party's constitution rules out a socialist economy or extensive nationalisation, although some nationalisation is theoretically possible. What is also ruled out is direct intervention in the economy, in the manner recommended by Keynesian economics, to solve unemployment or under-investment. The party is effectively committed to an efficient, competitive capitalist system. This is a very long way from traditional socialism. It remains to be seen to what extent a Blair government can create a different kind of economy, a stakeholder economy, without increasing public expenditure.

New Labour in power

On 1 May 1997 Tony Blair's new Labour won one of the biggest victories in British electoral history, gaining an overall majority of 179 seats. Policy decisions began to appear at a brisk pace. Most striking was the decision to give control of interest rates to the Bank of England in order to control inflation independently of political interference. This was a signal to financial markets and business that the Labour government was sincere in its conversion to supply-side economics that gives priority to the control of inflation. The message was further reinforced by the government's decision, promised during the election campaign, to stick to tough Conservative expenditure plans for two years, and not to increase income tax for the lifetime of the parliament.

These decisions have severely tied the government's hands in other areas, notably welfare. Traditionally, Labour governments have put more expenditure into welfare and education programmes, but the new government retained the Conservative regime of severe restraint. It has indeed made 'welfare reform' (widely regarded, especially on the left, as code for cuts in welfare), a major priority. The government has already agreed to charges for university education, and there is talk of new health charges of various sorts. It is argued that the government is preparing to reshape and slim down the welfare state in ways associated with Thatcherite conservatism, but to an extent that a Conservative government would not have dared. The reason for a slimming down of welfare provision is plain enough. With increasing life expectancy there is an expected increase in the proportion of people of pensionable age of vast proportions in the late-twentieth and early twenty-first centuries, which will increase demand for health and social security provision to far beyond what, the argument goes, the nation can afford.

Also worrying for the left is the government's insistence upon 'flexible employment markets' usually a code for the freedom of employers to hire and fire at will. That is, a diminution of employment protection measures. The government's argument is that this is more effective in dealing with unemployment, as shown by the growing American and British economies, than job protection, which is the less successful European model. The government claims to balance this with its signing of the Social Chapter of the Maastricht Treaty, which gives certain employment rights, together with its policy of a minimum wage.

More generally, employment policy and much of social policy – for example, in respect of single parents – is based on the idea that welfare dependency is bad for individuals and society, and that the emphasis of policy should be on making people employable and more ready to accept whatever work is available. An array of 'welfare to work measures' is designed for those with particular difficulties in finding employment. The best cure for poverty it is argued, is work. Settling down to a life on permanent welfare benefit should no longer be an option. A cut in benefit, although combined with a new scheme to help single parents to find work, provoked Blair's first back-bench revolt in December 1997.

Most of this attitude to the economy, welfare and employment would have been equally at home in the programme of a Thatcherite Conservative government. Indeed, the Conservative Party claims that New Labour has stolen its policies, while the Liberal Democrats claim that they are to the left of the Blair government. The left in the Labour Party are inclined to agree, and are unhappy. While it is recognised that new Labour socialism is meant to be a marriage of Thatcherite ideas (especially economic) and traditional socialist values, they claim the policies are Thatcherite, while only the rhetoric is socialist.

It is true that part of the New Labour 'project' is concerned with attitudes, some kind of national moral regeneration, but the overall aim is a change of society. The thinking begins with the perception that in the modern world a nation must have a competitive economy or face decline and irrelevance, and this involves the understanding that governments alone cannot simply decide to have high levels of employment and welfare created by high taxation without being severely penalised by the international economy. In this situation a job for life is a thing of the past, and security comes from the opportunities offered by a thriving economy. But if large numbers of people are not to live in constant fear in a less job-secure world there must be a strong society and strong infrastructure (education and training, etc.) to support the individual, who must have the confidence to change and develop within a secure society. These themes were emphasised in Tony Blair's speech to the Labour Party conference following the 1997 victory where he promised policies to re-establish the family as the bedrock of society and to encourage a compassionate society and an age of giving.

When Blair was first elected in 1997 he declared that his top priority was to ensure that Labour would be elected for a second term. This is connected with another major feature of the government's programme: that of constitutional reform. The proposed reforms – devolution for Scotland and Wales, removal of hereditary peers' voting rights in the House of Lords, proportional representation for assemblies in Scotland and Wales and for the European elections, and a referendum on proportional representation for Westminster, together with a revival of local government (with elected mayors for London, and perhaps elsewhere) – are all meant to give people a stronger say in their communities and encourage them to be more active citizens. At the same time, there is a strong link with the Liberal Democrats on these matters. The two parties worked together on constitutional reform both before the 1997 general election and after it. A left-of-centre alliance (especially in the context of a reformed electoral system) could keep new Labour in power for a very long time indeed.

Such a relationship with the Liberal Democrats would be more than a cynical manoeuvre to retain power. In his 1997 conference speech, Tony Blair pointed out that his political heroes were not just Ernest Bevin, Aneurin Bevan and Clement Attlee (the major figures of the post-war Labour government) but also the liberals, Beveridge, Keynes and Lloyd George. This is hardly an unusual thought, but it is highly unusual for a Labour leader to say so publicly. This is because of the tribalism of British politics (and most other politics) where a rival is never praised. But what Blair was implicitly drawing attention to, was first the ideological closeness of modern liberals and modern socialists, and also the argument that the two parties concerned have for most of the century accounted for a majority of the electorate, but in many cases their rivalry has allowed the Conservatives to be the dominant party of government. This is a situation that could conceivably be changed.

How socialist?

The extent to which new Labour's programme and aspirations can be described as socialist (or even social liberal) is a matter of some dispute and will remain so. The social democracy of the post-war world can be seen as a compromise between capitalism and socialism, perhaps an equal mixture of the two. In New Labour we have a second variety of liberal socialism in which it is clear that capitalism dominates the mixture much more. The question is whether the remaining socialist element amounts to anything other than pious words and good intentions.

Certainly the left are unconvinced and may be troublesome in the future. But a return to high-taxing, high-spending socialism seems not to be an option in the foreseeable future. The international markets would not accept it and neither would the electorate. On the other hand, the Labour government has enjoyed considerable economic fortune since coming to power in 1997. Should that change, as is inevitable at some stage, there could be a resurgence of the left. How significant a revival this would be would probably depend on whether it can offer a fresh analysis of the situation and new proposals.

In the meantime, Tony Blair sees New Labour socialism as evolving in office, just as Thatcherism did. He is still, as he puts it (using a phrase of Bill Clinton's) seeking a 'third way' between old left and New Right. Given the strong state of the economy when Labour took office, and the party's huge majority, the opportunity to develop new ideas could not be more favourable. A judgement on the extent of new Labour's socialism will need to be made as policies develop over time.

10

Nationalism and the politics of Europe

Since the Second World War, British politics has felt the direct impact of nationalism in a number of ways. The growth of nationalism within the British Empire was a major factor in Britain giving up that empire, but growth of nationalist feeling within Britain has also been important. There has been the growth of demand for independence or semi-independence in Scotland and Wales, while most difficult and long-standing of all has been the Irish question. Finally, Britain's membership of what is now the European Union has aroused a sense of British nationalism in some quarters not overtly expressed in the past except in relation to empire. We need to look at each in turn, but first some consideration is needed as to the nature of nationalism as a general doctrine.

The concept of nationalism

Among modern ideologies nationalism is the clearest, least theoretical and has the greatest hold on popular feeling. At its simplest, it is the belief that humanity is naturally divided up into nations and that all nations have the right to self-government and to determine their own destiny. Multi-national states and nations divided between states are, therefore, inherently wrong. Nationalists insist that is the nation-state alone that is the one legitimate type of sovereign political unit, and that the creation and preservation of national unity and national identity are primary objects of political action.

Origins of nationalism

What is perhaps surprising is just how recent such ideas are. They are very much the product of the French Revolution. This is despite the fact that a sense of national identity and national loyalty can be found as far back as the ancient world, while nation-states had been in existence for several hundred years before 1789. What the French Revolution did was fuse together these older phenomena with the new revolutionary notion of 'the people' as the ultimate source of legitimacy and authority. This was in deliberate contrast with ideas of royal authority and legitimacy based on tradition and religious sanction which made it perfectly proper for princes to have absolute rule over any territory they happened to inherit, irrespective of the wishes of the people who lived there.

The Jacobins used nationalist ideas to unite the French people in support of the Revolution. When the revolutionary armies went on the offensive, they saw themselves as on a crusade to bring freedom and self-determination to the nations of Europe. This provoked other forms of nationalist thought among peoples who resented French interference, including the Germans, Russians and Spanish. Their nationalist ideas were based more on the linguistic and cultural uniqueness of the nation and its and traditional ways of life. When the dust of the revolutionary period had settled, these different ideas of the nation came together to form the modern concept of nationalism that have inspired peoples around the world.

Problems with the concept

However, despite its simplicity and clarity, nationalist theory does in fact pose some awkward problems. In the first place, nationalist theorists (certainly the early ones) tend to take it for granted that humanity is clearly divided up into nations that are easy to identify. But this is not so. Clear criteria for deciding which group is or is not a nation simply do not exist. Ethnic homogeneity might, at first thought, be an essential precondition. Poles, Chinese and Egyptians are all clear ethnic groups. But many of the world's states are not like these. Many are mixed, with perhaps the Americans – among the most successful peoples of the modern world – being the most mongrel. Another criterion, which at first sight seems essential, is a common language. But here again, there are too many exceptions to make it decisive. We have only to look at the Swiss, a self-conscious nation of many centuries, but who speak no less than four languages: French, German, Italian and Romansch. In the end, all that we can say is that a certain group of people are a nation if they feel themselves to be so. Even this is problematic, for some may and some may not, as has been the case in Northern Ireland; some may feel their people properly belong to some different or wider grouping, with no way of determining who is right.

A second problem concerns the comprehensiveness of nationalist thought. Achieving national unification or independence is one thing, but how this new entity is to be organised and run is quite another. The nationalist cause has been espoused by socialists, liberals, conservatives and others, all with different ideas of the national society they wish to see develop. Often nationalists fall out over these issues once their primary objective has been achieved. Often too there is a related conflict between those who wish to preserve the traditional way of life of their nation, while others want their nation to build a modern state, a process that may be destructive of traditional ways. It is for these reasons that nationalism has sometimes been called an 'incomplete' ideology, one that needs to be supplemented by other ideas to make it complete.

Nationalism is still a highly potent force in international politics. We only have to look at some of the world's violent trouble spots – the Middle East, the Indian sub-continent and elsewhere – and to consider that nationalism (although sometimes combined with other religious and political doctrines) is the main source of the world's terrorism, to realise its importance. And, despite the growing internationalism of the world's politics, this is likely to continue. We can see this from the collapse of communist regimes in Eastern Europe. The huge Soviet empire is still disintegrating under the impact of nationalism, as is Yugoslavia. Even a rich, successful and peaceful country like Canada is threatened with dissolution under the impact of nationalist feeling.

In Britain there is a good deal of debate about the significance of nationalism and its potential for undermining the integrity of the United Kingdom.

Nationalism in Scotland and Wales

Nationalism in Great Britain (as distinct from the United Kingdom) has never been a major political force. It is a union of people of long-standing independence, and required no wave of nationalism to unite it or secure its freedom. Once established, the union of the English, Welsh and Scots has never been seriously threatened. Nevertheless, England has always been the dominant partner and this has, from time to time, produced resentments at what is seen as London's dominance and ignorance of the periphery. This has led in recent years to the growth of a body of opinion in Scotland, and to a lesser extent in Wales, in favour of some kind of autonomy, while some demand complete independence.

Scottish nationalism

Before the union with England and Wales in 1707, Scotland had been a successful independent nation-state. After the union it remained a self-sufficient entity with its own church, legal and education systems and its own economy. A Scottish 'home rule' movement at the end of the nineteenth century was the first significant emergence of nationalism, but it did not have much support.

An important change in Scotland's situation came in the 1920s and 1930s when the depression of those years severely and structurally debilitated the Scottish economy. Like Wales and the North of England, Scotland became a region of persistent unemployment in constant need of regional assistance. Ownership and control of parts of the Scottish economy came into English hands, with consequently less investment than might otherwise have been the case. It was what was perceived as English indifference to Scotland's plight that led to the creation of the Scottish National Party (SNP) by John McCormick in 1934. Several nationalist parties appeared around that time, but it was the SNP that survived and eventually prospered. Generally, it has been a left-of-centre party seeking to attract working-class members and votes. However, it has always contained a broad ideological spectrum, some-times united on the independence issue alone. The aim was for independence within the Commonwealth, recognising the Queen as head of state (similar to Canada or New Zealand).

It was not until the 1960s that the SNP began to attract serious electoral support. Again, it was economic failure, dependence on English government and firms, as well as foreign investment, that provoked resentment and sup-port for the idea that Scots would be better running their own affairs. Other factors helped, such as the British government's decision to site the Polaris submarine base on the Firth of Clyde, in the face of a good deal of Scottish opposition. Winning the Hamilton by-election of 1967, which gave the SNP its first MP, followed by success in local government elections, was the real breakthrough.

Several factors in the early 1970s combined to make the idea of Scottish independence more credible. A royal commission on the constitution, which had been sitting for several years, reported in 1973. The report (known as the 'Kilbrandon Report' after its chairman) advocated a legislative assembly for Scotland. Although this was not independence, it certainly gave a boost to thinking along those lines. Around the same time came the discovery of North Sea oil, most of which was discovered in what would be Scottish national waters. Hitherto there had been a strong anti-independence argu-ment to the effect that Scotland benefitted from being linked with the much stronger English economy, to the extent that an independent Scotland would have great difficulty in maintaining its standard of living. But 'Scottish oil', as the nationalists dubbed it, changed all that. Indeed, it suggested England's future dependence on Scotland. Finally, Britain's membership of the Euro-pean Community seemed to offer a framework within which small nations could be secure and thrive. The old aim of independence within the Com-monwealth was replaced by the new one of independence within Europe.

The economic difficulties of the early 1970s seemed to induce a general dis-illusionment with the main parties throughout the UK. The two general elec-tions of 1974 saw a big jump in support for 'third' parties generally, including the Nationalists. In the first election the SNP went from one seat and 11·4 per cent of the votes in Scotland to seven seats and 21·9 per cent and in the second election on to eleven seats and 30·4 per cent of the Scottish vote.

It was this jump in electoral support in the early 1970s that made the Nationalists a major factor in British politics generally. They suddenly became an electoral threat to the two major parties, who began paying serious attention to what they were saying. Hence the establishment of a Welsh office in 1974, and the subsequent interest of both major parties in the subject of devolution.

In 1979 there were referendums in both Scotland and Wales on the creation of legislative assemblies. The Welsh proposal was defeated outright, while the Scottish one fell because, although there was a small majority in favour of a Scottish assembly, a low turnout meant that it failed to meet the additional requirement that 40 per cent of the electorate be in favour. This failure was a considerable blow to the Nationalist cause. In the general election later in 1979, the SNP vote fell to 17.3 per cent and gained only two MPs. Only two seats were won again in 1983 with only 11.8 per cent of the Scottish vote. There was a small increase to three seats and 14 per cent in 1987, supplemented with another seat from a by-election in 1990. With the result of the 1992 election the SNP returned to just three seats, despite a considerable increase in their share of the vote, up to 21.4 per cent. However, with just a fraction more (21.9 per cent) representation jumped to six seats in 1997.

This was one indication of how massively unpopular the Conservative Party had become in Scotland. In the 1950s the Conservatives had a majority of Scotland's seventy-two parliamentary seats, but this steadily declined, and especially so in the 1980s. After the 1979 election there were still twenty-two Scottish Conservative MPs, but after 1987 there were only ten. The Scots firmly rejected Thatchersim. This led to talk of what was called, rather melodramatically, the 'doomsday scenario'. The idea was that the Conservative government had no mandate to govern Scotland. Thus, the Scots had every right to disrupt the government of Scotland until such time as at least a Scottish assembly was granted. The SNP was in favour. However, it was not the SNP that had benefitted from Conservative unpopularity in Scotland, but the Labour Party. And while Labour supported the idea of a Scottish assembly, it was not enthusiastic about tactics that might one day be used against a Labour government in the name of independence.

In the event the situation did not arise. In 1992 the Conservatives rather surprisingly increased their MPs by one, but then in 1997, following devastating losses in local government elections, the general election wiped out Conservative parliamentary representation in Scotland altogether. Apart from general unpopularity and a Scottish party seen to be split, the Conservatives resolutely opposed any suggestion of a devolved Scottish parliament. The Conservatives claimed that a Scottish parliament would threaten the union, and took their traditional stance as the party of the union. This was despite the popularity of the proposal. Before the election the Labour Party, the Liberal Party and the SNP had all co-operated in drawing up plans for a

Scottish parliament, even though they saw its significance in very different terms. The SNP saw it as a stepping stone to full independence; the Liberals as a step towards their favoured option of a federal system of government for the UK; while Labour saw the parliament as a way of satisfying a desire for autonomy and thereby preventing the development of demands for independence.

It was the Labour Party above all that was the beneficiary of the collapse of the Scottish Conservatives in 1997, and within months of taking office held a two-question referendum in Scotland on a Scottish parliament with tax raising powers which the Conservatives continued to oppose (although some Scottish Conservatives argued it was foolish to maintain a position the Scottish people had so plainly rejected). The result was a substantial majority in favour. On a 61.5 per cent turnout, 75 per cent were in favour of a parliament, and on the second question 63 per cent voted for the tax raising powers. The Scottish parliament will be in operation by 1999 and have 129 seats. It will control the budget of the Scottish office and, in addition, have the power to levy income tax at a different rate to the rest of the United Kingdom by up to 2 per cent. The new arrangement will make the leader of the largest party effectively prime minister of Scotland.

The new parliament will undoubtedly transform politics in Scotland and at least subtly alter the relationship between Scotland and the rest of the Union, but in what ways nobody knows. The main supporters have different and contrary hopes. Even the Conservatives can look forward to its establishment. This is because elections to it will be based on proportional representation, and thus there will almost inevitably be a substantial Conservative presence that they might have been denied had first-past-the-post been the chosen electoral method. Furthermore, the Conservatives may be proved right and there may be endless conflict with Westminster, which will weaken the union and foster nationalist feeling; or it may be as Labour hopes and the threat of Scottish nationalism to the union will be defused.

Welsh nationalism

Unlike the Scottish version, Welsh nationalism is more of the cultural and romantic kind: maintaining the ancient language, recording folk ways, and reviving lost artistic forms. Maintaining and encouraging the growth of the Welsh language is a major theme. Consequently, the Welsh nationalist party, Plaid Cymru (the Scottish nationalists never dreamt of calling their party by a Scottish Gaelic name), draws most of its support from the Welsh speaking areas of Wales; that is, the rural areas of northern and central Wales, rather than the more populous, urban and English-speaking south. Politically, like Scottish nationalists, Plaid Cymru tends to be anti-Conservative and generally to the moderate left (and since the advent of Blairite socialism, somewhat to the left of the Labour Party).

The declared aims of Plaid Cymru are to:

- secure self-government for Wales and a democratic Welsh state based upon socialist principles
- safeguard and promote the cultures, languages, traditions, environment and economy of Wales through decentralist socialist principles
- secure separate Welsh membership of the European Union and United Nations

The party was founded in 1924, but it was 1966 before it had its first MP. In 1970 it gained 11.4 per cent of the Welsh vote, but failed to win a single seat; while in subsequent elections it gained fewer votes but more seats. In February 1974, 10.7 per cent gained two seats; in October 1974, 10.8 per cent gained three seats; in 1979, 8.1 per cent gained two seats; in 1983, 7.8 per cent gained two seats; while in 1987, 7.3 per cent gained three seats. In 1992, the party gained four seats, as it did in 1997. These figures show the more restricted appeal of nationalism in Wales as compared with Scotland. In the 1997 election the Conservatives were wiped out in Wales, but as with Scotland it was the Labour Party that benefitted rather than the nationalists. The new Labour government immediately set in train a referendum on a Welsh assembly.

In 1979 the proposal for a Welsh assembly was defeated outright in a referendum, which was opposed by many Welsh Labour MPs in opposition to their own Labour government. In 1997 a new referendum was held in September and again, despite Labour being a much more disciplined party, not all Welsh Labour MPs backed the party line, some campaigning for a 'no' vote instead. The vote was even held a week after the Scottish referendum in the hope that a majority of Scots in favour of devolution would encourage the Welsh to vote the same way. The Welsh did in fact vote for a Welsh assembly, but by the slimmest of margins. Some 50.3 per cent voted in favour, while 49.7 per cent voted against.

The Welsh assembly is due to sit in 1999, as is the Scottish parliament, but they are very different. The Welsh assembly will have relatively little power, partly because the Welsh Office has far fewer responsibilities compared to its Scottish counterpart, but also the assembly is not to have tax raising powers. It will, its opponents claim, be little more than a talking shop, but one that could create a good deal of trouble and foment conflict between England and Wales. The Welsh nationalists would forever be demanding more powers. It would be an ideal platform for Plaid Cymru to make an impact on a bigger, Wales-wide stage, instead of, as at the moment, being confined to the less populated rural Welsh-speaking north.

As with Scotland, devolution will undoubtedly change politics in Wales, but to what extent and whether to the advantage of nationalism remains to be seen.

Irish nationalism

British rule in Ireland goes back to the eleventh century. It is a troubled history marked with misjudgements, tragedies and atrocities that have left a legacy of bitterness that still exists among some sections of the Irish people. The conflict between dominant power and subject people was compounded when Britain adopted Protestantism while Ireland remained Catholic. Some of the most tragic events and relationships stemmed from this religious difference: these include the settlement of Scottish Presbyterians on confiscated lands in Ulster in the early seventeenth century; the discrimination against Catholics; the depredations of English landlords; and, perhaps worst of all, the failure to help the starving population during the great potato famine in the 1840s.

The independence issue

Irish nationalism and the consequent call for independence was among the first in Europe. It began around the time of the French Revolution and developed during the following century. The great Liberal prime minister, William Gladstone, came to see the justice of the Irish cause and sought to give Ireland full independence. The northern Protestants were bitterly opposed, as were a substantial number of the House of Lords who owned lands in Ireland. It was these Lords who threw out Gladstone's Bills to give Ireland independence, despite their having been passed by the Commons. Gladstone also had trouble with some of his own party. A group calling themselves 'liberal unionists' led by Joseph Chamberlain left the party and joined the Conservatives in 1886. Thereafter, Unionism (maintaining the union between Ireland and Britain) became a fixed Conservative principle for a hundred years, and the Northern Ireland Unionists were formally linked to the Conservative Party.

By 1911 the power of the House of Lords had been destroyed and the opportunity arose for a Liberal government to grant Ireland its independence; but the First World War intervened. By 1918 the Liberal prime minister, David Lloyd George, had become entirely dependent on the Conservatives who would not countenance independence for all of Ireland. The result was an unsatisfactory compromise. Ireland was partitioned, with Northern Ireland remaining in the United Kingdom, but with a third of its inhabitants Catholic and nationalist. The North was given its own parliament at Storemont and its own government able to run its domestic affairs, with little interference from Britain. The result was that the Catholic population was heavily discriminated against and effectively denied many civil rights.

The Irish Republican Army, which had fought the British in the years before independence, attempted terrorist campaigns from time to time to persuade the British to leave Ireland altogether. But these were never remotely successful before the late 1960s. In 1968 a civil rights movement developed rapidly in the North to campaign for better treatment for Catholics. This provoked a Protestant backlash, which led to the sending of British troops to the province, which in turn provoked a renewal of nationalist violence led by a new version of the IRA, the Provisionals.

The Provisional IRA

After the civil war in Ireland following independence, IRA violence came in periodic bursts of activity for a few years that died away because of lack of success. The 1956–62 border campaign fizzled out in this way, and the organisation turned to revolutionary Marxist theory, in the form of traditional Marxism-Leninism. When the civil rights crisis flared up in 1968 the IRA were unprepared and were on the point of giving up terrorism for conventional politics. The movement split in 1969, with those convinced that only a 'military' campaign could be successful breaking away to form the 'Provisional' IRA. For a time the 'Official' IRA competed in violence with the Provisionals before withdrawing from the 'armed struggle'.

The Provisionals have never set much store by politics, let alone political theory. Patrick Bishop and Eamonn Mallie wrote: 'The Provisional IRA had been conceived in haste. The circumstances of its birth and early years meant that by the time of the hunger strikes it was politically backward, not to say retarded' (Bishop and Mallie 1987, p. 260). Insofar as it thought about what Ireland would be like after the British had left, the Provisionals spoke of a federal system with regional parliaments (thereby giving the Ulster Protestants a considerable degree of autonomy) and an IRA-dominated government in Dublin pursuing some rather vague version of democratic socialism at home and neutralism abroad. However, under the leadership of Gerry Adams, the Provisionals have developed a political strategy of standing in elections under the banner of a political party, Provisional Sinn Féin; while at the same time moving further left in their political outlook. Although they have not gone as far left as the Irish National Liberation Army (INLA) who are dedicated Marxist revolutionaries (like the Officials) but ferocious terrorists as well.

Although they have become more sophisticated in recent years, the Provisionals' ideology is basically very simple: the British have no right to be in Ireland; all the ills that have befallen the Irish people in the last four hundred years have been caused by the British 'occupation'; and that a new and better Ireland will be created when the British have been driven out. This does not involve any abstract theory or world-view, and is perfectly comprehensible to the most ill-educated recruit, whose political education consists of little more than an IRA version of Irish history, full of British atrocities and Irish martyrs. Unlike the New Left terrorist groups in Europe (like the Italian Red Brigades or the German Baader-Meinhoff gang), the Provisionals are mainly recruited from among the working-class youth with little education and few prospects. At the same time, the movement has many older followers, reflecting the longevity of the cause.

The Provisionals are, therefore, a rather narrow and traditional nationalist group which is not much concerned with the outside world, except when it can be of use. It has traditional links with Breton nationalists and the Basques (ETA), but more recently developed links with the Middle East, where arms have come from Colonel Gaddafi's Libya and where a few Provisionals have attended Palestinian training camps. There has also been some contact with European Marxist groups (especially in Holland) which have helped the IRA to attack the British Army in Germany.

The Provisionals' entry into Northern Ireland elections, through their 'front' organisation Provisional Sinn Fein, has not been a notable success. Although seats have been won, they have not displaced the moderate SDLP. The great majority of northern Catholics reject IRA violence, as do the overwhelming majority in the Irish Republic.

The SDLP

The civil rights movement of the 1960s, not only led to a renewal of violence, but also the establishment of a new party devoted to achieving a united Ireland by non-violent means. This is the Social Democratic and Labour Party (SDLP), founded in 1970. It has sought to negotiate with the British government to achieve power-sharing between Catholics and Protestants and to extend the links between the North and the Irish Republic, so that eventually the Northern Protestants will cease to fear closer ties with the South. The SDLP's most important achievement up to 1998 had been the Anglo-Irish Agreement of 1985, which required co-operation and regular consultation between London and Dublin and the Northern Ireland administration over the problems of the province. This infuriated the Unionists, while the recognition by all concerned that Norther Ireland would stay in the United Kingdom as long as the majority of the people of Northern Ireland wanted it to, ensured the hostility of the Provisionals. The SDLP hoped to demonstrate to the community that progress could be achieved by negotiation, while violence led nowhere.

Cease-fires and talks

In the late 1980s, after twenty years of war, some in the Republican community began to realise that while the IRA had by no means been defeated, the war against the British could not be won. There was a certain war-weariness, strengthened by the Loyalist paramilitaries' policy of sectarian killings. Although bombs and killings continued, secret talks began between Sinn Féin and the British government, with the encouragement of the SDLP. The coming to power of Albert Reynolds as Irish prime minister in 1992 gave further impetus to the process. He sought to embrace Sinn Féin in a wider nationalist alliance which would include the Dublin government and the SDLP which would, with American backing, negotiate a settlement with Britain and the Unionists of the North. Britain would not, as Reynolds hoped, act as a persuader of the Unionists to move towards a United Ireland, nor as the Sinn Féin hoped, base a settlement on an all-Ireland referendum (in which the Unionists would be in a minority).

The outcome was the Downing Street declaration of 1993 supported by both governments holding out the prospect of all-party talks on the future of Northern Ireland, to be submitted to parallel referendums, North and South, and to which paramilitaries would be invited provided they permanently renounced violence. The following year the IRA announced a cease-fire. However, no all-party talks began, and a little over a year later the IRA ended the cease-fire with massive bombs in London and Manchester. The nationalist claim that John Major dragged his feet because he was dependent on Unionist votes in the Commons was denied. The coming of a new Labour government with a massive majority in 1997 was quickly followed by a new cease-fire and the beginning of all-party talks. After months of intensive negotiations involving all parties (with the exception of Ian Paisley's Ulster Democratic party which refused to take part) an agreement was finally hammered out at Stormont on Good Friday, 10 April, 1998. It involved the creation of a new Northern Ireland parliament from whose representatives an all-party government would be formed. There would be cross-border bodies to deal with issues common to both north and south (such as tourism and economic development). The Irish government would seek to end the territorial claim to Northern Ireland that is contained in the Irish constitution. All sides would recognise that Northern Ireland would remain in the United Kingdom until a majority of its people decided otherwise. And the paramilitaries would give up violence and decommission their weapons.

The agreement had something for everybody, but also everybody had something that was hard to accept. Hard line Republicans and Unionists remain bitterly opposed, and the implementation of the Stormont agreement will be very difficult. But there is a widely held belief that it could be the basis of a lasting peace.

British nationalism and Europe

The United Kingdom is a multi-national state, yet while the nations that compose it have their own national identities, it is nevertheless fair to speak of a British nationalism embracing all of them. This is more a sense of identity than any conscious doctrine, if only because (unlike many other countries) there has been little historical need to assert such a doctrine.

Nationalistic feelings mainly find expression in such times as war, but occasionally at other times in relation to particular issues. The party that has tended to put particular emphasis on British sovereign independence and assertiveness, has been the Conservative Party.

In the late nineteenth century the Conservatives, in common with their European counterparts, discovered a source of popular support in nationalism. This was relatively mild in Britain compared to Europe and expressed itself in two themes especially associated with the Conservatives. The first was empire; it was the Conservatives who were the first to be, and long remained, the party of empire. It was Disraeli who particularly associated the Conservatives with imperial assertion, in contrast to the internationalism of the Liberals. The second theme was Unionism. This became important in relation to the problem of Ireland, but maintaining the Union has been an important conservative theme since the late nineteenth century. A recent manifestation was the staunch opposition to the devolution proposals of both the Labour Party and the Liberals for Scotland and Wales, by John Major in the 1992 and 1997 general elections.

However, the most important issue of recent years for British domestic politics, which has provoked the assertion of British nationalism, has been Britain's membership of the European Union (EU). Since joining the European Community (as it was then) in 1973 Britain's membership has been an increasingly important factor in government policy-making. It is a factor that is certain to increase in importance in the future as Europe moves towards ever closer co-operation and integration.

The idea of European integration

The idea of an economic community in Western Europe began to be discussed seriously after the Second World War. The aims were both economic and political. In the first place, to restore the prosperity of Europe within a free-market capitalist system. In the second place, and ultimately more importantly, to bring together the nations of Europe in such a way that the wars that had plagued European history, and had devastated the continent twice within a generation, would be prevented from happening ever again. If former enemies could be brought together in a common framework so that their economies were integrated, then armed conflict would be impossible. That is, in its political aspect the European Community was consciously designed as an antidote to aggressive nationalism.

The first step was to rebuild Europe's prosperity by replacing economic rivalry between states with co-operation. This began with the creation of a common market, followed by the introduction of common economic and social policies, to culminate in full economic integration. The final step would be some kind of political union, perhaps leading eventually to a federal United States of Europe with a federal president and cabinet.

The idea of a common market is fundamental. When firms export their goods to other countries they normally have to pay import duties (tariffs) which make their goods more expensive and harder to sell. Countries have these import barriers not just to raise revenue but also to protect their own industries against foreign competition. In this situation it is a great advantage for firms to have a large domestic market in which to grow in size and wealth, which in turn provides a strong foundation for competing in the rest of the world. A major reason why the USA is such a mighty economic power is that it has a very large domestic market of over 200 million people. Smaller countries are clearly at a disadvantage in this respect, and one way of overcoming it is for a group of countries to lower trade barriers among themselves and have uniform tariffs on goods coming from elsewhere, in order to create one large domestic market. In the case of the present EC area this amounts to some 320 million people, which is the largest single free market in the world.

However, the European Union version of this goes further in having a set of Community institutions independent of member governments, charged with running the Community and administering common policies. Common economic policies include those for agriculture, coal and steel, competition policy and regional policies. There are also common social policies, concerned with social benefits, equality of opportunity and other matters across the community. Consumer and environmental protection are also areas for common action. The hope is to extend these to monetary, taxation and other more general economic policies. However, these are controversial. It means governments handing over their right to make policy in ever more vital areas, which some are reluctant to do. The question is bound up with questions of national sovereignty and political integration. So far, political integration extends largely to a harmonisation of the policies of what remain independent sovereign states. All that has happened thus far involves a very limited pooling of sovereignty, but political integration implies a much greater loss of independence. By some it is considered worth it, for the sake of greater prosperity, political stability and communal influence in the world. Others, especially in Britain, are more doubtful.

The development of the European Community

France, West Germany, Italy and the Benelux countries (Belgium, Holland and Luxembourg) established the European Common Community when they signed the Treaty of Rome which set up the Common Market in 1957. They had been eager for Britain to be a founding member, but Britain stood aloof. The Common Market was soon seen to be a considerable success, with the economies of the member states growing rapidly. The British economy declined by comparison and it was soon apparent to many that Britain had made a mistake in not joining at the outset. By this time the French were no longer enthusiastic about British membership and blocked two applications before Edward Heath negotiated membership for Britain in 1973. The Republic of Ireland and Denmark joined at the same time. The nine member countries became ten in 1981 when Greece joined; and twelve in 1986 with the accession of Spain and Portugal. The fall of the Berlin Wall and subsequent reunification of Germany in 1990 enlarged the market without a further addition of members. In 1995 Austria, Finland and Sweden became members, making fifteen in all. Several other countries are negotiating membership, with more to follow. The larger the membership will create many difficulties. However, these are likely to be minor compared with the question of economic integration.

In the early 1980s there developed a strong feeling in the European Community that the energies of the organisation had been largely taken up with expanding the membership, to the neglect of institutional development. It was felt that the community would atrophy unless greater progress was made towards economic integration as had been envisioned when the organisation was founded.

The first step was the Single European Act agreed by heads of government, including Margaret Thatcher, and passed in 1986. The idea was to remove absolutely all barriers to the free flow of people, goods, services and capital within the EC. That is, taking the common market to its logical conclusion: a Europe without frontiers. This implied not just doing away with import duties and passports, but a whole range of changes. It implied the standardisation and harmonisation of technical regulations across the EC, so that, for example, Spanish electronic equipment has to meet the same requirements as in Belgium or any other country. It implied the standardisation and harmonisation of people's qualifications, so that the degrees, diplomas and certificates of one country are acceptable in all the others. It implied the ability of anyone to deposit and borrow money anywhere in the EC. It implied a whole range of legislative and administrative changes to ensure that conditions are the same in one country as in the others. To facilitate these changes, the Act introduced majority voting to prevent any state holding up the process with their own petty objections. The target set was the end of 1992 and much was achieved, although there were various exceptions, such as Britain's insistence upon maintaining passport controls.

However, implicit in the Single European Act was a commitment to a much more serious degree of economic integration, something Margaret Thatcher later claimed was not clear to her when she signed the Act. The single market implies a far greater integration of economic policy and institutions. Some argue that a common currency and a central bank and at least the beginnings of a centralised European government are inevitable consequences. Others, most notably Margaret Thatcher and the 'Thatcherite' wing of the Conservative Party, insist on preserving national sovereignty, which means national control over economic and monetary policy and the preservation of national currencies.

It was the cabinet that eventually overcame Margaret Thatcher's long-standing objection, and decided Britain should become a full member of the European Exchange Rate Mechanism (ERM), which links most EC currencies in a system of fixed exchange rates. But Margaret Thatcher and the 'Eurosceptics' remained fiercely opposed to further monetary and political integration, despite the fact that this was the way the rest of the EC wanted to go. To those in favour of closer links with Europe, this is little more than a blind assertion of an outdated nationalism, while the Thatcherites believe that the preservation of national independence is the primary duty of all governments.

Maastricht and Euroscepticism

When the single market programme was set in train it was agreed that further measures would be discussed at an inter-governmental conference (IGC) with a view to even closer integration. This occurred in December 1992 in the Dutch town of Maastricht. A whole raft of proposals were put forward concerning greater co-operation in foreign affairs and other matters, the change of name from the European Community to the European Union, to an agreement on workers' rights across the community (known as the Social Chapter) and a range of lesser matters. But by far the most important was an agreement to work towards a single currency, for the whole of the Union, to begin in 1999. Europe already had in place the ERM which linked all the currencies together in a set of fixed exchange rates. This would be built on, and the currencies would converge along with the economic measures needed to sustain the merging. But this was unacceptable to many in the Conservative Party, since it implied a European economic policy and a European government. In consequence, the British delegation led by John Major, by then prime minister, was the least enthusiastic and negotiated a series of opt-outs. Britain opted out of the Social Chapter completely, but also negotiated a special provision whereby it could participate in the setting up of the new currency but could opt out of actually joining at the last minute if it did not appear to be in its national interests to join.

All this was hailed as a triumph for John Major and seemed to allay the fears in his own party. But when the time came for a Commons vote on whether to sign the Maastricht Treaty the atmosphere had changed. A large section of the party was severely hostile and the government only forced through a 'yes' vote with the greatest difficulty. For the first time there was serious talk of Britain leaving the EU, hinted at by Norman Lamont the former chancellor of the exchequer, and echoed by many on the Thatcherite right of the party, such as Norman Tebbit; twelve Conservative MPs had the whip withdrawn (i.e. were expelled from the parliamentary party) for not supporting the party line on Maastricht and defying a vote of confidence. The atmosphere grew more heated and bitter between sceptics and pro-Europeans. The party, it was frequently said, was in a state of civil war. Things were not improved by Britain being forced out of the ERM in September 1992 (to the joy of the sceptics) and by the BSE crisis, when British beef was banned from the rest of Europe as unsafe to eat. A great deal of anti-European abuse was heard from some of the more outspoken sceptics.

The central demand of the Eurosceptics was the complete ruling out of Britain's membership of a single currency. The party was split and so was the cabinet. It was widely accepted that the chancellor of the exchequer, Kenneth Clark, would resign if membership was ruled out and he was frequently attacked by sceptics as preventing the party adopting a popular policy that could win the Conservatives the next election. During that election many Conservative MPs (including some junior ministers) openly declared their hostility in their personal manifestos, in defiance of party policy. During the election campaign John Major pleaded for unity in his own party, but with little response. The party's disarray over Europe undoubtedly contributed to their crushing general election defeat.

Since the 1997 election the divisions continued under the new Conservative leader, William Hague, who tried to bring together both Euro-enthusiasts and sceptics in his shadow cabinet. But a decision to rule out British membership for, effectively, at least ten years caused resignations and open conflict. In the meantime within the new Labour government there are also different levels of enthusiasm over Britain's entry. But sooner or later a decision must be made, although with what consequences nobody is sure.

Part III

The fringe

11

Green politics

The world-wide Green movement developed in the 1970s, flourished in the 1980s, but suffered something of a decline in the 1990s. The Green Party in Britain rather faded away after the 1992 general election, although it is still a political force in some countries, such as Germany. Yet despite its lesser prominence in recent years, the Green movement remains one of the most interesting political phenomena of the late twentieth century. It is easily the freshest and most original new ideology of our age and, given the right circumstances, has considerable potential for growth.

Threats to the environment

Concern for the environment has only been apparent since the turn of the nineteenth century. It has grown from a desire to preserve special places of particular beauty, to a serious and well-founded anxiety about the destruction of the planet as a setting for human life, and consequently about the survival of humankind.

Early concerns

It was the Industrial Revolution, and the huge growth in population and urbanisation that went with it, that provoked the first concerns about the destructive impact of human activity on the environment. Victorian social critics contrasted the healthy natural countryside with the ugliness and squalor of the new industrial towns. Pressure and action to protect the countryside began to develop. One example was the movement in America to create national parks, to prevent areas of unspoiled wilderness from being ravaged for commercial purposes, a concept that has gone around the world (British national parks are based on the different principle of preserving man-made working landscapes of great beauty). Such concerns led in time to comprehensive planning systems in Britain and elsewhere. Eventually it was to become clear that this was nothing like enough.

In the second half of the twentieth century, overpopulation, depletion of resources, destruction of the world's forests, the extinction of species, the poisoning of the land, sea and air, acid rain, the thinning of the ozone layer and global warming, not to mention the threat of nuclear annihilation of the planet, all pointed to the likelihood of some global catastrophe engulfing mankind. Such fears prompted the development of an environmental movement right across the developed world, to exert political pressure for preventative action to diminish the risks. However, for some it was simply too late to deal with the problems individually, and humankind can only be saved from catastrophe by a total transformation of human society and consciousness. Those who hold this view, and work to bring such changes about, belong to the 'ecology' or 'Green' movement.

Green politics

Ecology is one of the biological sciences that studies how living things interact and live together in a given environment. The ecology movement is not a movement of biologists, but of those who take the idea of ecology to have profound social and political implications for how people live and think about the world.

Many came into the Green movement from the New Left in the early 1970s, attracted by the radicalism of the cause. Indeed, many felt that Green ideas were a natural extension of New Left ideas (see Chapter 12) that rejected both capitalism and communism; that were suspicious of all bureaucracy and large-scale organisation; that strove to transform modern consciousness; and that experimented with alternative ways of living in communes and small anarchist groups, based on sharing and without domination or alienation. Not all of the early Greens came from the New Left, but some of the leading thinkers did, such as the German former-Marxist radical, Rudolph Bahro, and the American anarchist, Murray Bookchin. There are also important connections with other post-New Left causes, such as feminism. Bookchin, in *Post Scarcity Anarchism* (1972) and other works, has argued that 'authentic' Green thinking is the culmination of all the radical movements of the 1960s and 1970s, although this is a rather extreme claim.

The Green movement began as small groups and local parties in several countries. The first national political party, significantly called the 'Values Party', was formed in New Zealand in 1972. Britain's was formed the following year. It was initially called PEOPLE, then changed to the Ecology Party and finally, in 1985, the Green Party (see Parkin, 1989 p. 214).

It was the German ecologists who started to call themselves Greens (*Die Grünen*) and the name has now been almost universally adopted. The Green movement is now world-wide, with parties in just about every country. The most politically successful (in the narrow sense of winning elections) have been the German Greens. Although only founded in 1981, the party astonished Europe in 1983 by winning twenty-eight seats in the Bundestag, as well holding seats in many provincial and local assemblies. The party thus became a major force in Germany, Europe's most powerful economic nation, virtually overnight; it went on to win 8.3 per cent of the vote and forty-two seats in the 1987 general election. This success has, however, created problems of how to relate to other parties, a success which parties elsewhere have yet to experience.

Many countries in Europe and elsewhere now have Green MPs. Britain does not have any, although there are some Green local councillors. In the 1989 British elections for the European parliament the Greens gained a remarkable 15 per cent of the vote, but no seats. However, in the European elections of 1994 support dropped to 5.45 per cent. Support is even less in general elections, in the 1992 election 253 candidates averaged only 1.3 per cent of the vote. In 1997 the party fielded only ninety-five candidates. There was virtually no national campaign and it was left up local parties whether to put candidates up.

This decline partly results from conflicts within the party in the early 1990s, when some of its leading figures left amidst some acrimony. However, the 1989 European result does indicate potential support for Green policies; and there might be more support in general elections if Britain's electoral system did not penalise small parties. If a proportional electoral system were to be introduced in Britain, as now seems possible, the Greens might become a permanent feature of parliamentary politics. In the meantime it may still be said of the British Greens, what can be said of the world-wide movement, that while not a major factor in world politics, it is true that the environmental movement as a whole, of which they are part, has put the environment firmly on the agenda of world politics.

Green doctrine

Green ideas have developed rapidly and have already evolved into a number of significant variants. However, there is a range of basic ideas to which most Greens would subscribe.

Traditional attitudes to nature

Although the newest of ideologies, Green thinking claims to be discovering an ancient wisdom concerning the human being's place in nature. Philosophies of ancient India, China and elsewhere have emphasised the need to live in harmony with all natural things. It is implicit in a famous passage (much quoted by Green writers) in the reply of the Red Indian, Chief Seattle, to the request of the US government in 1885 to be allowed to purchase some of his tribe's traditional lands:

> How can you buy or sell the sky? We do not own the freshness of the air or the sparkle of the water. How then can you buy them from us? Every part of the earth is sacred to my people, holy in their memory and experience. We know that the white man does not understand our ways. He is a stranger who comes in the night, and takes from the land whatever he needs. The Earth is not his friend, but his enemy, and when he's conquered it, he moves on. He kidnaps the earth from his children. His appetite will devour the Earth and leave behind a desert. If all the beasts were gone we would die from a great loneliness of the spirit, for whatever happens to the beasts happens also to us. All things are connected. Whatever befalls the Earth, befalls the children of the Earth.

What is important here is the sense of humanity as not separate from nature but merely one part among others, as contrasted with the characteristic western attitudes which it rejects. It is understanding this contrast that Greens insist is the beginnings of genuine wisdom.

In contrast to the words of Chief Seattle are those of the Bible on the question of how human beings relate to nature: 'And God said, Let us make man in our image, after our likeness: and let them have dominion over the fish of the sea, and over the foul of the air, and over the cattle, and over all the earth' (Genesis I:26). This sets humanity apart and above nature, giving it dominion over nature and conceiving the natural world as being there solely for human benefit. It was a view reinforced by Aristotle, whose account of the natural world, as a great hierarchy in which the lower orders existed for the sake of the higher, largely dominated Western thinking until the nineteenth century. However, no great evil consequences for the environment could flow from such attitudes until humanity had vastly increased its power over nature. In all parts of the world and in all kinds of habitats, people adapted to their physical environment and of necessity lived in some kind of balance. It was when Western civilisation acquired unprecedented powers over nature that that balance became lost.

The impact of modernity

The process began with the development of physical science and an accompanying materialistic outlook, the eventual outcome of which was the Industrial Revolution. This gave human beings the potential to destroy nature as never before, and there was, in the West at least, no religious or ideological restraint on the process. Greater production, greater exploitation of resources and greater profits all became gods of the new age, and have continued to be so since.

The outcome is today's consumer society with its conspicuous consumption, massive waste and appalling consequences for the environment. Capitalism bears much of the blame, with its profits at any cost. But the communist world was no better in its attitude to production. The developing world has been bullied or persuaded to participate, industrialise and compete in world markets. And despite the fact that the world is beset by the social ills of poverty, starvation, unemployment, urban decay, even to the extent that some think that modern industrial society is breaking down, yet the solution of all contemporary ideologies of those in power, is the panacea of economic growth, which is, Greens insist, the root cause of all the problems anyway. Humanity is rushing towards an abyss and all the world's politicians can suggest is that we rush ever faster.

Industrialism and its alternative

Although Greens are perfectly aware of the differences between the main ideologies, they are more impressed by what they have in common. Conservatives, liberals, social democrats, democratic socialists and communists, are all and everywhere preoccupied with economic growth and technology and what they like to term 'progress'. For this reason Greens are inclined to see them as differing manifestations of the same 'super-ideology' which they call 'industrialism'.

The dominant 'super ideology'

The main features of this industrialism are:

- a devotion to economic growth and industrial expansion and continuous technical innovation
- a belief in the overriding importance of satisfying people's material needs
- large-scale centralised bureaucratic control
- scientific rationality being the only kind of reasoning that matters
- large-scale units – in industry, administration, etc. – are most efficient ('big is beautiful')
- a predominance of patriarchy and an emphasis on 'masculine' values of competition, aggression and assertiveness
- an anthropocentric view that sees the earth and all that lives on it as simply there to be exploited for any human purpose
- a hierarchical social structure where power and wealth is concentrated at the top
- economic considerations predominate in society and moral, social and artistic values are of lesser importance

Within this common framework, the predominant systems of East and West have their own horrors. Communism suppresses human freedom in the name of an inhuman system. And although communism has almost died out, the old Cold War rivalry produced a stock of nuclear weapons that could still destroy the planet many times over.

Western capitalist democracy has become triumphant within this 'super ideology'. But while, compared to communism, it has much to commend it in terms of liberty, Greens argue that it is even more ruthless in its destruction of the environment. On top of the industrialist feature it shares with communism it adds its own destructive characteristics. It is an outlook that favours aggressive individualism, competition and selfishness, that finds expression in a free market economy that is given free reign to make profit irrespective of the damage it causes. Profit is given priority over all things. The modern consumerism that the free market has created, positively encourages people to buy what they do not need and throw things away as soon as possible. Continuous consumption is deemed desirable, as good for the economy, no matter what resources it wastes. Free market capitalism has also created a world market which has given encouragement to the developing world to industrialise and compete in world markets, despite their severe disadvantages and the destruction of their traditional ways of life.

The most basic assumption – that economic growth, with ever greater production and consumption, is the solution to all ills – is the most destructive. We are so imbued with these assumptions, Greens claim, that it requires a considerable feat of imagination to break free of them. But break free we must if disaster is to be avoided.

The Green alternative

The first step is to realise that there is an alternative. The Green perspective is not just a set of solutions to environmental problems but a complete theory of the human and the social. There are variations, but all Greens would subscribe to the following.

First of all, human beings are part of nature and must live in harmony with nature or risk destruction. Green thinking is not anthropocentric but biocentric. What is good is not what is good for humankind in isolation, but good for the earth and all that live on it. Consequently, protection of the biosphere and the conservation of finite resources is a first priority; and to achieve this, international co-operation must replace competition and aggression between nation-states. There must be an end to both economic growth and population growth. Economic systems that recklessly exploit the earth's resources as though they were infinite are inherently wrong.

The giving up of such wasteful systems will necessitate a lower standard of living, with less growth and, for example, fewer cars and other consumer goods. Industrial society is breaking down, as is evidenced by such symptoms as chronic unemployment, inner city decay and general alienation. It needs to be replaced by a simpler and more satisfying way of life, one based upon more spiritual values rather than the material ones that dominate our world at present.

Most Greens would add the following principles. Patriarchal characteristics and values of aggression and competition must become much less important beside 'feminine' values such as co-operation and caring. There must be a massive redistribution of wealth; and not just between rich and poor within a society, but between continents and between generations (that is, we must not use up the earth's resources that future generations could benefit from). The Greens are not against private property as such, but against excessive wealth and power. Greens insist that any kind of decent society must be characterised by 'social justice', and be without discrimination or inequality. A world built upon such principles, it is argued, would be free, safe, humane and just.

Upon these broad principles Greens base their ideas as to what would be an ideal society, an 'ecotopia'. These vary, but generally they include a basis of small communities, where people know each other, where direct democracy can operate, and where everything is on a human scale. An economy made up of small-scale organic farming, small-scale industry and crafts, and based on co-operation rather than competition. All such industry should be labour-intensive and use the minimum of non-renewable resources. Great emphasis is put on self-sufficiency for community and region, so far as possible. No-one would be poor or disadvantaged.

Shades of Green

However, it must be said the while there is a good deal of consensus about what Greens are against, there is much less agreement about what Greens are for. There are considerable differences over detailed policies, strategy and tactics, and also over what kind of world would be possible or desirable.

Greens differ a good deal among themselves as to the exact place humanity has in nature and its ideal relationship with the natural world. For most, Green thinking must involve a spiritual element, and the salvation of mankind must involve some kind of spiritual renewal (see, for example, Jonathan Porritt's *Seeing Green: The Politics of Ecology Explained* (1984), or Sara Parkin's *Green Parties: An International Guide* (1989). For some, indeed, Greenism is a new religion. The earth is a goddess, Gaia, with whom we must be in tune, and so on. The most famous exponent of this view in Britain is David Icke, a former television presenter and former leading spokesman for the Green Party. He astonished the world in 1990 by announcing his religious beliefs (about him being the son of God and having a mission to save the world) which most people found decidedly eccentric. However strange Icke's beliefs may be, there is a large background to this kind of thinking, especially in America.

Other Greens see the need only for a greater reverence for nature, and greater humility in its presence, without any need for spirituality. Others still, dismiss all this as dubious metaphysics and emotionalism, and see nothing beyond the science of ecology as needed for a Green vision of the world.

There are other disagreements about what kind of world might be possible if and when humanity comes to its senses. What, for example, should be the role of technology? Some see our faith in science and technology as the root of our present crisis. Salvation lies, it is argued, in rejecting high technology and developing 'low-tech' solutions to practical problems that everyone can understand and operate. Yet others see modern communications and information technology as the key to a decentralised social life where people can work at home and live in small communities.

A major source of division in the Green movement is the development of various hybrids that synthesise Green ideas with older ideologies. Some have reworked traditional Marxist ideas to argue that capitalism is inherently the enemy of the environment, and that some form of communism is the only solution. Others have argued the feminist categories are the key to understanding the situation. Thus, male competitiveness and aggression are the source of the problem, which is essentially a side-effect of patriarchy; while it is female qualities of care and co-operation that must be the basis of a solution.

In many ways it is anarchism that is seen to have most affinity with Green ideas. The trend of Green thinking towards smaller, self-sufficient communities, as against large-scale modern industry, organisation and urban life is an inevitable consequence of any kind of Green approach, yet is strongly reminiscent of older anarchist ideas of federations of small communities in the writings of such as Proudhon, Kropotkin and William Morris, as well as of the more recent anarchism of the New Left (see Dobson, 1995 Chapter 5).

On one hand, Green ideas do not necessarily preclude quite different ideas, that involve hierarchy and authority. What for some may be a desire to create a viable post-industrial society, may for others be a desire to recreate a pre-industrial society based on social hierarchy and discipline. Writers like Edward Goldsmith, in *A Blueprint for Survival* (1972), see a Green programme in terms of preserving an essence of traditional Englishness in its rural purity. Then again, Green ideas can be consistent with fascism. One dimension of Nazi ideology was its 'blood and soil' with a nostalgia for a rural past of sturdy peasant life.

Support for Green ideas may thus come from very different and incompatible directions, but such differences usually matter little so long as the Greens do not hold political power. Once they do, differences tend to come to the fore. This has happened in Germany, where their electoral success has put them in a position of influence, and the consequent necessity of making hard political choices about who they can support. This had led to rows and splits within *Die Grünen*, and Greens in Britain have recently followed suit, with conflicts over strategy.

The British Green Party has deliberately pursued a policy of trying not to behave like other parties. They do not have a single leader; party conferences are a series of seminars; and so on. The point is to show that the Greens are not a party like other parties – that they are 'an anti-party party'. But some Greens feel such tactics are counter-productive, and considerable recrimination and acrimony followed the party's poor showing in the 1992 general election. Part of the problem was the perception by rank and file membership of a leadership developing which made the Greens increasingly look and behave like a conventional party. Others saw this as simply being politically effective. High profile leading figures such as Jonathan Porritt and Sarah Parkin left the party and, particularly after the 1992 election, the grass roots radicals have dominated the party. These are less interested in high-profile national politics, but more in direct action in relation to anti-road building, animal protection and other campaigns. There was almost no national campaign in the 1997 general election.

The variety and the differences within the Green movement may be exacerbated by the tendency to take on board radical causes which may not always fit with Green thinking. Unilateral nuclear disarmament and animal rights are causes that fit well. But Greens also tend to support feminism, gay rights, holistic medicine, the legalisation of cannabis and a good many other issues which may not fit quite so well and can be a cause of dissension.

Criticisms of Green ideas

The main criticism levelled against the Greens is not so much their variety and eclecticism, as their other-worldliness. The idea that we can simply de-industrialise the world and create some rural idyll, borne of nostalgia and a romantic imagination is, so it is claimed, a fantasy. We cannot forget science and disinvent industry. Greens counter this by insisting that we either do something drastic along these lines or we destroy ourselves. Besides, Greens insist, there is no desire on their part to recreate some mythical bucolic past. New technology is fine in its place, although not all Greens agree.

Perhaps a more telling criticism of Green ideas is along the lines of reconciling the freedom and equality that Greens insist upon, with the drastic transformation of society that they insist upon even more strongly. What if people do not want to live in small communities or change their lifestyle or co-operate with their neighbour? Will they have to conform? Will they be forced to be free?

Will there not need to be severe restrictions on people's economic activity? And who will enforce them? Many Greens reject the modern state. Yet it is possibly only the strong state that could enforce Green policies; and would certainly have a better chance of doing so than a network of self-governing communes. Greens often talk as though it is only necessary for people to understand the environmental dangers to stop them polluting rivers or destroying forests on the path to making money, or to stop them wanting cars or other goods. But the idea that all will be well once everyone sees things the right way, is one of the oldest of political illusions. How to stop people behaving in ways deemed undesirable, is a particular problem for Greens who reject authoritarianism.

Whatever answers to these problems the Greens come up with, it seems likely that Green ideas will become more important in the future. Sadly, it may take a major environmental catastrophe to raise the profile of 'dark green' politics again. However, short of this, the question of whether the future of Green parties will be one of greater strength and political success is difficult to answer. It may turn on whether the Greens can agree sufficiently on their ideas and learn to play the political game successfully, or whether ideas and energies will be dispersed among other parties and beliefs: Green socialists, Green liberals, Green conservatives, Green Marxists, Green Christians, and the rest. Either way, Green ideas seem set to make a major impact across the ideological spectrum.

12

The extremes and the fringe

The major political parties of Britain, those that are seriously concerned with winning elections and holding power, together represent a very broad spectrum of opinion. But beyond this spectrum there are other parties and groups whose views are, for the most part, unacceptable to the great majority of people and who stand virtually no chance of any kind of electoral success. These are the extreme parties of left and right.

At least part of the reason for their lack of popular support, and that which puts them beyond the normal spectrum, is that they are associated with the rejection of the parliamentary democracy that other parties take for granted. This is not to deny their claims to the contrary, or the fact that some do stand for parliamentary elections regularly; but it is to point to the fact that the doctrines they espouse are ultimately not compatible with the kind of liberal democracy existing in Britian. The far left has the greater number and variety of parties and groups, all more or less committed to revolutionary Marxism. The far right has fewer and less varied groups which are rather less open about their ideological commitments; but there is plenty of evidence of their devotion to fascist ideas.

However, there are other groups on the fringes of mainstream politics that hold views that are not so much extreme as narrowly focused, and this is indeed a borderline area between political parties and pressure groups pursuing various causes that they deem to be of overriding importance. We see this in Green politics as discussed in the last chapter. But it also applies to various forms of sexual politics, such as feminism and gay rights. Then there are various groups centred upon the European Union, moral issues and a miscellany of other matters that vary, in the public eye, from the responsible to the crazed; all contributing to the dense pattern of politics in Britain today.

The extreme left

The far left is highly complex and difficult to understand in any detail. This is largely because of their characteristic predilection for theory. Mainstream British political parties may be described as semi-ideological, in that they all embrace a wide range of belief and are far more concerned with gaining power than with having the right theoretical stance. Extreme left parties are, by comparison, preoccupied with the intricacies of Marxist theory (often compared in its complexity and abstruseness with medieval theology), the belief being that there is always a theoretically 'correct' analysis of any situation and a consequently 'correct' tactic to suit it. This emphasis on the correct line is combined with an emphasis (derived from Lenin) upon party discipline, with the leadership laying down the correct line and everyone accepting it or facing expulsion. The variety of Marxist theory and inevitable variety of opinion results in a wide range of groups (each with its party organisation and its weekly or monthly newspaper) and a tendency to split over doctrinal differences, so that there is a constantly shifting pattern.

The range of groups is also a reflection of the history of Marxism in the twentieth century: with orthodox communists, those influenced by the New Left Marxism of the 1960s, followers of Trotsky, of Mao Tse-tung, of Fidel Castro, and even of Enver Hoxha, who was leader of Albania up to 1985, and the last East European exponent of hard-line Stalinism. However, the main division is between orthodox communists and Trotskyists. To understand this we need a brief account of twentieth century communism.

Marx, Lenin and communism

Karl Marx believed that the periodic slumps of capitalism would become ever more severe until eventually the industrial working class (the proletariat) would rise in rebellion and take over the whole system. Once begun, he believed, the revolution would spread through the entire world. In each country the workers would replace the capitalists as the new ruling class, and so would begin a brief transitional phase which Marx called the 'dictatorship of the proletariat'. The historic task of this period of working-class rule was to prepare the way for a truly communist society, where there would be no more classes, no more rich or poor, no state apparatus and all would be free, equal and have all they needed for a full life.

What we now call 'communism' is a version of Marx's ideas developed by the Russian revolutionary, Lenin. It is the official doctrine of communist countries such as China and Cuba (and until 1989 the USSR and its East European satellites) where it is known as Marxism-Leninism. Lenin extended Marxist theory in two ways. In the first place he developed the theory of 'capitalist imperialism', which argued that capitalism's most advanced phase (which Marx could not have predicted) involved the exploitation of colonies, where the greatest profits were to be found. What the capitalists did was to use some of this to give workers back home a better standard of living. As a result, the true proletariat, which experienced the harshest exploitation, was in the world outside the advanced West, and therefore it was here that the communist revolution could be expected. What this theory did was to explain why there had been no revolution in the advanced capitalist countries, where Marx had expected it to be. It was because the workers there had been effectively 'bought off'. The theory also enabled Lenin to predict that the revolution would begin in Russia, which he regarded as a special and peculiarly vulnerable case of capitalist imperialism.

Lenin's second and more important addition to Marx's thinking (though many Marxists now call it a distortion) was his idea of the 'vanguard party'. In his pamphlet of 1902,*What is to be done?* Lenin argued that when left to itself the working class is never very interested in revolution, but only in better pay and conditions. What was needed was not a mass working-class party, but a small party of professional revolutionaries, who would prepare for the revolution, be masters of both the practice and the theory of revolution, and lead the masses when the time was right. There would be rigid discipline and everyone had to accept the 'correct line' from the leadership (called 'democratic centralism', although there is nothing very democratic about it).

Lenin created just such a party, the Bolsheviks, and when the Czarist regime collapsed because of the war (not any failure of capitalism) in 1917, Lenin led a Bolshevik seizure of power. The Bolsheviks became the Communist Party and all other parties were banned. As in other communist countries, the 'leading role' of the party was guaranteed by the Soviet constitution, which effectively meant that the party controlled everything. The party claimed to be the 'vanguard of the proletariat': that is, the most advanced and most self-conscious part of the working class, and this was supposed to entitle it to rule on behalf of the working class. The theory is that the communist countries are still stuck in the transitional phase of the dictatorship of the proletariat until the rest of the world has its own revolutions and catches up.

When Lenin died in 1924 he was expected to be succeeded by his most able colleague, Leon Trotsky. But Trotsky was outmanoeuvred and driven into exile by Stalin, who proceeded to terrorise the party and the Russian people into a massive industrialisation and an absolute submission to his personal dictatorship. Before his assassination by Stalin's agent in 1940, Trotsky wrote extensively to the effect that Stalin had distorted and betrayed the revolution and that the USSR was not the workers state that it claimed to be.

Following the Russian Revolution, communist parties were set up in every part of the world, all obediently following the 'Moscow line'. Initially, Lenin's theories of party and tactics were supposed to be tailor-made for the special circumstances of Russia, but having successfully prosecuted a revolution in Russia, Lenin insisted that all genuine Marxist parties follow his model and his lead. This led to many European parties splitting in two, with rivalry between a revolutionary communist party and a non-revolutionary social democratic party.

In a number of West European states, most notably Italy and France, communist parties controlled important trade unions and could muster millions of votes in democratic elections. Following the Second World War, communist governments took over in Eastern Europe and in China and put an end to democracy. However, the 'Cold War' and incidents such as the brutal suppression of the Hungarian uprising in 1956 disillusioned many, and party membership in the West dropped rapidly. Western European communist parties started to criticise Soviet policy and became more independent; a trend that came to be called 'Eurocommunism'.

The New Left and Trotskyism

Meanwhile Western youth was taking a fresh interest in Marxism, but rejected established communism as corrupt and totalitarian. In the 1960s there was new interest in Marx's early writings with their emphasis on alienation and transforming consciousness. This was the New Left that had a large student following in Western Europe and America.

The New Left of the 1960s was a largely Marxist movement, but based on a Marxism very different from and hostile to the official Marxism of the communist world. It was not in fact the Marxism of working-class parties and trade unions fighting capitalist oppression, waiting for capitalism to self-destruct because of its internal economic contradictions. In fact it was a Marxism based on Marx's early writings (especially the 'Paris Manuscripts' of 1884, only widely available in the mid-twentieth century) which stressed the alienation and dehumanisation of the capitalist system and how these could be overcome in socialism to achieve liberation for all.

This version of Marxism became popular not among the traditional working class but among the affluent middle-class university students in America and Europe. They were against the capitalist system (which in fact was providing a higher standard of living for the majority in a way thought inconceivable to previous generations) because of its psychological oppression: brainwashing everyone into bourgeois conformity and becoming consumer zombies. What people needed was liberation.

Liberation was here understood principally in psychological terms. The battle that interested the New Left was not the class war between workers and factory owners. Capitalism had moved beyond that simple kind of repression, to the position of oppressing people by manipulating their minds. It kept the workers happy in their exploitation through cheap commercial entertainment and consumer goods. This is why New Left Marxism (in works such as *One Dimensional Man*, [1960] (1968), by Herbert Marcuse) was linked with psychoanalysis, phenomenology and other psychological and semi-psychological theories. Liberation was thus a state of mind, a release from alienation, a transformation of consciousness. Once this had been achieved the oppressive capitalist system could be replaced and a decent society built.

Those young people who believed in a disciplined party working towards revolution looked to Trotsky as a source of inspiration, and small Trotskyite parties flourished as official communist ones declined. They argued that the communist countries were as much in need of a revolution as the West.

The fall of communism

In 1989 most of the communist regimes of Eastern Europe collapsed. These were the regimes from Poland down to Bulgaria that had been imposed by the Soviet army after the Second World War. Only in the Balkan states of Yugoslavia and Albania was Communism 'home grown' during resistance to the Nazis, but these regimes began to collapse soon after. In the Soviet Union itself, the 'leading role of the party' clause was only dropped from the constitution in 1990, and the party finally fell from power in 1991.

At the end of the twentieth century Communist regimes only exist in China, Vietnam, North Korea and Cuba. The latter two regimes are in serious difficulties and are not expected to last in their present form. China does represent a quarter of the world's population, and from that point of view, it could hardly be said that communism is dead. On the other hand, China is liberalising its economy at a tremendous rate and encouraging capitalism to flourish. All that communism now seems to mean is that the Chinese Communist Party will remain in power no matter what happens. The hope of the Chinese government (as in Vietnam) is that a highly productive capitalist economy can be combined with an authoritarian one-party politics as has been characteristic of the 'Asian tiger' economies of recent decades.

British communism

The Bolshevik Revolution of 1917 faced the Marxist parties of Europe with a choice. This was either to settle for being reformist parliamentary parties, that is, 'social democratic' parties; or else follow the Soviet example and become genuinely Marxist revolutionary, that is 'communist' parties, which meant accepting the discipline of Moscow and its ideology of Marxism-Leninism. The Communist Party of Great Britain (CPGB) was founded in 1920 largely out of existing Marxist groups, principally what had been H. M. Hyndman's Social Democratic Federation (although Hyndman himself had rejected Lenin's assumption that necessary historical stages could be jumped or telescoped so that Russia could miss out the stage of bourgeois capitalism). The CPGB soon gained several thousand members, but never became the major political force that similar parties became in some other Western European countries. In the inter-war years it was a loyal follower of the Moscow line, sometimes chopping and changing policy bewilderingly as Stalin decreed.

The party enjoyed greater popularity after the German invasion of Russia in 1943, when the Soviets became Britian's allies. Membership reached 55,000 and it even gained two parliamentary seats in the 1945 general election. But the coming of the Cold War put an end to any mass support, and the seats were lost again at the next election. The brutal Soviet invasion of Hungary in 1956, in order to suppress a movement towards independence, disillusioned many communists in Britain as elsewhere. In the aftermath of this event, many communist parties in Europe (especially the Italian) began to take a more independent line from Moscow, criticising Soviet policy from time to time. This phenomenon, known as 'Eurocommunism', became increasingly important in the 1960s and 1970s. The British party remained fairly orthodox, but began to develop the notion of a 'British road to Socialism' that argued that Britain could move towards the abolition of capitalism and the introduction of a socialist society without the necessity of a violent revolution and seizure of power. Its main strength was in the trade union movement, especially in mining, shipbuilding and car manufacture.

The obvious economic decline of the Soviet Union in the 1980s led to a good deal of criticism of the Soviet system from European communists and a further loosening of the ties with Moscow. The British party began to split into two broad factions. There were the old-style pro-Moscow-line communists who controlled the *Daily Star* (formerly the *Daily Worker*), the party's daily newspaper, and who tended to idealise Eastern Europe as a worker's paradise. The other faction, known as the 'Eurocommunists' were associated with the party's theoretical journal *Marxism Today*, and took a more independent line.

A fierce conflict led to the Eurocommunists taking control of the party. With the collapse of communist regimes in Eastern Europe and the Soviet Union itself disintegrating, the party has been moving away from communism altogether. It has given up what is now called the 'irrelevant trappings of Bolshevism' and become 'an open, democratic party of the new, pluralistic and radical left'. Like other West European parties it is dropping the word communism from its title, and becoming the Democratic Left, which is more a focus for radical discussion than a serious political party.

Militant Tendency

Trotsky had a following in Britain, as in other countries, even before his death in 1940, and by the 1950s there were several small Trotskyite groups. But it was the 1960s that saw the flourishing of Trotskyism in the West.

The most prominent Trotskyite group of the late twentieth century has been the Militant Tendency. Its leading figure, Ted Grant, has been a Trotskyite since the 1930s and involved in various small groups, such as the Militant Labour League and the Revolutionary Communist Party, that periodically fused and broke up and eventually became the Revolutionary Socialist League. Grant, who came from South Africa, was joined by Peter Taafe from Liverpool in 1964, and together they set up a newspaper called *The Militant*. The League then adopted the policy of 'entryism', which was one of the tactics Trotsky suggested that revolutionaries might adopt. It meant infiltrating democratic socialist parties that had a large following and using them as a cover for revolutionary activity. When the time was ripe the revolutionaries could seize the party and lead the workers in the overthrow of the state. Other Trotskyite groups in Britain have generally not pursued this line, at least not consistently.

As a consequence of its policy of infiltrating the Labour Party, followers of Grant and Taafe ceased to call themselves (in public) the Revolutionary Socialist League, or by any other name which would imply that they were a separate party with its own organisation and programme. This would be against Labour Party rules and be grounds for expulsion. Instead, they called themselves the Militant Tendency, since 'tendency' merely implied one point of view among the many that make up the Labour Party. What organisation they have is claimed to be merely for producing and distributing their newspaper, which falls within party rules. However, in the early 1980s the Militants effectively took over Liverpool City Council, and, led by Derek Hatton and Tony Mulhern, proceeded to confront the government and refuse to comply with government requirements. The resulting confrontation was a great embarrassment to the Labour Party, compounded by the fact that in 1983 two Militant supporters, Dave Nellist in Coventry and Terry Fields in Liverpool Broadgreen, were elected as Labour MPs.

Matters came to a head when Neil Kinnock sensationally condemned the activities of the Liverpool Militants at the 1985 Labour Party conference. It was followed by proceedings leading to the expulsion of leading Militant supporters, including Grant, Taafe, Mulhern and Hatton. This left a great many supporters of Militant in the party, who were gradually removed.

The policies which Militant wanted the Labour Party to adopt included: nationalisation of the top 200 firms, state control over the financial system, workers' control in nationalised industries and in firms threatening redundancies, abolition of the monarchy and the Lords, and withdrawal from the 'capitalist club' of the European Community. This, as a list of policies, is merely a more drastic version of policies others on the far left of the Labour Party believe in. However, unlike others on the Labour left these policies are not seen as part of a peaceful and democratic introduction of Socialism, but are 'transitional demands' that are part of a wider strategy that is not made public. The point of the 'transitional demands' is to provoke resistance from the ruling class, which would generate a revolutionary situation, in which the workers would demand policies like Militant's and Labour's right-wing leadership would be exposed and overthrown. Militant supporters within the Labour Party would then be strong and well organised enough to lead the workers in a general strike to install a genuine workers government. Either way, the workers' government would have to defend itself against 'counter-revolution', which rather implies the imposition of a 'dictatorship of the proletariat' as the Bolsheviks did in 1917.

Most people in the Labour Party thought all this was puerile fantasy which should be ignored, were it not for the fact that the Militants were bad for Labour's image; and since their ideas were quite alien to what Labour stood for they, should be removed.

Militant tended to appeal to the young and politically immature. Yet at the same time, Militant was curiously old-fashioned. They tended to exploit issues like strikes and the poll tax which can arouse popular feeling, rather than support gay, women's or black rights on principle; and they were less interested in the fashionable theoretical preoccupations of the 1960s New Left (like trying to combine Marxism with psycho-analysis). In 1992 Militant changed its name to Labour Militant but has faded into obscurity.

Workers' Revolutionary Party (WRP)

Like Militant, the origins of this group can be traced back to the Revolutionary Communist Party of the early 1940s. Gerry Healy broke away from this group in 1949 to join the Labour Party, but his attempts to develop Trotskyism within it led to his and his followers' expulsion in 1959. Healy thereafter rejected the tactic of entryism and concentrated on building up an independent Trotskyite party, which became the WRP. It grew significantly in the 1970s and attracted publicity by fighting parliamentary elections (for reasons of publicity) and by the membership of the actress Vanessa Redgrave and her brother Corin.

The WRP's main concern is the creation of a disciplined band of dedicated young revolutionaries, against the day when capitalism begins its inevitable collapse and the workers will need leadership. As with Militant, great stress is placed on hard work, discipline and 'politically correct' thinking. This party too is rather old-fashioned, being even more Marxist-Leninist-Trotskyist orthodox than Militant. It has little interest in other causes, such as feminism, and will have nothing to do with sophisticated New Left theorising. It has, however, expressed support for certain international causes, such as the plight of the Palestinians in Israel.

In recent years the WRP has been riven by splits, partly over tactics and partly over personalities.

Other groups

The above groups have been the most prominent, have fought elections and have each gathered support running into thousands. But there are a great many other groups with smaller followings. These include the Socialist Workers Party, strong on international links and part of the Anti-Nazi League; and the Socialist League, who grew out of the New Left, support women's and gay organisations and emphasise 'transforming consciousness' and overcoming 'alienation'. Smaller groups include the Workers' Socialist League, the Sparticist League and the Revolutionary Communist Group (see Coates *et al.* pp. 264–74). Beyond both Trotskyites and the former CPGB there are still further groups, each with some variation of theory or tactics or acknowledging the inspiration of some communist leader, Mao Tse-tung or Castro or Hoxha. These groups are often very small indeed.

The Socialist Labour Party

More recently, the coalminers' leader Arthur Scargill, having lost a rear-guard action to prevent the Labour Party dropping its commitment to nationalisation in 1995, formed a new party with the title of the Socialist Labour Party. Its programme is pure classical socialism: extensive nationalisation, state planning, guaranteed full employment, a four day week, abolition of monarchy and Lords and withdrawal from the EU. Within months of the announcement of the new party a by-election arose in Arthur Scargill's own heartland in the Yorkshire coalfield at Hemsworth, but at the poll (in February 1996) the party candidate received only a derisory 5.4 per cent of the vote.

This result as much as anything demonstrates that left-wing socialism is not serious politics at present, and perhaps may not be so again. There may be a future socialist revival, but this seems more likely to be of the Keynesian social democratic variety.

Fascism in Britain

Groups on the extreme right are associated with fascism. The term 'fascism' is often used as a term of vulgar political abuse, meaning roughly 'authoritarian' or 'totalitarian'. But properly used it refers to the two similar sets of beliefs developed by Mussolini and Hitler in the 1920s. Hitler's national socialist (Nazi) ideology added a very important extra dimension of racial hatred to Mussolini's basic fascism.

Fascist ideas

The main features common to both are:

- An extreme, aggressive, xenophobic nationalism.
- Worship of the state, to which the individual must be subordinated, and for which the individual must, if necessary, be sacrificed. There must be absolute unity.
- Contempt for liberal democracy, pluralism and toleration, because these lead to division and conflict. Instead there must be a totalitarian one-party state that controls everything and tells everyone what to think.
- Adulation of the leader as the embodiment of the nation's greatness, carefully orchestrated through constant propaganda. The leaders will is the nation's will.
- Social Darwinism which sees society and politics as a struggle for survival in which the best succeed. The leader and the party are therefore the 'natural' elite who have struggled to the top. The capacity to dominate is a sign of superiority.
- The same applies to relations between nations. War and conquest are justified, and indeed necessary for the health of the nation.

Hitler added to this unpleasant set of ideas an even worse one, that of racial superiority, based upon racist theories of the late nineteenth century:

- The European peoples are mostly descended from a noble race of conquerors, the Aryans, of which the Germans were the finest and purest remnant whose destiny was to conquer the world.
- Other races were to a greater or lesser degree inferior. But lowest of all were the Jews, the historic race-enemy of the Aryans, who must be destroyed.

Such ideas should not have found a serious following in any civilised country, but in the inter-war years Europe suffered from continuous economic distress and political instability, and the fear and insecurity that came with them (especially in Germany). People responded to the seemingly strong leader who promised to solve everything if given power. Mussolini and Hitler both came to power in this way and by the mid-1930s every country in Europe had a fascist party, including Britain.

Early fascism in Britain

The main fascist party in Britain was founded in 1932 by Oswald Mosley under the title of the British Union of Fascists. Mosley had been a Conservative, an Independent and a Labour MP (he was expelled from the Labour

Party in 1931). He finally came to believe that fascism was the answer to the persistent economic distress and crises of the 1920s and early 1930s. Initially he had been an admirer of Mussolini, but increasingly came to see Hitler as his model, his ideas becoming more racist as a result. Britain's problems, he thought, could only be solved by a charismatic leader (himself) substituting authority and discipline and a sense of national purpose, for the party bickering and class conflict common to the age.

In *The Greater Britain* (1932) Mosley argued that free market capitalism, backed by 'international finance' had failed. The world was moving towards protectionism and state intervention, and Britain should do the same. The state should supervise the economy to make sure all parts worked together in harmony like an organism, and workers and employers reconciled, all in the interests of the nation. Strikes and lock-outs would be banned. Corporatism, where representatives of workers and employers in different industries worked with government to plan the economy (as in Italy and Germany), combined with imperial self-sufficiency, was the answer to Britain's problems. This meant centralised direction and planning of a capitalist economy. It would be forbidden to import goods that could be made in Britain and the Empire would provide everything else. In this way the British Empire would be economically self-sufficient.

Mosley believed that the traditional parties ('the old gangs' as he referred to them) and the parliamentary system were useless and out of date. In keeping with his corporatism, he believed that the House of Commons should be elected on the basis of occupational groups. The first parliament with a fascist majority would grant the government extraordinary powers to introduce the corporate state. Thereafter parliament would have only an advisory role, while the Lords would be replaced with a new chamber made up of technical and managerial experts of various kinds that would be able to assist government. The government would then make periodic appeals to the people in the form of plebiscites to confirm its power. The party system could then be dispensed with. Mosley wrote: 'In such a system there is no place for parties and for politicians. We shall ask the people for a mandate to bring to an end the party system and the Parties. We invite them to enter a new civilisation. Parties and the party game belong to the old civilisation which has failed.' It would then be possible to end all divisions, merge everyone into the greater whole and ensure that everything is subordinated to the national purpose.

The failure of pre-war fascism

The nature of British politics, very different from Italy or Germany, required Mosley to be more circumspect in what he said. His anti-Semitism was usually expressed in metaphors ('alien influence', 'international finance') but everyone understood his meaning. He in fact envisaged depriving Jews of British citizenship and deporting any of whose activities he did not approve.

Ultimately, he wanted a place set aside for Jews in some barren area of the world to which they could all be sent.

Similarly, while he said he would govern with the help of parliament, and gain power with the consent of the British people, nobody doubted that, given the chance, he would establish a dictatorship, or that he would seize power in a coup. Certainly his methods were modelled on his heroes. Black-shirted para-military displays, great rallies, beating up opponents, and so on. But he never had the popular support, or the support of other groups in society, that continental fascists enjoyed; Britain's politics were far more stable than Italian or German politics. When war broke out in 1939 Mosley was locked up for the duration.

Hitler's aggression brought inevitable war and total defeat for himself and his allies. Furthermore, the discovery by Allied armies of Hitler's extermination camps where some six million Jews had been murdered, horrified the world. It was known that Hitler had persecuted the Jews and made them scapegoats for all Germany's ills, but no-one believed he had wanted to actually wipe out the Jewish population of Europe. The Holocaust, as it is sometimes called, was one of the most sickening crimes in human history. It entirely discredited fascism and any kind of racist thinking, which has no scientific or any other kind of rational basis.

The National Front and British National Party

It may seem astonishing that such ideas continue to have any following at all, but in the post-war world there have been parties with fascist sympathies. Normally these are tiny, and only gain modest public support when they disguise their real beliefs, which are still basically those of Mussolini and Hitler, and play on people's fears over issues like immigration and unemployment.

After the Second World War there were attempts by Oswald Mosley and his admirers to revive fascism as a national movement in Britain, but without success. Eventually, however, a party was created that managed to attract national support, and which became Britain's principal fascist grouping. This is the National Front (NF), founded in 1967.

At the levels of both policy and theory, race is central to NF thinking, although there are important differences between the two levels. At the policy level the central theme is colonial immigration. Ethnic minority Britons are blamed for every kind of social ill: poverty, crime, drugs, vandalism, bad housing, disease, unemployment and more. Worst of all, it is claimed, ethnic minorities pose the greatest threat to the British people through the mixing of blood. Thus, a member of the NF leadership wrote:

> The greatest danger this country has ever faced is that it has imported millions of aliens who are members of backward, primitive races, and whose large-scale racial intermixture with the indigenous Anglo-Saxons would not only put and end to the British as a distinct and unique ethnic entity, but would produce an

inferior mongrel breed and a regressive and degenerate culture of tropical squalor. (*Spearhead*, October, 1976)

One NF answer has been the compulsory repatriation of all ethnic minority Britons (although it hardlly makes sense to talk of 'repatriating' British citizens, born in Britain). Other NF supporters have advocated racial laws against marriage between 'Aryans' and 'non-Aryans' in order to preserve racial purity. Beyond this, there are conventional fascist concerns with national assertion and self-sufficiency (such as withdrawal from the EC). In public the racial hatred is played down, as is the contempt for democracy.

At the level of theory, however, the principal theme is not anti-ethnic minority but anti-Semitic. It is a slightly modernised version of the old Nazi theory of an international Jewish conspiracy. Thus, both 'international finance' and communism are instruments of a Jewish plot to destroy Western economies and society with recession and communism, and to destroy racial purity through internationalism, immigration and other forms of racial mixing. This is in order to subjugate the world to a world government based in Israel.

To the great majority of the population, such ideas are puerile and disgusting. Their main appeal in terms of membership is to those blinded by hatred or to those who are ignorant and young with a taste for violence (such as football hooligans). For electoral purposes, much of the uglier side of NF thinking (including its contempt for democracy) is not made public, and there is a more subtle appeal to fears and prejudices and to 'Britain first', which in times of economic difficulty has given them some national prominence.

The National Front was created through the amalgamation of a number of extreme right groups. Their collective membership amounted to around 4,000, but rapidly increased to its peak of around 17,500 in 1974. Elections in that year also gave the NF its highest ever popular vote of 0.6 per cent, although it came nowhere near winning any single seat. However, support for the NF began to wilt with the advent of Margaret Thatcher as a Conservative leader overtly wanting stricter controls on immigration and firmer policies on law and order and on Ulster. Many right-wing Conservative supporters returned to the fold. Perhaps also the true nature of the NF became better known. But for whatever reason the 1979 general election was a disaster for the NF. Within a couple of years its number were much as they were in 1967. The party split and new or resurrected groups were set up (such as the League of St George, the British National party and the National Socialist Action Group) producing an array of groups of various degrees of political nastiness.

In 1983 the NF split, and two distinct organisations emerged. A drastically reorganised 'new' National Front became a clandestine organisation concurring with terrorist methods, making contact with similar groups abroad. For a time it was a worrying development, but in the end it came to nothing.

The other new party was the British National Party (BNP) reviving the name of one of the groups that originally formed the National Front in the 1960s. This is a more conventional political party that is little different in its outlook and tactics from the old National Front. Occasionally it surfaces in times and in areas where there is particular racial tension for a time. In 1993 in the context of a particular racial dispute in Tower Hamlets in the East End of London the BNP won a local council seat, but it was quickly lost at the next election. Another example of its activities was at an international football match in Dublin in 1994 which was ruined by rioting. Perhaps because there are now much stricter immigration controls in Britain (whichever party is in power) there is much less scope for a far-right party as there is in France or Germany.

The non-extreme political fringe

Not all political parties and groups on the fringe of British politics belong to the extremes of left or right. The 1997 general election saw a remarkable array of small parties with programmes whose purposes ranged from promoting single issues of various kinds, to naked self-publicity, to the moral transformation of humankind. And beyond these parties there are a host of groups that do not form political parties, but are none-the-less important in relation to political issues, and may have a distinct ideological stance.

Small fringe parties

Among the strangest of parties to appear on the hustings at recent elections has been the Natural Law Party. In both the 1992 and 1997 general elections it fielded candidates all over the country but gained a derisory vote (a fraction of 1 per cent). The party believes in transcendental meditation as the answer to the world's problems. It will enable the world to regain its lost harmony. Fantastic claims are made for the efficacy of what they call 'yogic flying', which consists of leaping up from a cross-legged position. Such activity in Skelmersdale in 1987 was claimed as the cause of a subsequent fall in crime rates in Merseyside. Nonetheless, the party fights vigorously at elections despite being regarded as distinctly dotty.

The Monster Raving Loony Party has been a regular feature of British elections for many years. It is regularly seen at by-elections, usually represented by its leader and founder, Screaming Lord Sutch, a rock singer who normally stages a performance in the area. He claims he has ideas and policies representing the view of youth.

More seriously, single-issue parties were a feature of the 1997 election, representing causes ranging from gun control to anti-abortion. Much the most significant in terms of numbers of candidates, media attention and significant support, were those related to the European Union. The most important of these was founded and financed by the Anglo-French billionaire Sir James Goldsmith to campaign for a referendum on the Maastricht Treaty or on Britain's participation in a federal Europe. Once this referendum was completed (whatever the result), Sir James promised that the party be disbanded. This seems to imply that the party was not so much concerned with the outcome as long as the British people could make their own decision. In fact the party was overwhelmingly supported by people opposed to Britain's further involvement in Europe. Vast sums were spent on publicity and some high-profile supporters joined or expressed sympathy, including such prominent former Conservatives as Margaret Thatcher's former economic adviser, Professor Alan Walters and the Conservative Party's former treasurer, Lord McAlpine. In the event the party polled over 800,000 votes.

A more overtly anti-European party demanding Britain's withdrawal from Europe was the UK Independence Party which polled another 100,000 votes. It is calculated that the Conservatives may have lost some half a million votes to these two parties in the 1997 election.

Feminism and sexual politics

Since the 1970s feminism has become a significant ideological force in British politics, as in many other countries. There had in the past been important women's movements, above all the campaign to gain women the vote in the first two decades of the twentieth century. Feminist thought tended to fall into two categories, reflecting the main ideological divisions of 'progressive' thought. Liberal feminists saw feminist aims in terms of women enjoying the same rights as men within existing society. Socialist feminists on the other hand saw women's plight in terms of capitalist society, and their emancipation would only come as part of a wider emancipation of humankind from capitalism. However, the late 1960s saw a new wave of radical feminism, that was much more independent of other ideologies than older forms of feminism had been. Several versions of liberal, socialist and radical feminism have since existed side by side producing a complex pattern of belief.

The new feminism, beginning in the late 1960s, was known at the time as 'women's liberation', and this name reflects something of the New Left inspiration of the movement in its early stages. The New Left was a largely Marxist-inspired movement, but not the old Marxism of political economy and class war, but a new 'humanistic' Marxism concerned above all with alienation and liberation. It argued that capitalism oppresses us psychologically, by making us accept the system and conform to the roles it imposes upon us, and makes us feel guilty and inadequate when we do not. Liberation from this condition was above all a state of mind, a transformation of consciousness. This transformation could be achieved first of all by recognising one's oppression and alienation, and also by realising that one's feelings of inferiority and self-loathing are part of the oppressive system. An assertion of identity and self-worth, a 'raising of consciousness' was part of the process of liberation. Ultimately those doing the oppressing must be liberated, for they too are victims of the system that cuts them off from fellow human beings.

This analysis was initially developed in relation to society as a whole, but soon began to be applied to groups deemed victims of particular oppression. Hence an array of liberation movements: black liberation, women's liberation, gay liberation and so on. Black liberation was the first of these movements in the 1960s and provided much of the vocabulary and techniques for those that came after, especially women's liberation, which became the most extensive and influential. The oppression of women was analysed in terms of 'patriarchy', and women were deemed to be the victims of 'sexism'.

Whatever the origins of the women's liberation movement in Marxist revolutionary politics, it certainly struck a chord with vast numbers of women across America, Europe and beyond, and inspired women's organisations of all kinds. There were liberal, socialist and radical feminists, but there was a good deal of cross-influence and camaraderie in the initial stages when all women could share a common cause against discrimination and gross sexist attitudes. But with the increasing success of the women's movement in changing social attitudes (and such is the transformation that it is now difficult to realise the depth of prejudice, conscious and unconscious, that existed before), divergences have become increasingly prominent, and the movement in consequence has become more fragmented. Initially, feminists tended to range from the centre of the political spectrum to the far left, but now there is much more variety, with anarchist feminists, green feminists, conservative feminists and New Right feminists.

It is perhaps this degree of fragmentation that has prevented feminism becoming a unified movement in any organisational sense. There have been no feminist political parties, whereas the Green movement has found expression in political parties all over the world. Some women's groups undoubtedly see conventional politics as essentially a male activity concerned with power and domination. However, women's organisations that are active in the political system have preferred to engage in pressure group politics, working through exiting parties and institutions. In this sense they are active in all the main parties and can count many successes in terms of anti-discrimination and other issues.

A somewhat similar fragmentation has occurred within the gay movement, although the process is at an earlier stage when gays' organisations, allied to socialism, conservatism and other beliefs, can share common campaigns against particular forms of discrimination. Social attitudes are changing more slowly in this respect, although aided by a vigorous lead in anti-discrimination by the European Union and the European Court of

Human Rights, whose charter and precedents will now be part of English law.

Now all parties are committed to recruit more women MPs and to be more sympathetic to gay issues. This is especially striking in the Conservative Party since William Hague became leader. Thus, although the women's and gay movements have never formed political parties, their influence upon society, politics and political processes has been considerable.

Part IV

The future

13

Trends and prospects

When Tony Blair became prime minister in 1997 he faced a very different political world than that inherited by Margaret Thatcher in 1979. This was not just in the sense of a different political and social situation – the world had indeed moved on, as it always does – but the whole framework of politics in Britain and the wider world was shifting in unprecedented ways. Many of the taken-for-granted assumptions, parameters and certainties of post-war politics had disappeared or were being transformed, while the pace of change had quickened so that the future direction of politics in Britain and elsewhere was more unclear than at any time since 1945. This chapter looks at some of the trends and forces of change that have brought this situation about, and in the light of them discusses prospects for politics and ideology in Britain in the future.

In 1979 the Cold War was still fully in place, which, despite being based on a grotesque balance of terror, nonetheless did impose a certain discipline on international affairs. There were two hostile camps composed of groupings of states, with liberal democracies on the one side and communist regimes on the other, with a further block of neutral states in between, to be wooed or bullied by either side. Apart from those countries which had been conquered by Soviet armies at the end of the Second World War, most of these states were able to choose which of the two sides they supported, or whether to go their own way. There were organisations like the European Community, and multi-national corporations, which did not quite fit the basic pattern, but there was no question that the political world was a world of sovereign states, mostly nation-states, as it had been throughout modern history.

Within Britain, much also was of long standing. In particular the Union of the United Kingdom and its constitution. This was characterised by institutions and principles, seemingly so venerable and long-standing that significant change was inconceivable. The constitution had evolved gradually into a liberal democratic state dominated by mass parties holding differing ideological beliefs, competing for office by seeking to persuade the public of the rightness of their principles and policies.

Few in 1979 foresaw the dissolving or undermining of all of these certainties before the century was out; but this has been the case. The future of the sovereign nation-state, the basic unit of world politics, has been questioned. The most solid of institutions and constitutional arrangements are under scrutiny; the politics of mass parties is changing, and ideological politics as we have known them might be passing away. Some argue that we now live in a postmodern society with a postmodern culture, in which these structures, and the hierarchies and practices and ideologies that go with them, make less and less sense, and to which people have less and less loyalty or commitment.

Thus, the future looks uncertain not only terms of social and economic developments and the policies appropriate to them, but also the nature and frame of politics, both national and international, is in flux. Theories, explanations and prognoses abound, but nobody is really sure about where the world is going and what the implications might be for politics and ideology in Britain. We will look at two broad areas which are likely to influence future developments: the forces of globalisation and fragmentation which threaten the future of the state; and the social and cultural changes at the centre of the debate over the kind of society we may be moving towards.

The fading of the sovereign state

The collapse of Soviet communism as a threat to western liberal capitalism in the late 1980s seemed to offer the prospect of a 'new world order' of peace and stability. But the world has not been noticeably more peaceful, and it is far from stable. Indeed, the instability and volatility of the world in general seems to threaten the nation-state itself from both above and below.

Globalisation and the sovereign state

Undoubtedly the most important international development in recent years has been the growth of the global economy and its political impact. What is meant here by 'economic globalisation' is not merely the further growth of the international economy, but a qualitative change that is, in an important sense, replacing the concept of the international economy. 'International economy' implies economic relations between sovereign states, whereas the term 'global economy' is meant to suggest a network of economic relationships and processes beyond the responsibility or control of any state. The power of multi-national corporations, able to switch production from one country to another at will, has long been known. But the explosive growth of global communications has opened up global financial markets of enormous power.

In the mid-1970s, before international money markets were as powerful as they later became, a Labour government was forced to change its more radical policies in the face of a loss of confidence in the pound in international markets. A similar fate befell President Mitterand's socialist policies in the early 1980s. A more recent example of this power was Britain's withdrawal from the European Exchange Rate Mechanism in 1992 because the international markets thought the pound was overvalued. Billions were lost from Britain's reserves trying to prop up the pound to no avail.

What these examples show is not just that international markets are very powerful, but that there is an increasing tendency for international financial opinion to impose a kind of uniformity on states in terms of economic policies. This, of course, imposes restrictions on what policies a state can successfully pursue, what kind of economy it can have, what levels of public expenditure and taxation and therefore what social policies can be pursued. This has profound implications for parties and their ideologies, as well as profound implications for national sovereignty. The days when a government that is involved in the international economy (as, for example, Britain must be to survive) could decide entirely for itself its type of economy, levels of taxation and expenditure and welfare state, seem to be over. Hence the claim that the nation-state has, so to speak, been undermined from above.

An interesting question is raised here as to the power of regional groupings, most obviously in relation to Britain and the European Union. Those in British politics who are hostile to the EU on principle, fear the loss of identity and sovereignty implied in the idea of a federal state, a 'United States of Europe'. Whether or not they are right in believing that this would be the consequence of monetary union, it is not at all clear that life outside of the EU would be any more sovereign than inside it. It is possible that the Euro currency would be powerful enough to resist the pull and push of the markets in the way that no other individual currency could be. If that were so, governments within the EU would have far greater leeway to pursue the policies they wanted than those outside.

Cultural fragmentation and conformity

At the same time as there are forces of unity and conformity in the global economy that undermine the state from above, there are also forces of fragmentation working from below.

One of the first and most obvious consequences of the end of the Cold War and removal of the discipline of superpower rivalry has been the disintegration or weakening of multi-national states, particularly under the force of revived nationalism. The Soviet Union began to break up almost immediately, with outlying republics seeking independence and reviving old conflicts. The Russian Federation itself has also come under strain. Yugoslavia also disintegrated and wars broke out with a viciousness not seen since 1945. But states in other are as of the world and in quite different circumstances have also suffered threats of disintegration. India has suffered from Sikh and Tamil extremism; and even Canada, modern, prosperous and seemingly stable, has experienced an upsurge of Quebec nationalism that has threatened, and continues to threaten, the unity of the federation.

Such strains have also been felt in Western Europe. France (in Corsica), Spain (in Catalonia and the Basque areas) and Italy (with its separatist Northern League) are among those affected. The list also includes Britain. Irish nationalism has threatened the Union by unconstitutional means, while Scottish and Welsh nationalism does so by conventional politics. The United Kingdom since 1997 has embarked on a major experiment in devolution which some hope and some fear will lead to independence, while others have thought a measure of devolution necessary merely to preserve the Union.

A factor in this movement towards the assertion of regional identity and aspiration towards independence is the European Union. It suggests a framework within which smaller states may comfortably survive in a way not possible outside the EU. There is also a more widespread demand for greater devolution and more regional autonomy.

These demands may be connected with the globalised economy, in which an inability to compete can result in unemployment. This may affect peripheral regions, which the government feels it cannot help because of concern for the international markets and the value of the currency. This in turn may cause resentment and generate demands for the region's having a greater say in its own affairs, or even independence.

Other forces of fragmentation are more subtle, although in the longer terms perhaps more lethal. These are cultural forces that undermine the sense of the nation as a cultural unity with a shared way of life. Economic globalisation unleashes market forces which always have the tendency to dissolve established communities and traditional ways of life. Furthermore, global communication has great potential to undermine any cultural identity that a government or religion may wish to preserve. This can create a backlash where threatened cultural identity asserts itself and becomes aggressive. Islamic fundamentalists, for example, rail at the Americanisation of Islamic youth with pop music and television and consumer goods. More generally, non-Western nations may have little hope of quelling popular demand for goods that are seen by their citizens whether they want them to or not.

Another aspect of global communications is the internet and other information technologies whereby international communications between citizens are possible in ways that are impossible to regulate. It would seem that it is quite technically feasible for someone living in Barnsley to work from home for a firm in, say, Buenos Aires or Brisbane. Again, a host of relationships and exchanges of information are possible which governments cannot control.

Individualism, consumerism and community

But much more important is perhaps the more general growth of a kind of individualism that sees human beings as essentially creatures bent upon pursuing their own interests and satisfactions, with little reference to others or the community generally. It perhaps goes with the kind of individual-as-consumer picture particularly associated with the New Right.

Arguably the growth of communitarian ideas (see Chapter 9), which stress the individual's responsibility to the community, is a response to this decline of community in the face of this kind of individualism. Some say it is too little and too late; others that it is a disguised reassertion of a kind of social authoritarianism that is inappropriate to the age we live in. Others still point to the Eastern 'tiger' economies, and suggest it is precisely the stronger sense of family and community that has given these nations the economic edge because these provide most welfare rather than the state, and consequently there are far less social costs to their economies. One consequence is that the West may have to go the same way, putting more responsibility on families and local communities, in order to compete in the next century. Again, international pressures seem to dictate which national policies are going to be possible.

A further question is the effect of a self-regarding individualism upon social solidarity and national unity. The loss of a sense of community may be a step to a loosening of the overriding allegiance of the citizen to the state. There seem to be so many other links and relationships, and too many other identities in the modern world for one to override all others. The idea of a more fluid, plural, multicultural society where we have many identities and connections with nationality, ethnic group and sexual orientation, religious belief and so on, is bound up with the arguments surrounding the kind of society that is emerging in what is variously called our 'late modern', 'post-industrial', or 'postmodern' age.

Late modern or postmodern?

Such have been the economic, social and cultural changes of the closing decades of the twentieth century that is widely accepted by social theorists that we have now moved into a new phase of social development, sometimes called 'post-industrial' or 'late modern' society. Some go so far as to say we have moved into a new kind of society altogether, a 'postmodern' society. Either way there are important implications for the future of politics and ideology.

Late modern society and politics

Until relatively recently, we understood the modern world in which we lived as a society of mass production, mass workforces, and the standardised goods of modern industry, run by modern scientific management. And along with this industrial system went a notion of politics as organised into mass parties based upon the main divisions of industrial society, and reflecting, in the ideologies of liberalism, conservatism and socialism, the aspirations of those divisions.

However, we have moved steadily since the Second World War to a society based on consumerism. Consumption rather than production dominates the economy. It is a society with an abundance of consumer choice; a world driven by advertising, no longer dominated by standardised factory products, but by goods expressing image and lifestyle. It involves an economy where services are more important than industrial products; where key industries are knowledge- and information-technology based; perhaps above all, a world dominated by television.

It is arguable that television reduces everything to the same level, the important and the unimportant, high culture and low culture, information and entertainment. Everything becomes a commodity and subject to consumer choice, including tradition, politics, and institutions. It is perhaps summed up in the *Sunday Times* main headline 'Queen to appoint royal spin doctor to boost ratings' (22 February 1998).

The post-industrial world has seen a decline of mass political parties, both in terms of loss of membership and electoral support. The days of unthinking loyalty to one party for life (a common feature of electoral behaviour in the 1950s, as many studies pointed out) is long gone. Voters are more discriminating, more ready to switch support to another party, and more ready to vote for parties that are not expected to form governments. Despite the fact that the British electoral system is particularly harsh to smaller parties, there has been a considerable growth of them in British politics since the 1970s. Furthermore, many people have put their political energies into pressure groups, like environmental and community groups, and begun to campaign on issues that are important for them, rather than give generalised support for a major party. These issues are often characterised as being principally concerned with identity and lifestyle. One of the features of the 1997 General election campaign was the remarkable number of single-issue parties, concerned with, for example, Britain's relations with the EU, abortion, gun control and a variety of other matters.

All this suggest a politics that is becoming more consumerist, where citizens are understood as consumers of government goods (policies and services) in a political marketplace where parties offer competing wares, based upon market research and with little ideological content. Some argue that we are reaching this stage in British politics, and that the Labour Party won in 1997 partly because it understood the new consumerist political reality better than the Conservatives.

Postmodern society and politics

Some social theorists take these arguments concerning a changing society much further, and argue that modernity is over and that we now live in a postmodern world. Postmodernism is among the most diffuse and elusive of concepts, and embraces a wide variety of theories on many topics. The basic idea of a postmodern society, however, is that we now live in a world in which all the old certainties associated with the modern society, as we have known it in the twentieth century, have collapsed.

These certainties of modernity are to do with progress. The idea is that through the application of reason, in science and technology and rational organisation in government and the economy, there will be perpetual improvement of the human condition, with greater freedom and democracy, prosperity and the possibility of happiness for all. Modern industrial, urban society, prosperous and democratic, was seen as a model to all less advanced societies to make similar progress through modernisation.

But from the perspective of the late twentieth century, these hopes and expectations of universal progress leading to emancipation and happiness for humanity as a whole look absurd after a century of world wars, genocide, totalitarianism, world poverty and with modern technology threatening to wipe out mankind, either quickly through nuclear war, or slowly through industrial pollution. War, violence, drug abuse, crime and a host of other horrors seem to be growing rather than diminishing. The world to many seems less and less rational and organised than in the past, while at the same time we seem individually to be ever more subject to surveillance and control. It is perhaps not surprising that considerations like this lead some to the conclusion that the project of modernity has simply failed. Writers in the late twentieth century have questioned the objectivity and effectiveness of pure science, and even more the effectiveness of its applications to human organisation, such as rational planning and scientific management.

But if this postmodern analysis is correct, what does it mean for society, politics and ideology? On these questions postmodern theorists are much less agreed. The most extreme version of postmodern theory is that of the French thinker Jean Baudrillard. He argues that modernity was the era of production, but now we are in an era of reproduction. Television has taken over our lives: as he puts it, 'TV is the world'. We drift around in an endless stream of media images, that refer to nothing beyond themselves, with little capacity for ordering them in a meaningful way. These images have become far more real to us than real life. What has not been recorded on film or video, or reproduced in some way, cannot have happened. Our sense of reality has collapsed, and we have lost all sense of history. We can no longer distinguish between image and reality, the real and the unreal; and consequently we are simply lost in a world of images with no escape (Baudrillard, 1988). This is, perhaps, the gloomiest view, and it is difficult to see the role or the point of politics, or anything else, in such a world.

A more common, and more hopeful view among postmodernists, is that of another French thinker, Jean-François Lyotard. He suggested that all social and political activities justified by apparently universal truths no longer have any hold on us. We have, rejected grand theory, what he calls 'metanarratives', with their accompanying notions of universal human nature, human rights and human needs. This whole way of thinking is wrong. This of course, principally applies to ideologies: to various kinds of socialism, Marxism, fascism, liberalism and anarchism. Lyotard goes so far as to say that any attempt to impose one universal vision on anyone, not just Marxist or fascist, but liberal or national, is totalitarian and 'terroristic' (Lyotard, 1984). Instead we must learn to live in a world of shifting truths, of multiple points of view, where there is no means of determining who is right and who wrong. All is relativism and subjectivity. Truth is always 'local truth'; that is, only valid within the context of the group or community which generated it.

This view calls into question all kinds of authorities – political, scientific, intellectual, social – along with the hierarchies and justifications that go with them. It suggests modern society has to be pluralist and tolerant with a multitude of differing viewpoints from a multitude of groups, sections, social groups and individuals. In these circumstances, it is argued, it becomes impossible to impose, and morally wrong to try to impose, an ideology or any kind of mass identity, to do with class, nation, ethnicity, or whatever. The individual, so the theory goes, is recognised as having multiple identities, and resents ideological claims that one must be overriding, be it class or nation or gender or anything else. There is no fixed universal human identity, only accidental, historically specific identities.

For some this postmodern world is a liberating one, freeing us from traditional authorities, hierarchies and ideologies; a much more egalitarian and globally communicating world. They see a more fragmented and various society, no longer divided by simple and ideologically charged divisions like social class, and imagine much more the politics of social groups and associations based on age, gender, locality, nationality, ethnicity, sexual orientation, occupation, and other divisions. Politics of this kind is a matter of pressure groups and social movements, like the women's movement, gay rights and environmentalism. The base of mass parties, in Britain as elsewhere, has been eroding anyway. They have to appeal generally and not be tethered to sectional groups or classes. And, perhaps most significant of all, they cannot afford to be too ideological. They need to be flexible, pluralistic, and appeal across classes and to many identities, and be prepared to change as people's priorities change.

The future of politics and ideology

What late-modern and postmodern theories both suggest is an end to the class-based, mass-party ideological politics that we have traditionally known. Such politics is seen as a feature of the modern industrial society that it is claimed we are leaving behind. This decline of conventional politics re-inforces what has been said earlier about globalisation and fragmentation in relation to the sovereign state. On the one hand, there is globalisation's tendency to impose standard policies upon governments, which in turn re-inforces globalisation, which in turn suggests the death of ideological politics. On the other hand, globalisation would seem to be accompanied by a tendency to fragmentation by states and nations, with ever smaller units demanding their voice and their autonomy. And this too is echoed in the kind of cultural fragmentation suggested by late modern and postmodern theory. There is a tension between centrifugal and centripetal forces, which perhaps will shape the future of politics everywhere.

What might these trends mean for ideology? It might be said that there is a similar split between forces making for global standardisation on one level, while at the same time forces tending to fragmentation at other levels. On the one hand, there is the argument of Francis Fukuyama, who sees free-market liberalism as having triumphed over all rivals and now being accepted as the universal form of society for ever more (Fukuyama, 1989, 1992). On the other hand, developments within countries suggest the end of the politics of ideological mass parties and mass movement politics, claiming to liberate mankind; and more a fragmentation and proliferation of view-points. Late-modern/postmodern analysis implies rather a burgeoning of ideology, with an ideology for every human group and social distinction, every human difference and tendency, with no-one having the means to say that anyone else is right or wrong. As with politics generally, the future would seem to lie in the way these contrary forces will interact.

Bibliography

Background and general

Adams, Ian (1989) *The Logic of Political Belief: A Philosophical Analysis of Ideology*, Harvester Wheatsheaf.

Adams, Ian (1993) *Political Ideology Today*, Manchester University Press.

Adams, Ian and Jones, Bill (1996) *Concepts and Doctrines in British Politics*, PAVIC Publishing.

Barker, Rodney (1997) *Political Ideas in Modern Britain* (2nd edn), Routledge.

Butler, David and Kavanah, Dennis (1997) *The British General Election of 1997*, Macmillan.

Dickinson, H. T. (1977) *Liberty and Property: Political Ideology in Eighteenth-Century Britain*, Methuen.

Dickinson, H. T. (1985) *British Radicalism and the French Revolution 1789–1815*, Blackwell.

Dunleavy, Patrick *et al.* (eds) (1997) *Developments in British Politics 5*, Macmillan.

Dutton, D. (1997) *British Politics Since 1945* (2nd edn), Blackwell.

Eccleshall, R. *et al.* (1994) *Political Ideologies: An Introduction*, (2nd edn) Routledge.

Gamble, A. (1981) *An Introduction to Modern Social and Political Thought*, Macmillan.

Greenleaf, W. H. (1983) *The British Political Tradition*, vol. 2, *The Ideological Heritage*, Routledge.

Heywood, A. (1992) *Political Ideologies: An Introduction*, Macmillan.

Hielbroner, R. (1980) *The Worldly Philosophers* (5th edn), Penguin.

Hutton, Will (1995) *The State We're In*, Jonathan Cape.

Jones, Bill *et al.* (1998) *Politics UK* (3rd edn), Prentice Hall.

Kavanah, D. and Morris, P. (1989) *Consensus Politics from Attlee to Thatcher*, Blackwell.

Keynes, John Maynard [1936] (1983) *The General Theory of Employment, Interest and Money* to be found in *John Maynard Keynes Vol. VII Collected Writings*, Macmillan.

Leach, R. (1996) *British Political Ideologies* (2nd edn), Prentice Hall.

Lively, J. and Lively, A. (eds) (1994) *Democracy in Britain: A Reader*, Blackwell.

Marquand, David (1988) *The Unprincipled Society*, Jonathan Cape.

Marquand, David and Seldon, Anthony (1996) *The Ideas that Shaped Post-War Britain*, Fontana.

Miller, D. *et al.* (eds) (1991) *The Blackwell Encyclopaedia of Political Thought*, Blackwell.

Riff, M. A. (ed.) (1987) *Dictionary of Modern Political Ideologies*, Manchester University Press.

Scruton, R. (1996) *A Dictionary of Political Thought* (2nd edn), Macmillan.

Sharp, Andrew (ed.) (1983) *Political Ideas of the English Civil Wars 1641–1649*, Longman.

Smith, Adam [1776] (1970) *The Wealth of Nations*, Penguin.

Smith, David (1992) *From Boom to Bust: Trial and Error in British Economic Policy*, Penguin.

Stewart, M. (1972) *Keynes and After*, Penguin.

Tivey, L. and Wright, A. (1989) *Party Ideology in Britain*, Routledge.

de Tocqueville, Alexis [1840] (1968) *Democracy in America*, 2 vols, Fontana.

Vincent, Andrew (1995) *Modern Political Ideologies* (2nd edn), Blackwell.

Liberalism and democracy

Arblaster, Anthony (1984) *The Rise and Decline of Western Liberalism*, Blackwell.

Bentley, M. (1987) *The Climax of Liberal Politics, 1868–1918*, Edward Arnold.

Bogdanov, V. (ed.) (1983) *Liberal Party Politics*, Clarendon Press.

Bramsted, E. K. and Melhuish, K. J. (1978) *Western Liberalism*, Longman.

Bullock, Alan and Shock, Maurice (1956) *The Liberal Tradition: From Fox to Keynes*, Oxford University Press.

Eccleshall, Robert (ed.) (1986) *British Liberalism: Liberal Thought from the 1640s to 1980s*, Longman.

Freeden, Michael (1978) *The New Liberalism: An Ideology of Social Reform*, Oxford University Press.

Green, T. H. (1965) *The Political Theory of T. H. Green: Selected Writings*, Appleton-Century-Crofts.

Grimond, J. (1963) *The Liberal Challenge*, Hollis and Carter.

Heater, D. (1990) *Citizenship: The Civic Ideal in World History, Politics and Education*, Longman.

Hobhouse, L. T. [1911] (1964) *Liberalism*, Oxford University Press.

Hobson, H. J. (1974) *The Crisis of Liberalism*, Harvester-Wheatsheaf.

Locke, John (1965) *Two Treatise of Government*, Cambridge University Press.

MacIver, Don (ed.) (1996) *The Liberal Democrats*, Prentice Hall.

Malthus, Thomas [1798] (1971) *An Essay on the Principle of Population*, Penguin.

Mill, J. S. [1859] (1910) *Utilitarianism, Liberty, Representative Government*, Dent.

Paine, T. [1791] (1969) *The Rights of Man*, Penguin.

Parekh, B. (ed.) (1973) *Bentham's Political Thought*, Croom Helm.

Plamenatz, J. (1965) *Readings from Liberal Writers: English and French*, Allen & Unwin.

Rousseau, J. J. [1762] (1973) *The Social Contract and Discourses*, Dent.

Spencer, H. (1969) *Man versus the State*, Penguin.

Conservatism and the right

Adam Smith Institute (1986) *Privatisation Worldwide.*

Blake, Robert (1970) *The Conservative Party from Peel to Churchill,* Fontana.

Buck, P. W. (1975) *How Conservatives Think,* Penguin.

Burke, Edmund [1790] (1969) *Reflections on the Revolution in France,* Penguin.

Burke, Edmund (1908) *Speeches and Letters on American Affairs,* Dent.

Clarke, P. and Graham, G. (1986) *The New Enlightenment: The Rebirth of Liberalism,* Macmillan in association with Channel 4.

Duncan, Alan and Hobson, Dominic (1995) *Saturn's Children: How the State Devours Liberty, Prosperity and Virtue,* Sinclair-Stevenson.

Eccleshall, R. (ed.) (1990) *English Conservatism Since the Restoration,* Unwin Hyman.

Evans, B. and Taylor, A. (1996) *From Salisbury to Thatcher: Continuity and Change in Conservative Politics,* Manchester University Press.

Friedman, M. and Friedman, R. (1980) *Free to Choose,* Penguin.

Gamble, A. (1988) *The Free Economy and the Strong State: The Politics of Thatcherism,* Macmillan.

Gilmour, Ian (1978) *Inside Right: A Study of Conservatism,* Quartet.

Gilmour, Ian (1997) *Whatever Happened to the Tories: The Conservatives Since 1945,* Fourth Estate.

Gray, John and Willetts, David (1997) *Is Conservatism Dead?,* Profile Books in association with Social Market Foundation.

Green, D. G. (1987) *The New Right: The Counter Revolution in Political, Social and Economic Thought,* Wheatsheaf.

Hayek, F. A. (1944) *The Road to Serfdom,* Routledge and Kegan Paul.

Hogg, Quinton (1959) *The Conservative Case,* Penguin.

Joseph, Keith and Sumption, J. (1979) *Equality,* John Murray.

Kavanagh, Dennis and Seldon, A. (1994) *The Major Effect,* Macmillan.

Keegan, W. (1985) *Mrs Thatcher's Economic Experiment,* Penguin.

King, D. S. (1987) *The New Right: Politics, Markets and Citizenship,* Macmillan.

Lawson, Nigel (1992) *The View From No. 11: Memoirs of a Tory Radical,* Bantam.

Levitas, R. (1986) *The Ideology of the New Right,* Polity,.

Ludlam, S. and Smith, M. (eds.) (1996) *Contemporary British Conservatism,* Macmillan.

Macmillan, Harold (1938) *The Middle Way,* Macmillan.

Nozick, R. (1974) *Anarchy, State and Utopia,* Blackwell.

O'Gorman, F. (ed.) (1986) *British Conservatism: Conservative Thought from Burke to Thatcher,* Longman.

O'Sullivan, N. (1976) *Conservatism,* Dent.

Quinton, A. (1978) *The Politics of Imperfection,* Faber.

Sampson, G. (1984) *An End to Allegiance: Individual Freedom and the New Politics,* Temple Smith.

Skidelsky, Robert (ed.) (1988) *Thatcherism,* Blackwell.

Thatcher, Margaret (1993) *The Downing Street Years,* HarperCollins.

White, R. J. (1950) *The Conservative Tradition,* Kaye.

Young, Hugo (1989) *One of Us,* Macmillan.

Socialism and Labour

Anderson, P. and Mann, N. (1997) *Safety First: The Making of New Labour*, Granta.

Beer, M. (1929) *A History of British Socialism*, (2 vols) Bell.

Bellamy, Edward [1888] (1986) *Looking Backward*, Penguin.

Benn, Tony (1980) *Arguments for Socialism*, Penguin.

Benn, Tony (1981) *Arguments for Democracy*, Jonathan Cape.

Berki, R. N. (1975) *Socialism*, Dent.

Blatchford [1894] (1976) *Merrie England*, Journeyman Press.

Callaghan, J. (1990) *Socialism in Britain Since 1884*, Blackwell.

Crick, B. (1987) *Socialism*, Open University Press.

Crosland, C. A. R. (1964) *The Future of Socialism*, Jonathan Cape.

Crosland, C. A. R. (1974) *Socialism Now*, Jonathan Cape.

Fielding, S. (1995) *Labour: Decline and Renewal*, Baseline.

Foote, G. (1986) *The Labour Party's Political Thought: A History*, Croom Helm.

Glasier, J. B. and St. John Conway, K (1890) *The Religon of Socialism*, Labour Press Society.

Hattersley, Roy (1987) *Choose Freedom: The Future for Democratic Socialism*, Michael Joseph.

Heffer, Eric (1986) *Labour's Future: Socialist or SDP Mark 2?*, Verso.

Hyndman (1881) *The Textbook of Democracy: England For All*, E. W. Allen.

Jones, Bill (1977) *The Russia Complex*, Manchester University Press.

Gould, Bryan (1985) *Socialism and Freedom*, Macmillan.

Le Grand, J. and Estrin, S. (eds) (1989) *Market Socialism*, Oxford University Press.

Liddle, Roger and Mandelson, Peter (1996) *The Blair Revolution: Can New Labour Deliver?*, Faber.

Macdonald, J. Ramsay (1911) *The Socialist Movement*, Williams and Norgate.

MacKenzie, N. (1966) *Socialism: A Short History* (2nd edn), Hutchinson.

MacKenzie, N. and MacKenzie, J. (1977) *The First Fabians*, Quartet.

Macmurray, John (1961) *Persons in Relation*, Humanities Press International.

Macmurray, John (1991) *The Self as Agent*, Faber.

More, Thomas [1516] (1991) *Utopia*, Cambridge University Press.

Morris, William [1886] (1887) *A Dream of John ball and A King's Lesson*, Reeves & Turner.

Morris, William [1890] (1993) *News From Nowhere*, Penguin.

Morris, William (1973) *Political Writings of William Morris*, Lawrence & Wishart.

Owen, Robert (1969) *Report to the County of Lanark* [1821] and *A New View of Society* [1814], Penguin.

Pelling, H. and Reid, A. (1996) *A Short History of the Labour Party* (11th edn), Macmillan.

Pimlot, Ben (ed.) (1984) *Fabian Essays in Socialist Thought*, Heinemann.

Rentoul, J. (1995) *Tony Blair*, Little, Brown & Co.

Sassoon, Donald (1996) *One Hundred Years of Socialism: The West European Left in the Twentieth Century*, Fontana.

Seyd, P. (1987) *The Rise and Fall of the Labour Left*, Macmillan.

Shaw, G. B. (ed.) [1889] (1911) *Fabian Essays in Socialism*, Walter Scott Co.

Shaw, Eric (1996) *The Labour Party Since 1945*, Blackwell.

Sopel, Jon (1995) *Tony Blair: The Moderniser*, Michael Joseph.

Tawney, R. H. [1921] (1964) *The Aquisitive Society*, Fontana.
Tawney, R. H. [1926] (1938) *Religion and the Rise of Capitalism*, Penguin.
Tawney, R. H. [1931] (1964) *Equality*, Unwin.
Taylor, K. (1982) *The Political Ideas of the Utopian Socialists*, Frank Cass.
Webb, Sidney (1893) *Socialism in England*, Swan Sonnenschein.
Wright, A. (ed.) (1983) *British Socialism: Socialist Thought from the 1880s to 1960s*, Longman.
Wright, A. (1986) *Socialisms: Theories and Practices*, Oxford University Press.

Nationalism and internationalism

Alter, P. (1985) *Nationalism*, Edward Arnold.
Aughey, A. and Morrow, D. (eds) (1996) *Northern Ireland Politics*, Longmans.
Bishop, P. and Mallie, E. (1987) *The Provisional IRA*, Heinemann.
Crick, Bernard (ed.) (1991) *National Identities*, Blackwell in association with Political Quarterly.
George, S. (1991) *Britain and European Integration Since 1945*, Blackwell.
Hobsbawm, E. J. (1990) *Nations and Nationalism Since 1780*, Cambridge University Press.
Kedourie, E. (1966) *Nationalism* (3rd edn), Hutchinson.
Marr, Andrew (1995) *The Battle for Scotland*, Penguin.
Minogue, K. R. (1967) *Nationalism*, Methuen.
Pilkington, C. (1995) *Britain in the European Union Today*, Manchester University Press.
Smith, A. D. (1991) *National Identity*, Penguin.

Green ideas

Bahro, R. (1984) *From Red to Green*, Verso.
Bookchin, Murray (1972) *Post Scarcity Anarchism*, Black Rose Books.
Dobson, A. (1995) *Green Political Thought* (2nd edn), Routledge.
Goldsmith, Edward (1972) *A Blueprint for Survival*, Tom Stacey.
Parkin, S. (1989) *Green Parties: An International Guide*, Heretic Books.
Porritt, J. (1984) *Seeing Green: The Politics of Ecology Explained*, Blackwell.
Roskak, T. (1981) *Person/Planet*, Granada.
Schumacher, F. (1974) *Small is Beautiful*, Abacus.
Ward, B. and Dubois, R. (1972) *Only One Earth*, Pelican.

Extremes and the fringe

Benewick, R. (1972) *The Fascist Movement in Britain* (2nd edn), Allen Lane.
Berlin, I. (1963) *Karl Marx* (3rd edn), Oxford University Press.
Bouchier, D. (1983) *The Feminist Challenge: The Movement for Women's Liberation in Britain and the United States*, Macmillan.

Callaghan, J. (1987) *The Far Left in British Politics*, Blackwell.

Charvet, J. (1982) *Feminism*, Dent.

Clarke, P. and Linzey, A.(1990) *Political Theory and Animal Rights*, Pluto Press.

Coates, D. *et al.* (eds) (1985) *A Socialist Anatomy of Britain*, Polity.

Crick, Michael (1986) *The March of Militant*, Faber.

Cruikshank, Margaret (1992) *The Gay and Lesbian Liberation Movement*, Routledge.

Eisentein, H. (1984) *Contemporary Feminist Thought*, Unwin.

Fielding, N. (1981) *The National Front*, Routledge & Kegan Paul.

Greer, G. (1971) *The Female Eunuch*, Paladin.

Henshaw, D. (1989) *Animal Warfare: The Story of the Animal Liberation Front*, Fontana.

Humm, Maggie (ed.) (1992) *Feminisms: A Reader*, Harvester Wheatsheaf.

Icke, D. (1991) *The Truth Vibrations*, HarperCollins.

Lenin, V. I. [1902] *What is to be Done?*, in *V. I. Lenin: Selected Works*, Lawrence & Wishard, 1968.

Marcuse, Herbert [1960] (1968) *One Dimensional Man*, Sphere Books.

McLellan, (1980) *The Thought of Karl Marx* (2nd edn), Macmillan.

Mosley, Oswald (1932) *The Greater Britain*, BUF Publications.

Singer, P. (1983) *Animal Liberation: Towards and End to Man's Inhumanity to Animals*, Thorsons.

Thurlow, R. (1988) *Fascism in Britain* (2nd edn), I. B. Tauris.

Weeks, J. (1977) *Coming Out: Homosexual Politics in Britian, from the Nineteenth Century to the Present*, Quartet.

Wilkinson, P. (1983) *The New Fascists* (2nd edn), Pan.

The future

Adams, Ian (1991) 'Can History Be Finished?', *Politics*, vol. 11, no. 2, October.

Baudrillard, Jean (1988) *Selected Writings*, Polity.

Fukuyama, Francis (1989) 'The End of History?', *The National Interest*, Summer, 3–18.

Fukuyama, Francis (1992) *The End of History and the Last Man*, Hamish Hamilton.

Lyon, David (1994) *Postmodernity*, Open University Press.

Lyotard, Jean-François (1984) *The Postmodern Condition: A Report on Knowledge*, Manchester University Press.

Mulgan, Geoff (1994) *Politics in an Antipolitical Age*, Polity.

Mulgan, Geoff (ed.) (1997) *Life after Politics: New Thinking for the Twenty-First Century*, Fontana.

Index

218